THE
POLITICAL
CONSTRUCTION
OF EDUCATION

THE
POLITICAL
CONSTRUCTION
OF EDUCATION

The State, School Expansion, and Economic Change

Edited by
Bruce Fuller
and
Richard Rubinson

PRAEGER

New York
Westport, Connecticut
London

Copyright Acknowledgment

Chapter 4 draws on arguments made in *New Citizens for a New Society: The Institutional Origins of Mass Schooling in Sweden* by John Boli. Copyright 1989. Reprinted with permission of Pergamon Press PLC.

Library of Congress Cataloging-in-Publication Data

The political construction of education : the state, school expansion,
   and economic change / edited by Bruce Fuller and Richard
   Rubinson.
       p.   cm.
   Includes bibliographical references and index.
   ISBN 0-275-93831-X (alk. paper)
   1. Education and state. 2. Education—Political aspects.
   3. Education—Economic aspects.   I. Fuller, Bruce. II. Rubinson,
   Richard.
   LC75.P65   1992
   379—dc20   91-33893

British Library Cataloguing in Publication Data is available.

Library of Congress Catalog Card Number: 91-33893
ISBN: 0-275-93831-X

First published in 1992

Praeger Publishers, One Madison Avenue, New York, NY 10010
An imprint of Greenwood Publishing Group, Inc.

Printed in the United States of America

The paper used in this book complies with the
Permanent Paper Standard issued by the National
Information Standards Organization (Z39.48-1984).

10 9 8 7 6 5 4 3 2 1

To Deborah and Susan. And to our children: Claude, Paul, Emily, Max, Dylan, and Caitlin. We hope that our critical questions will aid in the recrafting of schools so that our children's offspring will grow up within institutions that are more thoughtfully created and more respectful of their joy-filled curiosity.

Contents

Preface

For three centuries, Western society has celebrated the medicinal magic of mass schooling. Whatever the economic or social ill—sluggish productivity, the erosion of community, intractable inequality, even sexual discontent—it can seemingly be remedied by more education. God is not dead but living in the bodies of education ministers.

When the miracle cure is swallowed by policymakers and citizens of industrialized nations and the patient fails to improve, concern grows as to why schooling did not boost economic growth, reduce class conflict, or smooth over cultural rough spots. In contrast, the spread of mass schooling in some developing countries occurs at a breathtaking pace, spurring both modernization and social disintegration. In these settings, schooling efficaciously transforms society and constructs novel conceptions of the individual. Yet critics wonder whether these visible effects are desirable, even controllable.

Whether the school's influence is minuscule or monumental, another question arises, which is the subject of this book: *What forces are driving the spread of mass schooling?*

The contribution of schooling to economic growth and social change was formalized in the late 1950s by human capital theorists. The forces driving popular demand for school were wrapped up in the institution's alleged effects: An increase in parents' propensity to express demand for more schooling paralleled the rise in expected (economic and status) returns to their children. This upward-spiraling faith in the Western system of schooling was driven by the claim that more schooling would boost individual (and national) productivity. By the mid–1970s, however, it was clear that heightened investment in schooling within industrialized countries guaranteed neither continued economic expansion nor a reduction in inequality (as human capital proponents would have it). But if massive school expansion does not consistently yield the theorized economic effects, *why do educational institutions keep growing, enrolling more children, and receiving more and more public and private resources*?

Over the past fifteen years, a great deal of empirical research has focused on this question. The revival of class-conflict theory fueled interpretations that ran counter to functionalist human capital arguments: Schooling expanded to legitimate present inequalities, allowing advantaged classes to retain their jobs and cultural forms through a seemingly fair, meritocratic system. Here, the central state does not functionally expand mass schooling to pursue society's "common good." Instead, political actors, captured by elites, serve to reinforce and reproduce economic and cultural differences.

In recent years, world institution theorists have argued that mass schooling spreads like a social movement, allowing the state to signal that it is modern and efficacious and allowing the constructed individual to claim membership in Western institutions. The fact that the system may originally have been pieced together by elites is no longer the salient point. Now everyone accepts the credibility of modern schools, states, and workplaces: These provide understood rules for achievement, common paths toward higher status, and seemingly just ways of distributing material goods. The spread of mass schooling is both an expression of and method for reinforcing these institutionalized arrangements. Faith in a particular agency—be it the family, the state, or the structure of labor—is dwarfed by popular ideological faith in the miracles of mass schooling. When the miracle antidote fails to cure society's ills, the remedy is simply to buy and consume more of this tasty medicine.

EVIDENCE AND COMPETING MODELS OF SCHOOL EXPANSION

The rise of theories aimed at pinpointing the forces that drive the spread of schooling has far outpaced empirical investigation. More than a decade ago, however, focused empirical work on competing models of school expansion was begun by economists, historians, and sociologists. A subset of these scholars began meeting in 1985 to compare findings and to discuss (1) which elements of which causal theories could be substantiated and (2) which ones lacked solid evidence. This book is the result of the School Expansion Workgroup's annual meetings.

The chapters—spanning a variety of historical periods and national settings—focus on different institutions that may drive either popular demand for, or the organized supply of, mass schooling. Several chapters emphasize the political construction of schooling, which is linked to the rise of the secular state. Under certain conditions, political actors shape the family's preference for more schooling. As popular demand grows, the state supplies more schools and teachers. A number of questions flow from this analysis. Does the state act independently of elite interests? Can it put a damper on popular demand once the mass school institution gains legitimacy and momentum? Does the spread of schooling itself serve as a civic stage upon which political agencies demonstrate a central raison d'être in modern society?

The state is simply one player in this thrust to expand schooling. The family may press government to broaden educational opportunity. Particular social groups (competing for economic mobility, status, or cultural cohesion) may drive up school enrollments whether or not the central state has the resources to keep pace with demand. Changing forms of work and labor demand alter opportunities for school-age youth, cause adjustments in the types of skills required, and link occupational mobility to school credentials. Other social organizations, especially the church, may push for school expansion in ways that are independent of the ideals and socialization modes of the spiritless state. Chapters in this volume examine the strength of these various institutional forces under different national and historical conditions.

A FOUR-PART STORY

We begin this volume by reviewing what is known about the state's clout in expanding schooling. We distinguish competing theoretical frameworks, detail extant evidence, and suggest several steps in building theory that is sensitive to different political-economic conditions. Until conditions are more clearly specified under which particular institutions drive school expansion, scholarly camps will remain divided and guidance for policymakers and activists will remain hazy at best.

Part I of the book focuses on how popular demand for more schooling is constructed, largely but not exclusively by political actors. Economist David Mitch argues that the post-Reformation rise of demand for literacy skills is attributable to various decentralized forces. Francisco Ramirez and Marc Ventresca demonstrate how the rising Western state incorporated and formalized a diverse array of schools through a remarkably similar institution-building process around the world. John Boli emphasizes the role of mass schooling in nineteenth-century Europe: It helped to erode community-based forms of authority and substituted the individual's formal loyalty to the state. William Morgan and J. Michael Armer show how family demands in the African context often bridge traditional forms of religious training with the Western school's relentless incursion. Sorca O'Connor, arguing from a feminist perspective, reviews different justifications for state incorporation of younger children and the daycare organizations that serve them.

Part II focuses on relationships between education and the economy. First we review institution-level research on education and national economic growth. We argue that the right question to ask is, Under what conditions does education increase economic growth? We then develop a theoretical model that specifies these conditions, and we demonstrate how the three grand theories may operate simultaneously with fluctuating levels of causal strength. Aaron Benavot then moves from the national to the international level in studying the effects of education on economic growth. He finds that these effects are conditional on global cycles and a country's position in the world economy. Walter McMahon uses a general economic model of investments in education to analyze both the growth and the decline of school enrollments. His analysis of the recent erosion in African enrollment rates signals that we cannot take continual educational expansion for granted.

Part III focuses on how the state and other institutions endeavor to supply mass schooling. Jerald Hage and Maurice Garnier highlight how the relatively strong French state has historically controlled growth in school supply, especially for the children of elites, while the relatively weak Italian state holds little ability to check rising popular demand. Pamela Walters contrasts the political-economic conditions found in the North and South after the American Civil War: Differing class structures and economic demands placed very different pressures on local states, resulting in different rates of school supply and expansion. David Baker reveals how a non-state agency like the Catholic Church can provide a counter-supply of mass schooling while building its own legitimacy by constructing schools that look increasingly like their secular counterparts. John Richardson examines how the state defines *common schooling* and its close link to the constructed meaning of "deviance."

In Part IV, John Meyer concludes the volume with a provocative question: What institutional conditions allow central agents (like the state) to become credible actors in expanding and reinforcing the authority of mass schooling? Meyer is less interested in the material causes and consequences of mass schooling than in the underlying faith that legitimates central actors when they argue for the virtue—indeed, the apparent necessity—of building more schools.

ACKNOWLEDGMENTS

Special thanks are due the American Sociological Association and the committee that oversees the Advancement of the Discipline Fund (supported by the National Science Foundation). They provided critical support as we were pulling together empirical work and delineating concrete steps toward building theory. Early support also came from the World Bank, where Steve Heyneman and George Psacharopoulos continue to appreciate the value of different disciplinary viewpoints. National Science Foundation funding for our independent work also has significantly spurred this collective project.

Steve Slaner at Harvard spent many hours helping to edit and improve the chapters. Lisa Gerloff and Betty Walker prepared the figures and tables. Norma Diala generously provided extra staff for our project while other work waited.

Anne Kiefer and John Roberts at Praeger have been patient, supportive, and candid editors.

Finally, thanks to John Meyer for opening up this field of study twenty years ago and for letting no claim about the causes and consequences of school expansion go unquestioned.

THE
POLITICAL
CONSTRUCTION
OF EDUCATION

Does the State Expand Schooling? Review of the Evidence

Bruce Fuller and Richard Rubinson

TURNING TO THE STATE?

The state's proper role and actual influence within Western society has been loudly debated since the birth of this modern institution two centuries ago. Can politicians and bureaucrats guide nations more rationally, equitably, and humanely than market forces? Can government organizations backstop the steady erosion of local institutions that traditionally have defined the individual and community: the family, church, and village authorities? Can the state reinforce a "common good" and shared moral tenets within nations that are growing more pluralistic culturally and more stratified economically?

One important target of active states is the school institution and its influence over how children are socialized. But are government activists efficacious in constructing and expanding the institution of schooling? Since the Reformation, civic leaders have made grand claims about the magical effects of mass schooling and the secular state's power to expand it. But only in the past decade has research matured on both the causes and economic consequences of school expansion. This book aims to clarify the causal models implicit in these grand claims and then to present empirical evidence as to their validity.

This opening chapter tries to circumscribe the feisty, growing field that links the state, school expansion, and economic change. First, we describe the remarkable phenomenon of school expansion that is sweeping outward from Europe to the New World, East Asia, and the Third World. Second, we briefly review the major theories advanced by civic activists and scholars regarding the relative force of the state vis-à-vis the economy, the church, and the family in pushing and shaping the bullish institution of schooling. Third, we detail the burgeoning evidence on which institutions drive the spread of mass schooling across different nations and political-economic conditions.

In Chapter 7 we focus on evidence regarding the next step in this causal chain: when and how school expansion boosts economic growth.

We emphasize that the validity of each (competing) explanation of school expansion, and claimed economic benefits, depends upon the institutional and economic conditions present within a country and a historical period. We are not proposing a new theory. Instead, with our contributors, we delineate the specific settings under which major processes linking the state, school expansion, and economic change become stronger or weaker.

Political Faith and Costly Ignorance

Like the unstoppable spread of blue jeans, the school institution first burst from Europe and the United States and now steadily moves across all nations, oozing into every cultural nook and cranny. The secular school may be tailored to local tastes, may even be accommodated within earlier forms of child rearing and socialization. But the Western school's basic organizational form—its lines, fabric, and signaled meaning—looks remarkably similar as it creeps around the globe, papering over enormous differences in how children once were raised.

Ironically, until recently we have known little about what institutions and economic forces have driven, and continue to energize, the relentless spread of modern schooling. Civic leaders recurrently express hope that state actors, business leaders, community groups, and parents can spark or reinforce political support for expanding education. Yet evidence pinning down specific institutions and economic forces has been surprisingly scarce. Since we hold such strong faith in the magic of schooling, we have been slow to question the claimed power of ideologies and organizations that allegedly spur school expansion.

The state, under modern social rules, is immediately implicated whenever civic activists talk of altering the pace or character of school expansion. Contemporary debates illustrate the gap between faithful affection (or distaste) for government action and evidence about the state's actual efficacy.

Political actors in Washington struggle to boost subsidies for preschools and child care, despite the fact that evolving labor patterns, women's social roles, and private services already have boosted demand and prompted increases in organizational supply. Is the state really a key actor?

In Britain, civic leaders recurrently debate the utility of expanding both higher education and vocational training, despite empirical evidence showing that neither form of schooling yields consistent economic effects within postindustrial conditions (Meyer and Hannan 1979; Psacharopoulos 1989; Chapter 8, this volume). Are political activists behaving rationally?

In Africa and much of Asia, governments and international agencies are searching for effective ways of boosting young girls' demand for basic schooling. The central state presumably is the key actor. But do economic and institutional forces that have successfully driven growth in male enrollments operate similarly on young females' expressed demand for schooling?

In each case, despite civic leaders' ignorance regarding the likely force of different institutions (the state, economic firms, churches, or the family) in boosting school expansion, expensive social policies and private strategies are mounted. Quite often these well-meaning efforts fail to raise popular demand for schooling, to increase school supply, or to boost economic growth. Only then do we question the state's efficacy and hunt for alternative organizations that might hasten, slow, or alter the character of school expansion.

THE STATE BUILDS INSTITUTIONS: THREE CENTRAL QUESTIONS

We begin the story by focusing on the state, which is seen by many as the pivotal actor in spreading mass schooling and in reaping subsequent economic benefits. This tale quickly becomes more complex, taking on several subplots: the early role of churches and commercial elites in starting the first schools, often creating a post-Reformation class of private tutors; later, the schizophrenic forces of economic organizations, simultaneously competing with schools for young labor while backing improvements in the quality of human capital; and the now two-century-old influence of the school institution itself, bullishly legitimating and reproducing its role within the broader polity's commitment to individual development, material opportunity, meritocratic forms of status, and economic expansion.

Despite these diverse institutional forces, we argue that the state plays a strong role in constructing the school institution under a variety of conditions. Governments around the world spend enormous amounts of resources to boost the supply of classrooms and teachers, sparking even greater legitimacy and popular demand for more schooling among disenfranchised groups. Governments in Europe and the United States strive to attract more children to school for longer periods of time; they are struggling to reduce the number of high school dropouts, pulling infants and tiny children into bureaucratic forms of socialization, even preaching the spiritual virtues of "life-long learning" (in school, of course). Political leaders habitually turn to the school as the institutional antidote for a variety of social ills and as a stage upon which Western ideals and moral commitments can be debated and ritualistically enacted (Durkheim 1956).

In addition, the state acts powerfully in constructing demand for literate and "educated" citizens. Simply to be a member of the modern political economy requires that individuals receive large doses of mass schooling. The state creates large numbers of white-collar jobs, legitimates urban forms of work and knowledge, and sanctions school credentials through a variety of licensing and employment rules (Meyer 1977). Thus, employment opportunities and social status become interwoven with the formal school institution.

Third World states similarly hold the school institution as sacred; they regard it as being *the* organizational mechanism for delivering mass opportunity, economic growth, and national integration. The school is one cornerstone of the state's drive to construct and reinforce modern institutions. Third World governments, nudged by their international bankers and benefactors, must build more classrooms, hire more teachers, enroll more children. The heretical nation-state that chooses not to expand mass schooling quickly becomes the object of criticism within the international press and diplomatic circles. The state allegedly plays a pivotal role in expanding mass education and ensuring that the school yields miraculous economic and social benefits (Boli et al. 1985; Fuller 1991).

The school's capacity to attract and shape children comes into question when nations go through periods of economic adjustment or unsettling cultural divergence. The state is pushed sharply by various interests to boost popular demand for education and to deepen the school's imprint (technical or moral) upon children's hearts and minds. When domestic economies decline or face stiffening international competition, political leaders turn to the schools, either to share the blame or to become part of the policy remedies. But again, such faith-filled political advocacy is rarely informed by evidence on the state's actual influence in expanding school opportunities or in crafting greater economic effects.

This book frames the state's possible influence as a set of empirical questions. If you are among the faithful, we ask that you temporarily suspend your sacred belief in the modern state's efficacy. This book indulges the profane by focusing on three researchable issues:

- Can state actors boost enrollments by shaping the supply of schooling or by raising popular demand for education? If so, under what political-economic conditions and through what organizational means is the state most forceful?

- What is the state's actual force relative to the influence of other institutions and economic organizations (the church, family, firms, and school itself)? How does variation in a nation's (or region's) economic and cultural organization enhance or constrain the state's influence?

- Does the expansion of mass schooling spur economic and institutional change (or simply reinforce existing structures and rules)? If school expansion does yield economic and organizational change, under what conditions and for what social groups are these effects most consistently felt?

Clear and universal answers to these questions have proven to be more elusive than school advocates and critics once claimed. To inform these issues we begin with three fundamental theories, advanced both by civic leaders and scholars, that attempt to reveal the institutions that efficaciously push school expansion and the economic benefits that allegedly result. From these competing models—technical functionalism, class conflict, and world institutions—we move to the accelerating flow of recent research findings that empirically assess claims made by each theory. As the universal character of the grand theories breaks down, we attempt to delineate the conditions under which the basic models may hold, and when they do not. For instance, when is the state more likely to boost school enrollments, independent of competing economic forces? Or, under what institutional conditions are economic gains from school expansion more likely to be observed? These theoretical frameworks will become more useful in policy settings only when they are bounded and applied to local conditions.

THE RISE OF MASS SCHOOLING:
TWO CENTURIES OF INSTITUTION BUILDING

Most children two hundred years ago labored alongside their parents in the fields, the household, or small shops. Literacy was passed on to a fraction of children by the local church, by private tutors, or within affluent families. European political leaders and urban elites were wary of what French revolutionaries were labeling the *petite école,* or what irreverent Americans termed the *common school.* Organized schools certainly played a role in training priests and military leaders, or in saving souls in distant colonized lands. But traditional groups argued that building schools for the rising middle class or for peasant families could raise explosive expectations of attaining higher social status and broader economic opportunity.[1]

Nevertheless, like a smoldering, inextinguishable grass fire creeping across the African savanna, the institution of mass schooling has spread across continents and national boundaries for over two centuries. By 1980, three-fourths of all school-age children worldwide were enrolled in a primary school. Today, over one-fifth of the world's population attends school. Between 1950 and the year 2000, school enrollments will quadruple to one billion young people. In the Third World, school enrollments will increase sevenfold (Unesco 1983).

Enrollment growth in mass schooling since 1870 is illustrated in Figure 1.1. Early growth in secular primary schooling had already occurred by mid-century in Northern Europe and the United States, spurred by churches' interest in literacy, rising aspirations of the petite bourgeoisie, and interest by state actors in aligning themselves with national versions of the common school movement. By 1870 over half of all children were at least registered for school, although actual attendance often was erratic. Enrollment rates lagged behind in southern Europe but have caught up since World War II.

Enrollment rates were lower a century ago within late-industrializing countries, including Japan. Participation in formal schooling remained low throughout most of the Third World, even in Latin American nations that had gained political independence by the mid-nineteenth century. In 1940 no more than 30 percent of all Central American children were enrolled in primary school. Yet in the postwar period, enrollment rates have climbed dramatically in both Latin America and sub-Saharan Africa.

Defining School Expansion

A few definitional statements help clarify how we delimit and frame the major historical event of school expansion. First, this book focuses on the growth of

Figure 1.1
Growth in Primary School Enrollment Rates, 1870–1990

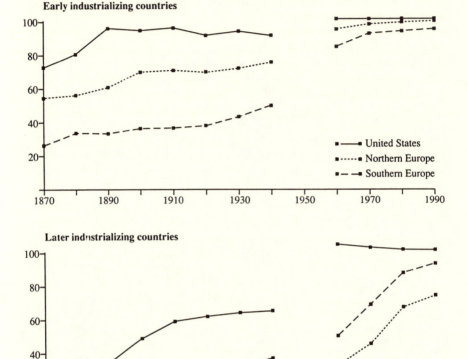

Notes: Rates for pre–1940 and post–1950 periods are not precisely comparable. The number of children age five to fourteen years is used in the denominator for the first period; the age cohort six to eleven years is used for the second period. Countries also vary slightly in the regional groupings. Data are from Unesco (1983), Benavot and Riddle (1988), and Lockheed and Verspoor (1991).

school enrollments from the early nineteenth century onward. Chapters by sociologists Francisco Ramirez and Marc Ventresca and economist David Mitch emphasize how popular support for formal instruction, rarely sponsored by the state, had already gained significant momentum as modern Europe advanced into the nineteenth century. These chapters speak to subsequent political construction of popular demand for, and institutional supply of, secular mass schooling. Remaining chapters look at the quickening expansion of schooling in Europe, the New World, and—most recently—the Third World.

Second, our general model of school expansion assumes that by the early nineteenth century many families in Europe preferred to enroll their children in formal schooling (Figure 1.2). Popular support for mass schooling grew rapidly in the mid-nineteenth century within commercial centers, even in rural areas where Calvinist commitments to literacy and formal (moral) socialization ran high (Archer 1979; Graff 1987). However, popular preference for schooling (like any good or social service) does not equate with expressed demand. The politically constructed supply of schools, pricing, and constructed institutional rules for entering mass education—set by the central state, church, economic elites, and/or the school itself—intervenes to determine the frequency with which family preferences translate into expressed demand. The central state may prefer to expand school enrollments. But its capacity to boost supply, decrease direct and opportunity costs to families, and institutionally widen access to quality schools conditions the extent to which political preferences will lead to a rise in enrollments. Chapter 2 by David Mitch details the implications of this point. Strong institutions also may forcefully attempt to block or divert families from expressing their demand for a certain form of schooling. The state, for instance, may try to contain the educational aspirations of working-class families (see Chapter 10). Similarly, churches in the First and Third World often attempt to draw children away from state-sponsored secular schools (see Chapter 12).

Third, the term *mass schooling* refers to secular primary schools that are open to children from a variety of backgrounds. In many countries completion of secondary school (or at least lower secondary in the Third World) is now required to enter the modern polity and economy. The nineteenth-century shift in Europe away from seminaries and private tutors, and toward formal schools financed by secular municipal governments, represented the initial drift toward mass schooling. In the Third World, newly independent states usually have wrested control of primary schooling from churches or colonial administrations, and then they have greatly expanded the number of schools and access to them. This pattern also represents the West's shift toward schooling for the mass of children, regardless of family background, caste, or ascribed characteristics.

Fourth, we define *school expansion* simply as growth in enrollments, usually linked to child counts conducted by schools at the beginning of each year. We do not assume that attendance is regular throughout the school year.[2] Nor do we assume that enrollment growth within a nation parallels rising aggregate levels of literacy or achievement. Literacy spread via churches and tutors in northern Europe well prior to the advent of state-sponsored schooling. In contrast, contemporary Third World governments have rapidly built and legitimated mass schooling, spurring enormous enrollment growth in the past half-century; but corresponding gains in literacy are difficult to substantiate, largely due to the state's ambivalence toward educational quality (Lockheed et al. 1991).

School expansion often is associated with growth in education expenditures. We prefer to see school spending as a possible determinant of enrollment growth, not as a co-occurring outcome. School spending (public or private) may move

Figure 1.2
General Model of School Expansion

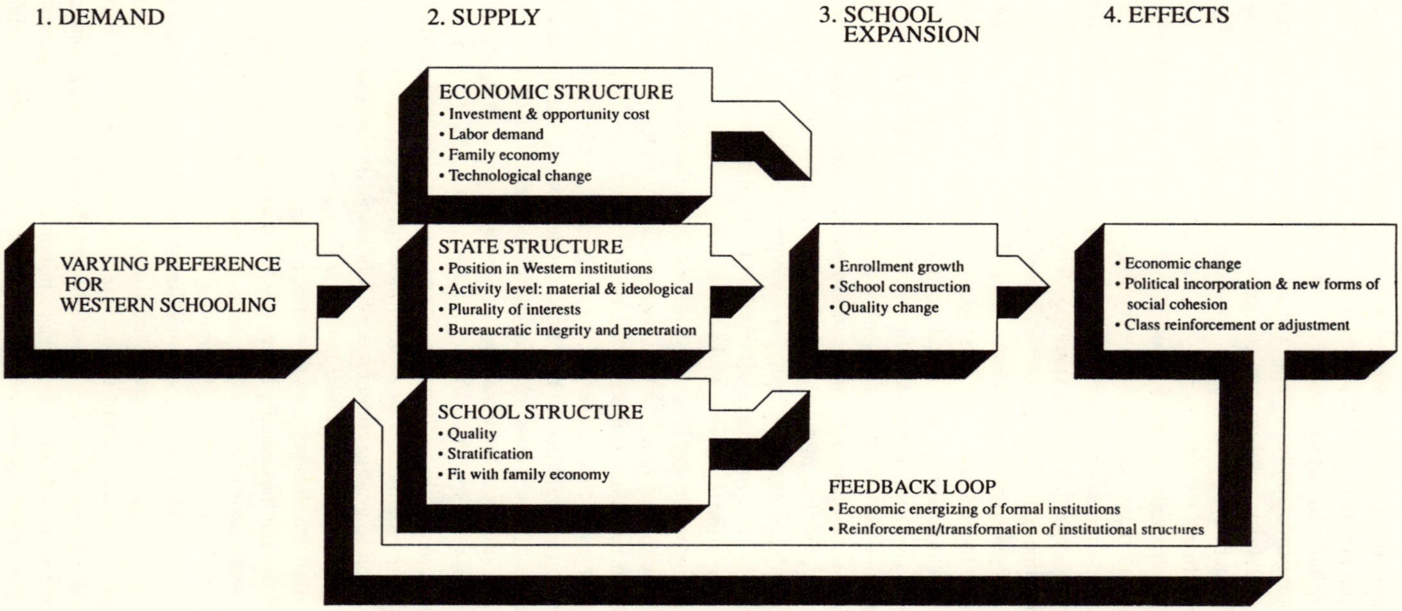

1. DEMAND 2. SUPPLY 3. SCHOOL 4. EFFECTS
EXPANSION

VARYING PREFERENCE FOR WESTERN SCHOOLING

ECONOMIC STRUCTURE
• Investment & opportunity cost
• Labor demand
• Family economy
• Technological change

STATE STRUCTURE
• Position in Western institutions
• Activity level: material & ideological
• Plurality of interests
• Bureaucratic integrity and penetration

SCHOOL STRUCTURE
• Quality
• Stratification
• Fit with family economy

• Enrollment growth
• School construction
• Quality change

• Economic change
• Political incorporation & new forms of social cohesion
• Class reinforcement or adjustment

FEEDBACK LOOP
• Economic energizing of formal institutions
• Reinforcement/transformation of institutional structures

independently of enrollment growth. Real education spending in the United States, for instance, has steadily increased over the past three decades, but this has done little to affect enrollments of low-income children. In contrast, enrollment rates continue to climb in most Third World countries, even as per capita education spending declines. Spending action by the state or family represents just one way of boosting institutional supply that does not necessarily raise enrollment.

Finally, we gaze into the school expansion phenomenon from different levels of analysis. Several of our contributors have pioneered the world institution perspective, emphasizing that Western ideological and organizational forms have leaped across national boundaries over the past two centuries. Other authors focus on regional variation within a particular nation in the waxing and waning strength of different economic and social institutions. Our economists emphasize the "choices" of individuals, families, or governments, seen as volitional actors. The reader may feel a bit dizzy from this movement across levels of analysis. Yet looking into the school expansion phenomenon from different angles provides fresh views of institutional action—sources of authority, methods of influence, alleged and real effects of competing organizational initiatives.

WHAT INSTITUTIONS DRIVE SCHOOL EXPANSION?

We rarely think consciously about the organizations, ideologies, and economic forces that precede or drive the expansion of schooling. More important in the eyes of parents, politicians, and business elites is whether enrolling one's children in school or boosting financial support of education yields the intended effects. Yet when the effects of schooling are difficult to observe or are disappointing in magnitude, civic leaders and scholars ask why the robust school institution continues to grow beyond its apparent utility. In the 1960s, liberals and centrists in the United States criticized the overly optimistic assumption that expanding schools (enrollments and spending) would reduce poverty. This fueled criticism of functionalist views of schooling and bolstered the class-conflict perspective. Many Third World countries have seen little economic growth over the past three decades despite massive school expansion. Why does mass education grow if anticipated benefits are not felt?

Alternatively, the school may be seen as quite effective—but in undesirable ways. In France, conservative town council leaders opposed expansion of secular primary schools during much of the nineteenth century. They feared that mass schooling would feed rising social expectations held by the working class and rural peasants. Here the school was seen as potent in a politically threatening way. The tactical question then became how to manipulate institutional and economic levers to slow the growth of school enrollments (Gildea 1983). This is a contemporary issue in the United States, where the state lacks the resources and political will to keep pace with rising popular demand for child care and preschools. The problem of slowing demand also is common in developing countries where massive underemployment of secondary school graduates can destabilize a government. The conserving political question becomes how to "cool out" social demand without undercutting the state's popularity. Again, civic leaders and scholars search for a causal theory (even a little evidence) as to which specific institutions and economic forces are influencing popular demand for schooling.

Grand Explanations of School Expansion and Economic Growth

Western philosophers have never been shy about their claims regarding the effects of formal schooling, although they have differed dramatically over the character of ideal benefits and to which social classes they should flow. Aristotle advocated explicit socialization of elite children to advance their moral strength, cognitive proficiency, and the city-state's democratic rules. Post-Enlightenment thinking brought more varied claims about both the school's effects and the institutions (civic and private) that should play an antecedent role in expanding formal education. Diverse philosophers and social theorists—including Rousseau, Adam Smith, Dewey, and Durkheim—claimed individual and national benefits from schooling. Social theory in the early nineteenth century foresaw a greater role for the modernizing state in boosting schooling, emphasizing that secular schooling could serve the technical-economic interests of modest, yet rising capitalists (for Europe, see Prost 1968; for the United States, Tyack 1974).

Here we confine ourselves to a review of three basic theories: *technical-functional*, *class-conflict*, and *world institution* models. Our review provides a framework for sorting out the empirical work reported in the remaining section of this chapter. These theories have been reviewed elsewhere in greater detail (Craig 1981; Rubinson 1986). Proponents of each model have addressed, to a certain extent, the empirical weaknesses of previous models. Contributors to the present volume explore facets of each theory in more depth.

The *technical-functional model* argues that productive technology and economic organization become more complex as Western societies "modernize." Novel and differentiated skills required for transforming an economy can best be provided by a bureaucratic formal school. Traditional agencies of socialization are inadequate. An increasingly differentiated social structure requires rationalized efforts at integration. Local institutions—the family, church, and village authorities—are grounded in local particulars. Social and economic integration on a nationwide scale requires a universal, managed form of socialization (Durkheim 1956).

Human capital theory is an influential variant of technical functionalism. Here theorists assume that economic structures are moving toward higher levels of value-added industrial production, bringing gains in wages and real income. Formal schools presumably provide modern skills that provide entry to higher paying, more productive jobs; therefore, the individual youth or family rationally sees the economic incentive for entering and persisting through school. In turn, the spread of mass schooling and aggregate accumulation of human capital should boost nation-level productivity and income (Schultz 1961; Harbison and Myers 1964). Recent versions argue that schooling also contributes to farm productivity as better-schooled growers become open to, and more knowledgeable of, innovative practices (Lockheed, Jamison, and Lau 1980).

The *class-conflict model* argues that mass schooling represents one way in which society's dominant tribe or elites attempt to impose their economic structure or cultural commitments on less powerful groups. Schools can be seen as obtrusive agents of control in that they legitimate and impart skills, language, and attitudes that help fit youngsters into firms and market relations (Bowles and Gintis 1976; Carnoy and Levin 1985).

The school may operate more subtly, legitimating a seemingly fair meritocratic achievement structure. Universal schooling presumably gives all children, regardless of ascribed characteristics, an equal chance to achieve in school and later within the occupational structure. Rational and secular control of schooling is intended to eliminate particularistic advantages based on tribal affiliation or family background. Class-imposition theorists assume that central agencies, be they comprised of political or economic elites, wield considerable influence over the expansion, form, and content of schooling.

It is important to note that historical evidence from weak states (the United States) and strong postcolonial regimes (Mexico) shows that school enrollments often grew prior to strong state involvement in education. Even assuming that economic elites act in a concerted fashion, their collective influence on enrollment growth (linked to labor demand or rising income) appears to be substantial only when an economy's commercial or industrial sectors are expanding rapidly. Such challenges to general theory are documented in our subsequent discussion and in the chapters that follow.

One emerging variant of the class-conflict model sees both the state and school as contested terrain—fluid collections of actors and interests that vie for dominance over long stretches of time. Elite groups and high-status tribes, of course, tend to hold legitimacy and organized power within many snapshots across historical eras. But pluralistic groups and their ideologies often challenge elites' interests. Thus, the organizational form and content of government programs and schools (linked or decoupled from the state) may reflect a mosaic of, even institutionalized compromises among, contradictory ideals and conflicting material interests (Offe 1984; Hogan 1985; Fuller 1991).

A third viewpoint, *world institution theory*, argues against viewing modern society as vertically or laterally differentiated, characterized by centers of institutional power that are able to dominate or bargain with other groups. Here theorists argue that mass schooling represents a higher level of collective authority—really, a worldwide social movement that is linked more to ideals of Western progress than to any specific economic or political organization (Meyer 1977; Chapter 14, this volume). Mass schooling is viewed as one way in which the Western polity attempts to rationalize the individual's development, fitting the individual into the grand project of nation building. The school historically preceded the emergence of consolidated capital and the bureaucratic state; thus, it is best seen as a concomitant manifestation of Western ideology, not as a dependent agent of economic or state organization. The individual must be pulled away from local affiliations and "intermediate collectives"—village authority, the church, the family. Instead, loyalty to institutions of national scope—the state, the firm, and markets—is required if mass economic opportunity and meritocratic rules of status are to be successfully constructed by the polity and pursued by the individual (Nisbet 1980; Boli et al. 1985).

World institution theorists offer crossnational evidence suggesting that mass schooling expands everywhere, independent of a country's economic wealth, political structure, or ideological commitments (Meyer and Hannan 1979). This intellectual camp recently has advanced several hypotheses on how variation in nation-specific conditions may slow, albeit temporarily, this deterministic drive to expand schooling (Meyer et al. 1991).

BIG PROCESSES, LOCAL CONDITIONS:
BUILDING THEORY ABOUT SCHOOL EXPANSION

After reviewing the growing body of empirical evidence, you may feel quite overwhelmed, even confused. Sharp images and causal steps, so vividly outlined in the three grand theories, begin to blur. Indeed, the sound of universal theories shattering into jagged pieces, like a light bulb dropped on concrete, sends shivers down the spines of many Western scholars.

As with other young fields, these early models of school expansion and state formation manifest a universal and deterministic outlook. The study of institutions has yet to clearly specify the political and economic conditions under which basic organizations arise, transform, or die. Our approach to building theory avoids the conceptual abyss of historicism. This latter approach yields little knowledge useful to either scholars or activists who seek to understand the patterned ways in which institutional forces cause schools to grow, or when economic effects from school expansion are more likely to be observed. Yet political-economic conditions do vary over historical periods and among different societies. Three conceptual devices may help sort out how the three major processes operate under these different conditions.

1. The three general theories can be seen as simultaneous *oscillating processes*, each operating within a given society but with varying strength over long stretches of time. Take, for example, recent evidence from the United States showing that technological change did contribute to school expansion in the early twentieth century. These findings, of course, please the human capital caucus within the functionalist school. But by the mid-twentieth century this effect had disappeared, as mass schooling became fully legitimated, a nondiscretionary institution from the family's viewpoint. At this point neither variation in technology nor labor

demand significantly influenced enrollment rates. The school itself, and rising credentialism, displaced earlier influence from economic institutions.

2. Both *ideological and material forces* of institutions must be recognized. Past theories tend to look either at symbolic or technical-economic forces that may drive educational expansion. The interaction between moral commitments and material forces should be highlighted as we build a theory of school expansion. We often assume that the antecedents and subsequent effects of school expansion come as tight-knit bundles of signals and economic action. But the two may operate independently. States, for instance, often act aggressively to expand enrollments independently of labor demands.

3. We should *clearly distinguish between fluctuating actions of specific actors versus underlying, slower-changing institutional structures*. We tend to examine the influence over time of one antecedent force, such as the state or demand from families. We rarely look at the relative strength of different institutional actors and then seek deeper conditions that help explain the relative strength of competing actors (which may oscillate over historical periods). Intensified demand for white-collar workers, for instance, appears to consistently boost early school expansion. Here the state can manipulate early school enrollment levels through various fiscal measures, especially by building more classrooms and schools. But once the previously foreign school becomes institutionalized, fluctuation in state action may hold little effect.

Next we review the recent empirical literature on how different institutions may drive the spread of mass schooling. Our review is organized around the major institutional players that stimulate or depress school expansion: economic organizations, the state, and the school itself.

THE INFLUENCE OF ECONOMIC INSTITUTIONS

Early models of school expansion advanced by economists defined formal education as a consumption good. Families and governments hold a strong preference for schooling, given its presumed economic and social benefits. Provided that tastes and costs of schooling remain constant, expressed demand for mass schooling should rise as real income climbs, according to household economics. At the individual level, demand models continue to see family wealth, the public cost of schooling, and prices faced by parents as the principal forces driving enrollment growth (McMahon 1970).

Wealth, Investment, and Opportunity Costs

These early demand models portray wealth (or industrial growth) as inevitably associated with school expansion. Initial empirical work by economist Albert Fishlow (1966) challenged this general model. He found that nineteenth-century school enrollments across the United States were highest in rural agricultural states, not within urban industrial areas. Fishlow suggested that schooling was demanded by certain social groups in order to reinforce their position in the status structure, independent of absolute levels of family income and expected wage returns. More recent research uncovers higher enrollment rates for children from wealthier farming families (Soltow and Stevens 1981). Yet the structure of family economies, their match with school calendars, cultural (Protestant) commitments, and implications for the perceived opportunity cost of entering school all represent forces that Fishlow's work helped to introduce. Fishlow's findings also prompted work on how rising industrial labor demand often suppresses school enrollment as urban children go to work at a young age (detailed in our subsequent discussion).

Human capital theory, arising in the 1960s as an influential model, argues that enrollment rates should be higher within industrializing regions since (1) demand for skilled workers should be higher and (2) the family's rate of return for keeping children in school rises as the number of higher-paying industrial jobs increases (Becker 1964).

Fishlow's counterintuitive finding, however, helped to shift attention to the immediate opportunity costs associated with staying in school as perceived by families and children. Human capital functionalists continue to assume that a high level of rationality occurs within families, whereby the long-run benefits of school enrollment are weighed against opportunity costs. But if immediate earnings are relatively high for children working in factories or within the informal urban sector, then short-run opportunity costs appear to swamp this more complex choice process.

Present choice, however, is constrained by the immediate structure of economic opportunities as well as by expected social roles to be filled by sons and daughters. Recent evidence from the Third World, for instance, reveals that enrollment rates in the poorest farming areas are at times higher than those in more productive rural communities. Wealth and cash income must be considered within local conditions before one assumes that they are positively related to school expansion. Where the school institution competes head-on with labor demand or higher status organizations (like the family farm or factory), then higher income levels may be negatively associated with school enrollment (Harbison and Hanushek 1990). Similarly, where wage-labor demand is highly constrained for certain subgroups (for example, adolescent girls in Africa), their enrollments are found to be higher than for groups (males) that enjoy wider work opportunities (Duncan 1989). African parents engaged in trade at times report significant losses in cash income when their child stays in school rather than representing the household at the market. Salient opportunity costs of staying in school are embedded in local family economies as well as within the society's broader wage structure, a topic to which we will return.

This overarching set of opportunities may be reinforced or transformed by central elites as well as by local actors with ties to central organizations. For instance, as the state becomes stronger and more independent of economic elites, child labor legislation often is enacted that helps to legitimate the school, not the workplace, as the normative place for youth to be. When the range of roles children can assume in the modern polity is restricted, the opportunity cost of staying in school drops dramatically. Thus, state manipulation of the labor structure indirectly shapes the pace of school expansion.

In early periods of nation building, the state can either perpetuate or reshape feudal patterns of land ownership and caste-like social structures. The secular state commonly signals that wage labor found in the city holds higher status than limited opportunities found in the rural village. Enrollment effects of rising income will be observed only in this context, and for groups that experience expanding job or status opportunities. Until the 1960s, for example, the French state maintained two separate school systems, one for working-class and one for middle-class children. It is interesting that economic incentives and changing labor demand patterns helped boost growth in the middle-class schools, where the opportunity structure was more open for graduates, but had little effect on working-class enrollment growth (Garnier et al. 1989). In the Third World, expansion of the modern economic sector may hold little influence on school enrollment decisions by lower castes, be they defined by ethnicity, landlessness, or low cash income. Until the opportunity structure opens and low-status groups are allocated wage jobs and status, the family's "choice" of whether to keep their children in school remains highly constrained.[3]

Parents' perceived opportunity cost of keeping a child in school is, in large part, socially constructed. In subsistence household economies, the eldest child (especially the eldest daughter) often must perform many more domestic and farming tasks. The perceived opportunity cost for this child is greater than for later-born offspring (Hyde 1989). Research from western Europe also suggests that nineteenth-century acceleration of enrollment is attributable in part to declining fertility rates and parents' preference to raise fewer children (Craig 1981). This ideological shift toward quality of child rearing over quantity may occur independently of change in or the static character of the family economy.

Labor Demand

We have mentioned the negative school enrollment effect of early industrial growth and factory employment. Both functional and class-conflict theories assume a close positive correspondence between industrial modernization and school expansion. Yet evidence revealing this negative relationship is now available, in various periods and under diverse political-economic conditions, from the United States (Field 1976; Fuller 1983; Walters and O'Connell 1988), England (Graff 1987), and Mexico (Fuller et al. 1990). In the Third World, growth in unskilled trade and service jobs also constrains the spread of mass schooling. The casual visitor to any Third World city observes children filling many jobs as marketers, clerks, street vendors, street sweepers, and errand runners. Political and business leaders invest heavily in urban development; higher status and labels of modernity are assigned to urban institutions and social customs. But as rural dwellers flock to the city, they often find little work in the modern wage sector. Initial findings from the Third World suggest that high rates of urbanization—driven by the state's desire to look more modern—lead to employment structures that pull young children out of school (Fiala and Ramirez 1984). Here labor demands compete with the school for children's loyalty, and the state unwittingly exerts contradictory pressures by boosting urbanization and then expanding mass schooling to absorb rising numbers of children.

This recent evidence on the enrollment effects of labor demand points to three important institutional conditions. First, the influence of wage-labor demands may change dramatically over historical periods. The negative enrollment effect from early growth in industrial employment may diminish as wealth generated from value-added production trickles down to the working class. As demand for child labor declines, the state can normatively define the school as the legitimate location for children and youth.

Second, labor demand effects are conditioned by levels of literacy and school attainment, two manifestations of the school institution's own legitimacy. Labor demand patterns in parts of Europe and the United States, for instance, may have held less influence in shaping school expansion, since the school held an independent status and momentum prior to the (post–eighteenth century) modern period. In contrast, written literacy and formal schooling are not firmly established institutions in many Third World societies. Under these conditions, since access to a small wage sector is linked to school credentials, labor demand patterns more strongly influence school expansion. In later periods of nation building, the school becomes a more institutionalized organization. Once the school becomes the normal location for children and youth, labor structures, technological change, and even unemployment rates exert much less influence on school expansion (Rubinson and Ralph 1984).

Third, the effect of labor demand on school expansion is conditioned by the interrelated distribution of job skills demanded and aggregate levels of school attainment. During early or quickening periods of growth in the modern economic sector, youth with technical skills and high-status social customs (language, hip dress, a savvy capacity to work within bureaucracies, and a desire to achieve) are in great demand. Youth with more schooling fit these demands better than traditional village youth. This high rate of return declines as demand for skilled labor dwindles or as mean school attainment rises (Psacharopoulos 1989).

Schooling may retain its signaling value to employers, independent of whether job-skill requirements are actually increasing. Retail clerks now must have a college degree, since all job applicants have finished high school. Youth stay in school longer to retain their position in the long, competitive queue to enter the best jobs. Note that neither aggregate labor demand nor technical skill levels need to change. Expansion of schooling is driven simply by the competitive desire by some social classes and families to remain at, or move toward, the front of the line (Berg 1971; Collins 1979). Here the (lack of) fit between a static labor structure and expanding enrollments feeds successive generations of school expansion and heightened credentialism.

Family Economy

The conditions under which labor demand shapes school expansion also are defined by the structure of the family's economic activity. The character of work obviously differs, for example, between a subsistence farming family and an urban middle-class family. Of particular import is that the forms of opportunity facing children vary enormously. The family's economic structure within both settings represents a long-term condition that defines how variation in labor demand (within the specific context) operates on school enrollment growth. Walters and O'Connell (1988), for instance, show that rural enrollment rates (but not necessarily daily attendance) were higher than those in more urban manufacturing states. Within the farming family, children had idle time between planting and harvest seasons to attend school, whereas urban working-class kids had to choose between seeking full-time employment in the factory or going to school. Here the structure of work alternatives available to the family, and its compatibility with school attendance, lay down conditions that mediate any covariance between labor demand and school expansion.

In developing countries, both the family economy and gender continue to condition the process by which labor demand may shape school expansion. In subsistence farming economies, parents' demand for their sons' labor often slackens if a boy appears to have the potential to pass the primary school-leaving exam with marks high enough to enter secondary school. Boys are given the chance to find their way into the modern cash economy. In contrast, girls in some urban areas of Latin America persist longer in school than boys. Here it appears that boys leave school to earn money for the family, usually in the informal trade and service economy. Largely for cultural reasons, girls are expected to perform chores in the household, and this economic contribution is compatible with staying in school—but only on condition that discretionary time is available and schooling imposes no social opportunity cost. When demand for daughters' labor is high or socially constructed facets of opportunity costs of staying in school are high (lowering bride price, for instance), then female enrollments likely will be lower. Again we see labor structure effects, but they are conditioned by the salient opportunity structure as defined by types of available work, legitimate gender roles, and compatibilities with the school's calendar and organizational structure (Duncan 1989; Hyde 1989).

Technological Change

Central to functionalist modernization theory is the claim that industrial development involves change in the technical production of goods and services.

In turn, more highly skilled workers are required to support the use of more complex technology. Human capital improvements must match physical capital gains. Schooling allegedly provides these more complex skills. Families and youth demand more schooling as they observe that higher-paying jobs are allocated to "better educated" (presumably more highly skilled) workers. Technological change also has played a central role in class-conflict theory. Here technical change in the production process is linked to the interests of economic elites, including their desire to control workers and to lower dependence on human labor by substituting machines.

Over time technological change renders the labor of youth redundant, which puts pressure on the state to "warehouse" them in schools, divorced from the production process as well as adult roles. Credentialing theorists further argue that as labor scarcity in the modern economic sector recedes into history, school-allocated credentials become even more important signals of merit and status in the competitive struggle to find a good job. Technological change thus begins a sequential process whereby labor shortages lessen; the school becomes the legitimate place for children; and the school gains legitimacy as the agency for awarding skills and attributes that serve to allocate youth into a class-structured hierarchy of jobs (for different interpretations of this process, see Durkheim 1956; Carnoy and Levin 1985).

What evidence exists to support these competing claims regarding the force of technological change? Only a handful of empirical studies have been conducted. Variation in the mechanization of agriculture across local counties in the United States, for example, was found to be related to school enrollment during the early twentieth century. Both school attendance and formalization of the school organization (such as length of the school year) also were related to levels of farm ownership and land improvement (Guest and Tolnay 1985).

Looking over the period 1890–1970, Richard Rubinson and John Ralph (1984) found significant effects on school expansion from technological change in the United States. Rather than looking at variation across states or counties, they used national time-series data. Rubinson and Ralph emphasize a point highlighted throughout this book: Both the school institution and written literacy were spreading with significant momentum prior to the industrial revolution that moved outward from Britain. Rubinson and Ralph focus on how pre-industrial expansion of schooling blended with heightened capital accumulation and technological change to boost secondary enrollments. But after setting postprimary school expansion in motion (by the early twentieth century), later changes in technology and productivity did little to boost further enrollment growth. With the consent of its political patrons, and fed by intensifying credentialism, the school bullishly reproduced itself, independent of technical change.

Prior to the industrial period, schooling helped mediate the status competition process. Here relative position among ethnic, occupational, and regional groups could be legitimated by certain practices, including one's level of literacy, classical schooling, and religious (Protestant) convictions. But technical progress

and industrialization led to an increasing emphasis on gaining skills and knowledge associated with "modern forms" of production and work.[4]

THE STATE'S INFLUENCE

Over the past 150 years the state has become the major supplier of mass
schooling.[5] Since the French Revolution, debate over the modern state's appropriate level of authority has often involved the question of what form of political
agency should expand and control local schools. Most functionalist theorists now
see the central state as the provider of more schooling; they usually define the
school as a basic element of the polity's infrastructure. Class-conflict theorists
reply that mass schooling fails to serve a common good but instead inculcates
the language, customs, and skills embedded in the economic interests and social
ideals of the elite groups. By expanding mass schooling, the central state reinforces dominant class interests. World institution theorists recognize that the
school enables the state to incorporate various groups into a socially homogeneous
and economically integrated polity. Yet they ask the provocative question of
whether, in fact, the school is an organized instrument of the modern state.
Given its historically earlier origins, we might better see the school as an independent social movement displaying ideals and symbols that often are co-
opted by political elites to advance the secular state's own legitimacy.

Despite these theoretical developments, little empirical research has examined
the state's independent influence on school expansion. Much has been written
about the exceptionally "weak state" within the United States. Contrary to the
functionalists' normative hope that the central state pushes school expansion,
and class-conflict theorists' interpretation that it does so in a heavy-handed
manner, the North American state exerted little influence historically. Municipal
political elites certainly played a role in making the form of urban schools more
bureaucratic. But common school enrollment rates in the United States were
very high prior to the formation of central government education offices. A
highly institutionalized faith in secular schooling and its link to republican nation
building appear to better explain early enrollment growth, according to John W.
Meyer (1989) and fellow institutionalists.[6]

As research on school expansion moves beyond the infamously weak North
American state, a more differentiated view of political actors is beginning to
emerge. Next we will suggest how (1) forces emanating from political elites and
state agencies and (2) underlying conditions can be more clearly specified.

Relational Position of State and School

One could argue that the North American state's limited influence on school
expansion had nothing to do with the internal political economy of the United
States. The young republic simply borrowed England's highly institutionalized
faith in secular schooling and two ideological structures that reproduced the

school's popular legitimacy: Protestant churches, which placed a moral premium on literacy, and a secular republican distaste for centralized government. Or take the case of England. Here David Mitch (see Chapter 2) demonstrates that state policy did have a significant impact on school expansion, primarily by boosting subsidies for local schools and reducing pupil fees. Yet the magnitude of this effect was small compared to the actual rise in enrollment through the nineteenth century. Broad-based demand for schooling already had gained momentum well before the advent of formal government policies. This cultural movement then traveled within British church and secular institutions across more than one ocean to colonized societies.

Similarly, in France school enrollments grew to one-third of the primary school-age cohort prior to formation of an effective central state. Here middle-class demand for schooling blended with the Church's relentless effort to control child socialization and the local political structure. The competitive process among the three estates, and eventually a coalescing state organization—not the dominant force of any one institution—spurred growth in school supply (Archer 1979; Gildea 1983).

Newly independent African states provide a sharp contrast in the school's historical level of credibility relative to the central state. Over the past three decades, nationalist leaders have taken over colonial administrations that usually operated limited, segregated school systems. Some indigenous peoples living in rural villages have experienced limited exposure to formal schooling, usually through Western missionaries. Under these conditions state formation precedes rapid expansion of mass schooling. The fragile nationalist state becomes the institution driving the growth of schooling (Fuller 1991).

Rapid expansion of secular schooling serves two important agendas for fragile African states. First, building schools clearly signals nation building, "progress," and a swift opening of the opportunity structure. This modern school, previously open only to colonial elites and certain blacks, is now extended to all. Individual effort and mobility become more defined by one's effort and achievement, not by ascribed characteristics. Second, by building schools political elites demonstrate their authority and look just like legitimate actors within other modern states. Nationalist leaders promise change, enfranchisement, and mass opportunity. To advance their credibility they must deliver something, and the symbolic value of building more schools buys considerable political capital. Opening the school to mass participation, just like opening the old colonial golf club, sends out signals that are consonant with Western nation-building ideals.

The state's level of authority relative to economic actors also sets an important condition that mediates political actors' influence on school expansion. Most states hold sufficient legitimacy to create jobs in the public sector, or to devise rules of entry to private sector jobs. This political construction of labor demand, in turn, influences popular demand for schooling. Even weak states ally themselves with the school to define requisite credentials for entry into a variety of occupations and professions (Meyer 1977). Third World states often hold even greater authority, including the power to construct credential requirements in parastatal firms, which, along with government jobs, may comprise a majority of all wage sector jobs. Schooling becomes economically functional, but within a labor structure largely created by political and educational elites.

The State's Material and Ideological Force

While the central government in the United States was not historically influential in boosting enrollment growth, the influence of state government spending has been observed. Rural states with lower fiscal resources overall experienced higher growth in common schools. But over the late nineteenth and early twentieth centuries, state governments that spent more on public schooling per capita had higher secondary school enrollments, after the effects of prior common school enrollments and state-level indicators of wealth are removed (Fuller 1983; Walters and O'Connell 1988). Here competition among state governments may have conditioned the effects of state expenditures.

State action is not limited only to spending. Policies enacted by civic elites signal alleged benefits of school attendance: economic opportunity, individual development, membership in the modern project of nation building. Few researchers have disentangled fiscal from ideological action of the state. Recent historical findings from France do suggest that legislation and ideological signals manifest in regulation can hold real consequences, independent of actual spending levels. Expenditures aimed at raising the school's apparent quality and credibility also may influence growth. Enrollments increased in France as the central state and local councils boosted the quality of schooling by reducing the number of pupils per teacher (Garnier et al. 1989). A contemporary study from the Philippines and Malaysia found that school construction and policy action by central states sharply influenced enrollment rates, after the effects of family income are removed. This effect operated mainly through new school construction, thereby reducing the distance rural children traveled to school. In Malaysia, but not in the Philippines, these state actions also lessened the prior inequity as to which families benefitted from increased school participation (King and Lillard 1987).

Plural Interests within the State?

Advocates for the liberal, capitalist state argue that political elites push for mass schooling to enfranchise diverse groups into national organizations and the modern economy. Historically, of course, all Western states have not been so classically liberal. The French state maintained two school systems well into the 1960s, one for the working class and one for the middle class. By carefully rationing admissions into middle-class schools, the government limited opportunities for youth to enter high-status civil service or private sector jobs (Garnier et al. 1989). When the central state is not dominated by a particular group or holds little authority, competition among classes may spur enrollment growth

(Archer 1979). Cultural conflict, even following modern state formation, may spur school expansion as an explicit political strategy for encouraging assimilation and civic stability. For instance, levels of immigration to the United States help to explain enrollment growth over the twentieth century, controlling on a variety of economic factors (Ralph and Rubinson 1980).

Conflict within the state may contribute to enrollment growth within elite secondary schools. Even though "local states" in Britain have played a more influential role than the central regime, leftist voting in national elections has been historically associated with expansion of the (eroding) elite secondary school system (Hage and Garnier 1990). Urbanization and growth in trade and service jobs have driven expansion of mass secondary schools. But leftist strength has contributed to the convergence of these two systems.

The State's Organizational Integrity and Penetration

In the Third World, colonial administrations held little interest in fully enfranchising all groups into the modern polity. The labor of indigenous people and low-status immigrants was certainly in demand, especially in the mines, on the haciendas, or for building rail lines and government buildings. Postcolonial societies continue to experience one important legacy of imperial administration: a modern elite defined by their government or corporate employment, surrounded by a largely disenfranchised peasant class. Third World states thus attempt to build institutions that attempt to allow vertical mobility and lateral integration, pulling in low-status groups from rural hinterlands and urban shantytowns. But does the central state hold sufficient administrative capacity and fiscal resources to penetrate peripheral areas and social classes? And does this outward attempt to incorporate pluralistic groups actually lead to expansion of mass schooling?

Work on postrevolutionary Mexico looks specifically at this issue of state penetration. Following its revolutionary civil war in 1918, the central state was somewhat successful in rapidly boosting primary school enrollment among rural peasants and the fledgling working class. This was accomplished through direct investment in modest government services: one-room schoolhouses, post offices, train stops, and rural community organizations (led by government workers who were often based in the village school). Despite a very modest industrial base and incremental commercial growth, the central state represented literacy as a sign of modern progress, literally promising salvation through rural schooling. The structure of material opportunity, in fact, improved very slowly for people in the rural hinterlands and for migrants moving into towns. Income per capita leveled off in the period 1920–1940 as an increasingly socialist state became alienated from a world economy that moved into depression. Yet the symbolic appearance of opportunity, via the mass school movement, spread across rural and urban areas. Whether these schools were of sufficient quality to boost literacy substantially remains an open question. Change in Mexico's labor structure and economic growth in commercial centers have been empirically observed, and they stemmed in part from state penetration (Fuller et al. 1986). The most remarkable aspect of this story is the Mexican state's capacity to penetrate various groups and successfully raise their expectations and school enrollment (for review, see Fuller et al. 1990).

Many contemporary Third World states simply lack the administrative or fiscal capacity to build more schools. And the rhetorical association of schooling with economic opportunity, advanced by political leaders, may be shattered by material realities. After fifteen years of erratic world economic conditions, many contemporary African states are undergoing severe economic downturns: declining prices for raw commodity exports, rapidly declining currency values, mounting foreign debts, and a drying up of capital and investment. Over time, these economic factors narrow the opportunity structure, limit upward mobility, and constrain the state's capacity to incorporate rural tribes and urban peasants. Popular preference for schooling may persist. But eroding expectations regarding the benefits of staying in school threaten the stability of already fragile states. In Chapter 9, Walter McMahon looks at the economic causes of falling enrollment rates.

The question of when the state effectively "penetrates" local institutions assumes that local elites and households are resisting pressure from the political center. Yet the process of (secular) state formation may occur locally. In the United States, for example, local elites varied enormously among regions in the extent to which common schools were built and staffed, even into the twentieth century. Class, labor, and ethnic interests—and their consonance with expanding school supply—differed sharply among the Northeast, the Midwest, and the South (James and Walters 1990). The rise of liberal secular interests locally outpaced political rationalization centrally during much of the nineteenth century in France, with corresponding local pressure for mass schooling. And school supply often was spurred in Third World settings by relentless missionary activity. Here colonial administrations sanctioned expansion of school supply, leaving subsequent nationalist governments the easier task of simply incorporating well-established school networks (Fuller 1991).

The initial studies reviewed here suggest that the state's fiscal and ideological activities naturally play a role in increasing the supply of schooling. But the exogenous forces of rising real income, the changing structure of labor demand, or the school institution's own prior momentum may be more influential under certain conditions. We must better understand the state's fiscal and organizational capacities, its ideological voices and signals, and the complex class interests from which these actions spring. Once we sort out these elements of action by state elites, we should be better able to see how and with what force the state independently drives the expansion of mass schooling.

THE SCHOOL INSTITUTION'S INFLUENCE

In Europe, since the late eighteenth century, the school institution has demonstrated a bullish momentum of its own. Time-series models beginning as early as the mid–1800s, for instance, reveal that prior enrollment levels predict subsequent school expansion more strongly than the appearance of novel forces, such as rapid commercial growth, industrial job demand, and the modern state's rise and penetration into the hinterlands. The ideological faith and economic factors that sparked early growth in elite secular schooling appear to intensify as the school becomes a mass institution (Archer 1979; Meyer and Hannan 1979).

Three facets of the school itself may quicken the pace of enrollment growth. First, the *quality of education* may spur families to express demand for more schooling. Historically in the United States, private school enrollments have been higher where state governments spend less per pupil (a rough indicator of school quality). The direction of causality is difficult to sort out. But the competitiveness of public mass schooling is undoubtedly influenced by its quality. In the Third World, an active private school sector for the children of urban elites draws them out of government schools. In other settings, self-help village schools have lower-quality teachers and fewer instructional materials compared to better-funded government schools. In both cases, quality differences are clear in the eyes of parents, and effects on enrollment levels in ''government schools'' are often significant (Jimenez and Lockheed 1991).

School quality also may be defined in terms of the character or content of schooling. Many urban parents in North America often prefer the tight cohesion and shared mission found in Catholic schools, compared to the looser discipline commonly perceived within public schools. In the Third World, the structure of schooling may be critical. For instance, whether school breaks occur during planting and harvesting seasons likely plays a role in school attendance patterns. Many schools start early in the morning and end by noon, allowing children to work in the afternoons. Unfortunately, little empirical work has been done on how such structural aspects of the school encourage greater participation (Lockheed et al. 1991).

Second, the *stratified structure of schooling* certainly helps shape enrollment levels and the distribution of school participation across different types of families. This stratification of separate school systems (in the case of France, for example) is often legitimated by the larger political structure. As we have mentioned, the French state tightly controlled the number of seats available in the middle-class secondary school system. This became untenable in the 1960s. The government created comprehensive high schools that were less restricted on the basis of class, significantly boosting enrollment rates (Prost 1968).

In developing countries, urban schools often receive the bulk of government support, and rural schools continue to exhibit low quality. This may depress rural enrollments, especially where domestic demand for child labor is high and where kids must walk many kilometers to the nearest village school. Yet lower school quality may not cut into urban enrollments, or among particular ethnic groups, where demand for education has been strong historically.

Third, the *uniformity or plural character of school organization* may influence the pace of enrollment expansion. Margaret Archer's (1979) work suggests that where ideological conflict was great in nineteenth-century Europe, mostly between church and secular elites, this competition spurred enrollment growth. The surface debate was over who should control and which ideals should define the context of local schools. But local political battles implicitly helped to legitimate socialization within the formal school. In Chapter 12 of this volume, which examines the United States, David Baker argues that the growing presence of Catholic schools in the nineteenth century attracted many working-class children who would not otherwise have entered Protestant-controlled common schools. And contemporary government efforts to incorporate and formalize the colorful array of child care providers have run into stiff resistance from advocates who view local organizational diversity as a positive force in raising daycare enrollments. In each case, the diversity of schooling forms may be linked to higher enrollments. The school's capacity to fit local ideologies or political organizations is linked to greater institutional legitimacy and enrollment demand (for postrevolutionary France, see Gildea 1983; for postrevolutionary Mexico, see Fuller et al. 1986).

SUMMARY: THE POLITICAL CONSTRUCTION OF SCHOOLING?

Let's return to two basic issues posed early in this chapter: Can state actors boost enrollments by raising the supply of, or local demand for, education? How influential is political action relative to the strength of economic forces and action by other institutions? In summarizing major empirical findings, we should keep in mind that the state's influence on school expansion is enhanced or constrained by underlying political-economic conditions. And the state's role—as variously portrayed by the three grand theories—may be observed with oscillating salience as conditions change over long stretches of time. We must keep our eye on both (1) covariation between state action and school expansion and (2) how long-term political-economic conditions mediate this relationship.

Empirical evidence to date suggests that state actions—material and symbolic—can influence school enrollments under certain conditions. To review, the forms of effective action may include the political crafting of labor structures; opening the opportunity structure and signaling that more schooling will yield economic returns; directly raising the supply of schools and pupil places; linking schooling to broader Western ideals regarding enfranchisement, national integration, and individual development; and lowering perceived opportunity costs by restricting child labor and legitimating the school as the normative location for socialization.

These actions can be effectively mounted only by "strong states." And underlying political-economic conditions define the likelihood that strong actions can be legitimately pursued and that they will hold actual effects on school expansion. After Mexico's civil war, for instance, the central state emerged as the dominant institutional actor. This was conditioned by an environment in which economic elites had lost authority, incorporation of rural peasants became a principal political objective, and secular institutions gained enormous credibility vis-à-vis traditional church and village organizations. Yet conditions would shift again in the postwar period, as the credibility of firms and market ideals rebounded, the opportunity structure widened, levels of social integration rose, and institutionalization of the secular primary school occurred in most rural areas. At this point, the Mexican state's independent influence on the further expansion of schooling began to erode.

Political-economic conditions can evolve in very different ways. In nineteenth-century France, as we discussed, the village school had gained substantial legitimacy, boosted by earlier advocacy of the *petite école* by French revolutionaries. State formation, however, was so slow that when Parisian politicos finally held sufficient legitimacy to act, they simply pursued ways of incorporating an already large network of schools filled with pupils. Early local demands by commercial employers, and contention between church and republican activists, largely explained expansion of primary school growth. These local factors could only be efficacious under the following conditions: a fragile, contested central state; low capital accumulation and industrialization; a persistently low level of economic integration; and relentless strength of the Church and its traditional allies. Only when these contextual constraints on the state lessened would construction of schooling by the central political actors be possible.

The three grand processes of school expansion—technical-functional, class-conflict, and world institution—all suggest a role for the state. Yet here the state's actions and force depend on technical change in the economy, the credibility of elite interests, or an implicit drive to conform to worldwide expectations of how the modern state is supposed to act.

Finally, there is another way to visualize why political action rises with greater visibility to efficaciously construct mass schooling. These three big processes, oscillating in strength over time, act to variably enhance or constrain political actors' capacity to operate with some degree of independence. Beyond this threshold the state organization acts through various methods, and with varying proficiency, to affect the growth of schooling. When these conditions allow or encourage state-crafters to move out on their own—independent of demands exerted by economic actors and other social institutions—the political construction of education can proceed. These pressures from employers, families, churches, and civic groups, however, can sweep back in with a vengeance. Then the state must react to, and express, the social ideals and economic interests originating from outside the political apparatus per se. School construction continues. But state actors are no longer the master craftsmen.

NOTES

This chapter has benefited greatly from discussions with the School Expansion Workgroup, a wandering troupe that has met annually since 1985. We received early support from the World Bank and the National Science Foundation. Bruce Fuller's collaboration with Maurice Garnier, Jerry Hage, and Max Sawicky has greatly informed our view of the interaction between state, school, and economy.

1. The modern institutions of state and secular school were brought together, in part, by their mutual interest in eroding traditional forms of ascriptive status and caste-like restrictions on economic mobility while protecting the cultural commitments and interests of certain classes or social groups (Durkheim 1956; Parsons 1951; Nisbet 1980).

2. During planting and harvest seasons, rural children's school attendance in the Third World may drop 20 to 30 percent. Similarly, Walters and O'Connell (1988) found that at the turn of the twentieth century, urban enrollment rates in U.S. cities were lower than rural rates, but attendance was more consistent in urban schools.

3. National levels of wealth have had little influence on school expansion if we look across nations in the postwar period. The distribution of enrollment and school attainment within countries does depend upon the family's social class, resources, and perceived opportunity costs. And across nations, vast differences in the quality of schooling exist between countries in the West and the Third World. But aggregate enrollment rates, particularly in primary schools, vary independently of national wealth (Meyer and Hannan 1979; Meyer et al. 1991). This important finding supports the contention of world institution theorists that schooling is a broad social movement, repeatedly taken up by central states as they eagerly try to build a modern-looking polity. It certainly raises the following question: Under what conditions does wealth give way to the state's institutional (material and ideological) force in shaping the taste for mass schooling?

4. Thus, Rubinson and Ralph found that as the primary school and then the secondary school were becoming mass organizations, technological change did influence the rate of school expansion. They point out, however, that this effect can be interpreted in two ways. As more technical skills are demanded of all classes, not just of elites, families figure this out and children stay in school longer. "Skills" that are demanded may include basic cognitive proficiencies, social behaviors, or manual competencies. The point is simply that skill changes associated with technological improvements appear to bolster the shift of schooling from an elite to a mass institution.

The second and not incompatible interpretation is that the appearance of acquiring "skills" becomes an important process for retaining an advantage in the status competition game. Whereas this process of class conflict was earlier arbitrated by particularistic religious or cultural affiliations and related forms of achievement, the rise of industrial production calls for signals of merit that are more closely associated with "modern skills" and secular social rules. These modern symbols of merit are then awarded by the modern-looking school. Children may, in part, learn skills that are materially useful in technology-intensive workplaces. But more important is the fact that children simply become members of the school, given the institution's symbolic fit with modern forms of achievement and virtue.

5. We define the state to include those political actors and government organizations that engage in economic and ideological action under some form of civil authority. Images of the modern state emphasize actors within the central government. Yet we see municipal elites and local government agencies as important members of the state institution.

6. This claim must be amended, however, by more recent research showing how in (nonindustrial) midwestern communities the class structure mirrored variation in school

attendance. Institutionalized faith in this social movement called schooling was not evenly distributed across social classes in rural areas. The state apparatus was not necessarily mature enough to manifest and reinforce these class advantages. Indeed, the lack of state strength in the education arena may have served to blur class lines (Rubinson 1986).

Rising Demand for Schooling: Institutional Origins and Political Accommodations

The Rise of Popular Literacy in Europe

David Mitch

Before 1500 only a small minority of Europeans could read and write, perhaps no more than 10 percent of the adult population.[1] At the time of the Norman conquest of England, for instance, some members of the nobility were illiterate, as were many judges in thirteenth-century Venice (Cipolla 1969; Wormald 1977).[2] Even such oases of civilization as Renaissance Florence and Venice had adult literacy rates of less than 40 percent (Graff 1987). By 1900, however, northwest Europe was on the verge of universal adult literacy and both southern and eastern Europe were making rapid progress in lowering the proportion of adults unable to read or write. Table 2.1 summarizes evidence on the timing of this transition. Its recency and speed are striking.

The dramatic transition from largely illiterate societies to widespread mass literacy in Europe roughly corresponded to the early rise of the nation-state. Furthermore, in twentieth-century Europe, provision of elementary schooling and instruction in reading and writing was administered by the state and major religious denominations. It is not surprising that historians have commonly attributed the rise of mass education to the formation and growing strength of the state (Cubberly 1920; Blaug 1970).

However, large segments of society had become literate throughout much of Europe by 1800, well before centralized efforts by church or state were undertaken to promote mass primary schooling and literacy. In part this resulted from local endeavors by landowners, merchants, and other elites to support schools through endowments and ongoing subscriptions (Simon 1968; Maynes 1985). Yet even more humble community members pooled support for basic instruction. In Baden in the eighteenth century, for example, teachers were compensated by

Table 2.1
Literacy Rates in European Countries at Various Dates

| | Percent Literate | | | | | | |
	1500	1600	1700	1750	1800	1850	1900
England							
Men	10	25	40	60	65	67	97
Women	2	8	25	35	40	50	97
Scotland							
Men						89	98
Women						77	97
Ireland						47	86
France							
Grooms			29	47		69	95
Brides			14	27		54	94
Moklinta,Sweden		21		89			
Iceland				50	90		
Amsterdam							
Grooms			70		85		
Brides			44		64		

	1870	1880	1890	1900	1910	1920	1930	1940	1950
Austrian Empire									
Males				79					
Females				75					
Russia				21		40			
Italy									
Males	38				67				
Females	24				58				
Spain									
Males		51			59		75		
Females		27			41		60		
Portugal			24	26	30	34	38	51	60
Greece									
Males							77		
Females							43		

Note: For a number of countries only approximate dates are indicated for the literacy estimates. For the exact years involved see the sources cited below.

Sources: England, estimates based on court depositions and marriage register signature rates (Cressy 1980); Scotland, nineteenth-century estimates based on marriage register signature rates; Ireland, based on census surveys of those over the age of five who could read and write; France, based on marriage register signature rates; Moklinta, Sweden, based on examination of reading ability taken in 1705; Iceland, based on examination of reading ability for those over the age of twelve; Amsterdam, based on marriage register signature rates (Graff 1987); Austrian Empire, based on adult population who could read or write (Cipolla, 1969); Russia, based on those over the age of ten who could read or write (Brooks 1985); Italy, based on those over the age of six who could read or write (Graff 1987); Spain, based on those who could read or write (Cipolla 1969; Gallagher 1979); Portugal, based on those over the age of seven who could read or write (Monica 1978); Greece, Atonakaki 1955.

the so-called *Wandertisch*, whereby parents of pupils would alternate in providing meals or small payments for witnessing baptisms, marriages, and funerals (Maynes 1979). Such local "public" effort was undertaken for motives other than personal gain or the well-being of immediate relatives.[3]

In contrast, the early rise of popular literacy may be explained by rising private demand for literacy—demand by individuals for their own education or that of their children. The growth of private demand was reinforced by motives ranging from religious piety to commercial gain. These two alternative explanations, voluntary public educational efforts and private demand, are not mutually exclusive. Their relative importance, of course, was subject to considerable variation across time and space given the diversity of political-economic conditions across Europe.

In short, I address the questions of why literacy rose at such a steady pace and whether state provision of formal schooling institutions was really an antecedent factor contributing to the spread of mass literacy. Could all of Europe have been taught to read and write solely through private for-profit instruction? Would popular demand for reading and writing have risen sufficiently to lead most Europeans to acquire literacy by the mid-twentieth century in the absence of government intervention? How effective were religious and philanthropic groups in promoting literacy over and above what the private market in literacy instruction would have accomplished? This chapter surveys the educational history of Europe since 1500 in order to address these questions.

PRIVATE SUPPLY OF LITERACY INSTRUCTION

Centralized state provision of schooling in Europe dates largely from the nineteenth century, by which time literacy was already widespread. Therefore, effective alternatives to state provision must have existed before 1800. Private instruction may have been one efficacious method. Could the attainment of near universal adult literacy by many European nations after 1800 have been accomplished solely by private means of instruction?

In assessing private provision, it is important to note that before 1800 literacy was frequently acquired either with no formal schooling or with spells of formal schooling interspersed with less formal tutoring. Consider the case of Thomas Tryon, born in 1634 in Oxfordshire, England, the son of a village tiler and plasterer. Tryon was sent to school at the age of five but was quickly taken out of school and put to work. Tryon provided the following account of how he learned to read and write:

All this while, tho' now about Thirteen Years Old, I could not Read; then thinking of the vast usefulness of Reading, I bought me a Primer, and got now one, then another, to teach me to Spell, and so learn'd to Read imperfectly, my Teachers themselves not being ready Readers: But in a little time having learn't to Read competently well, I was desirous to learn to Write, but was at a great loss for Master, none of my Fellow-Shepherds being able to teach me. At last, I bethought myself of a lame young Man who taught some poor People's Children to Read and Write and having by this time got two Sheep of my own, I applied myself to him, and agreed with him to give him one of my Sheep to teach me to make the Letters, and Joyn them together (Spufford 1979, p. 416)

Tryon was an unusually motivated learner. But there are indications that such informal instruction was widespread in Europe through the nineteenth century. For example, a survey of forty small villages in the Vorenezh district of Russia at the turn of the twentieth century found that among peasants surveyed who could read, only 6 percent had learned to read in school (Eklof 1986). Other studies reveal the importance of informal instruction in nineteenth-century France and England as well (Furet and Ozouf [1977] 1982; Mitch 1982). The widespread use of informal instruction to acquire literacy suggests the importance of popular demand for literacy and individual persistence in seeking literacy instruction. This is evident in autobiographies of those who pursued informal methods of instruction (e.g., Laqueur 1976).

Eighteenth-century Sweden in particular was able to make successful use of informal instruction. The national church, with the prompting of the king, undertook a campaign to promote instruction in reading and basic mastery of the catechism. The campaign was based on home instruction and was reinforced by examinations given by the clergy. This campaign increased the proportion able to pass basic reading examinations from 20 percent in the seventeenth century to over 80 percent by the early nineteenth century (Johansson 1981).[4] The Swedish case suggests that when public agencies were willing to put enough energy and resources into literacy campaigns, they could produce marked increases in popular literacy. And this could be done without providing formal schools.

Indeed, formal schooling can be a barrier to directly reaching the masses; after all, one has to first get people into schools. This point has resurfaced in twentieth-century literacy campaigns in Cuba, Nicaragua, Tanzania, and Vietnam. In these campaigns the direct personal contact of field workers, reinforced by threats of heavy fines and other forms of coercion, make it possible to spread literacy to large segments of these countries' populations in a matter of months (Leiner 1987).

However, the disadvantage of relying on nonschool forms of literacy instruction is that skills acquired are commonly based on rote memory and often are forgotten or remain undeveloped when not reinforced by daily demands for literacy (Arnove and Graff 1987). Informal instruction also seems especially difficult in communities with initially low literacy levels, and where few tutors are available to convey literacy. Nonschool methods are likely to be ineffective in reaching groups with little motivation to acquire literacy, thus lacking in the persistence that informal methods would seem to require. The general tendency to shift from informal methods to formal schooling in the teaching of literacy during the late eighteenth century may have reflected the organizational superiority of formal schooling as a method of instruction (Blaug 1970; Mitch 1982).

But this shift also reflected efforts of various interest groups to link indoctrination in assorted moral, political, and religious ideologies with instruction in literacy. Could the problems of informal instruction be avoided through the private provision of formal schooling?

Private Supply of Formal Schooling

A common concern of advocates of state intervention was that many areas had no schools whatever. The evidence is clear that during the eighteenth and nineteenth centuries variation in the availability of schooling was quite wide across Europe (Maynes 1985).

This variation in the presence of schools did not necessarily reflect variation in the presence of private teachers willing to supply their services to select families. If a village had no school, this may have been because few or no parents demanded school instruction. Nevertheless, at least some European communities had no schools because of the basic supply problems created by low population density. Those living in small communities and areas of scattered settlement frequently did not have enough students to cover the cost of a full-time teacher (Vovelle 1975). As Weber's estimates of urbanization indicate, in 1800 almost 90 percent of all Europeans lived in settlements with fewer than 5,000 people; in 1850 more than half lived in settlements with fewer than 2,000 people (Weber [1899] 1963). These estimates suggest that low population density may have precluded establishing resident schools throughout much of Europe.

Viable alternatives to a resident school do seem to have been available in some communities with low population density. Informal instruction through parents and neighbors was the most obvious solution, although it also would have required some initial foothold of literacy to make progress. Such methods were clearly viable in Sweden because of religious pressures and in Iceland because of popular enthusiasm for literature (Graff 1987). Traveling teachers also provided instruction in rural communities with low population density (Furet and Ozouf [1977] 1982). Easing the constraint of low density would not have required universal use of state-administered schools. Population growth and urbanization would have improved the ability of the private sector as well as the public sector to provide instruction to increasingly larger proportions of children. And centralized bureaucracies had difficulties in providing instruction to isolated rural areas. Private teachers may have been more effective in supplying instruction to these areas because they had more flexibility than centralized state or church organizations (Sutherland 1971).

The Cost of Instruction

Would student fees in schools financed solely by charges to parents have been so high as to preclude widespread popular attendance? Fees in European private schools varied widely depending on teacher qualifications, facilities, materials, and the type of clientele. However, for a fee that most working-class families could afford, instruction by experienced teachers in buildings devoted primarily to education was available throughout much of Europe between 1500 and 1850 (Briggs 1978; Mitch 1982).

Would private school fees have risen beyond what working-class families would have been willing to pay if public schools had been unavailable? To what extent would the upward pressure on fees have been exacerbated by the markedly rising proportion of working-class children attending school, a rise that in fact was accommodated largely through the provision of more state-supported schools? Expenditures and fees per pupil in *public* schools did rise over time (Tropp 1950). Yet private schools would not have been constrained by the bureaucratic standards imposed on public schools for the recruitment of teachers and thus were less subject to cost increases over time. England was able to achieve marked increases in literacy and school attendance even though the percentage of its labor force in teaching rose from only 0.9 percent in 1841 to 1.7 percent in 1891 (Armstrong 1972). A marked increase in the number of private teachers could have bid up their supply price. But the wide range of previous occupations and activities reported by private school teachers would suggest an abundant pool of possible entrants (*British Parliamentary Papers* 1861, vol. 21).

The contribution of public schools to keeping student fees below the level that would have prevailed with purely private provision of schools should not be dismissed. Although fees in private schools were not necessarily beyond the reach of working-class budgets, the level of fees does appear to have influenced school attendance for certain social groups (Maynes 1979; Gildea 1983).

Did Private Schools Impart Literacy?

"[T]he refuse of other callings, discarded servants or ruined tradesmen . . . men . . . whom no gentleman would entrust the key to his cellar and no tradesman would send of a message." This is how Thomas Macaulay characterized school-teachers in early Victorian England (*Hansard's Parliamentary Debates* 1847, pp. 1016–17). Other observers of early European education shared his disdain for working-class private schools. Teachers allegedly lacked any training; on occasion teachers were unable to write themselves, let alone teach basic literacy. Classes were frequently conducted at home in extremely cramped quarters; instructional materials were scarce and of poor quality.

Private schools were frequently said to exist primarily for child minding rather than with any intent of offering instruction (Hurt 1971). This emphasis may have reflected what parents demanded rather than an inherent defect in private school supply (Gardner 1984). The basic force ensuring that parents seeking effective instruction found it was competition. Schools and teachers that did not provide what parents wanted were driven out of business by those that did satisfy parental demands (*British Parliamentary Papers* 1861; Eklof 1986).

The most common objection of civic leaders to private schools was that such schools were not socializing children in accord with political, moral, or religious values that reformers thought important. Poor instruction in literacy was much less frequently mentioned as grounds for reform. In Baden the official 1834 school code stated that "Children are to be impressed with the duty of loyalty to the Grand Duke, love of fatherland, obedience to laws and ordinances, attentiveness to religious and secular authorities . . . and to their duties toward their fellow citizens." (Maynes 1985, p. 50). In nineteenth-century Russia, peasant-sponsored schools were labeled by government officials as "wild schools." A Russian finance minister asserted that "the fact that literacy was growing more rapidly than the school system represented a major political danger" (Eklof 1986).

In sum, private elementary schools in most areas of nineteenth-century Europe were providing instruction in accord with parental demands at a price within reach of most working-class households. Low population density did restrict the private supply of schooling in some regions, particularly in the Mediterranean, but low popular demand may have been the fundamental problem (Briggs 1978). The evidence reviewed here suggests that Europe's steps toward universal literacy during the nineteenth century could have been largely accommodated by private means of instruction.

DOES GROWTH IN POPULAR DEMAND EXPLAIN THE RISE OF LITERACY?

A private market for schooling might have effectively provided instruction to most Europeans. But would European parents or young adults have demanded such basic teaching? What forces might have led the European masses to acquire literacy by 1900 without any push from elite segments of society? Three forces are commonly cited: (1) the impact of industrialization and commercial development on the demand for a literate work force, (2) rising living standards, and (3) the increasing importance of literacy in popular culture.

Was Demand for Literate Workers Growing?

The European labor force, since the mid-eighteenth century, has shifted from agriculture to manufacturing, commercial, and service activities. If this shift increased demand for literate workers, incentives to learn to read and write should have risen. However, the record is mixed on trends in the demand for literate workers in European economies over the last three centuries. Several studies of industrializing areas in Europe reveal that literacy rates declined as the manufacturing sector expanded (Sanderson 1972; Graff 1987). But the impact of the much earlier commercial revolution was surely positive.

Increased commercial activity and production for markets between 1500 and 1800 provided important incentives for acquiring literacy among merchants, tradesmen, and farmers. As early as the thirteenth and fourteenth centuries, the rise of long-distance trade with the Orient required considerable correspondence by Italian merchants (Hyde 1979). From the sixteenth through the eighteenth century, the use of written records and correspondence also became more common among smaller merchants, craftsmen, and farmers. Simultaneously, literacy rates rose substantially among these groups (Smith [1776] 1976, vol. 1; Houston 1985). Growth of the putting-out system during the early modern period may have further encouraged written accounts. Merchants using this system had incentives to keep accounts to protect against embezzlement of raw materials and to determine what to pay for completed production. And workers dealing with such merchants would have a strong incentive to keep careful records (Grafteaux [1975] 1985).

Despite any adverse literacy effects of early industrialization on literacy rates, by the second half of the nineteenth century the composition of the European economy was again shifting toward work that demanded the basic capacity to read and write. The share of the labor force in commerce and transport rose at a faster pace than that of manufacturing during the last half of the nineteenth century in Europe (Kaelble 1989). In the case of England, however, only 20 percent of observed increases in literacy can be accounted for by changes in occupational composition during the second half of the nineteenth century (Mitch 1991). The most marked increases in literacy rates during this period were for unskilled laborers and miners, occupations for which literacy would seem to have provided no economic advantage (Vincent 1989). It is thus unlikely that a rising demand for literate workers was the sole force driving gains in literacy during the second half of the nineteenth century.

The nineteenth-century European labor market does appear to have offered rewards for acquiring literacy, even if the influence of these rewards on literacy trends was primarily to reinforce the impact of other incentives for acquiring literacy. Thus, recent research on nineteenth-century England and France indicates that (after controlling for social origins) literate workers tended to enter higher-status occupations than illiterate workers (Sewell 1985).

Literacy was certainly no guarantee of upward mobility. For one sample of laborers' sons in England in the 1840s, 50 percent of all literates were laborers at time of marriage compared with 80 percent of illiterates (Mitch 1991). Surveys of Russian peasants and workers in the late nineteenth century indicate that many believed literacy did little to improve economic prospects (Eklof 1986). These studies raise the question of how much the improved prospects that literates experienced were due to literacy as such or were instead linked to other factors correlated with literacy, such as innate intelligence or ambition.

Advertisements in English newspapers in the mid–1800s did often list openings for quite humble positions that required applicants to "write a clear hand" or gave other direct indications that literacy was expected.[5] The labor market contribution to literacy may have been modest. But in many situations it would clearly have improved prospects for advancement. Even when labor demand did not change markedly in the median term, it did reinforce the impact of other factors lowering costs or raising the benefits of acquiring literacy.

Did Rising Family Income Spur Literacy Increases?

Living standards among the working class were far higher in 1900 than in 1500 for most areas of Europe (DeVries 1976). Rising family income would have eased the pressures to send children out to work and the burden of school fees. However, available evidence does not indicate that the standard of living was necessarily an important influence on literacy rates.

West (1975) has found that educational expenditures for a number of Western countries in the late nineteenth century tended to rise at a faster rate than incomes. However, such evidence does not necessarily imply that rising income levels were the cause of climbing literacy rates. Numerous other factors could have contributed to rising educational expenditures, including increased state involvement in education. Furthermore, aggregate evidence fails to capture how demands of individuals and families for education responded to changes in personal income. Studies from a variety of countries do indicate systematic variation in literacy rates across occupational categories, with those in higher-status, and thus presumably better-paying, occupations more likely to have been literate (Graff 1987). (1) Yet a simple positive correlation between literacy rates and adult income for individuals across occupational categories does not directly capture the impact of parental income on the literacy of their children.

Other evidence shows that income levels had a relatively weak influence on literacy rates (Fishlow 1966; Mitch 1982). In communities where little value was placed on literacy, living standards appear to have had little influence on whether literacy was acquired. English miners, for instance, were notoriously indifferent to education either for themselves or for their children, despite earning relatively high wages (*British Parliamentary Papers* 1861; 1899). In many cases highly motivated individuals were willing to pursue the acquisition of literacy despite their own poverty, as the case of Thomas Tryon illustrates. Still, those with more modest motivations to acquire literacy either for themselves or their children may have been partially influenced by their level of income.

Rising living standards could have influenced literacy trends indirectly through increasing life expectancy and reducing birth rates. Gains in life expectancy would have increased the expected value of "investing" in literacy by increasing the expected length of time that literacy would yield benefits. Limited evidence suggests possible links between falling fertility and mortality and rising educational attainment (Tilly 1973). However, the rise in literacy in western Europe was well under way before European populations began to undergo transitions to lower fertility and mortality (Flinn 1981).

THE INFLUENCE OF POPULAR CULTURE ON LITERACY

A number of cultural forces were at work increasing the popular demand for literacy from 1500 onward. Some Protestant sects emphasized the ability of individual believers to read, first hand, the word of God; other sects emphasized mastery of a printed catechism (Houston 1985). The emergence of new religious movements spurred sharp theological debate, expressed in a burgeoning pamphlet literature. These pamphlets in turn generated a desire to read among at least some of working-class origin (Laqueur 1976). Urbanization could have encouraged literacy by increasing contact with written and printed matter and by generating more situations where record keeping was important. Increases in migration would have increased the proportion of individuals who desired to maintain written contact with those they had left behind. And improvements in printing and paper making lowered the cost of publications and letter writing, making these media accessible to broader segments of society.

Protestant areas of Europe tended to have higher literacy rates than Catholic areas: Compare, for example, Scotland, Sweden, and Lutheran areas of Germany with Spain, Italy, and France. But detailed local studies indicate a less certain connection between religion and literacy (Fleury and Valmary 1957; Maynes 1977). Differences in literacy rates among occupational categories for a given religious group were often greater than differences among religious groups for a given occupational category (van der Woude 1980; Houston 1985). The political consequences of Protestantism may have had a stronger influence on primary schooling than did strictly religious factors. In areas subject to Protestant influence in sixteenth-century Germany, both Catholic and Protestant rulers sought to ensure religious homogeneity through education. In Scotland and Sweden, purely religious efforts by Protestant groups accomplished little until bolstered by efforts of the central state (Houston 1985). The influence of local religious motivations should not be dismissed entirely. Studies of England and Scotland, for example, have detected a positive influence of religious motivation on the decision to acquire literacy (Kaestle 1985). However, in general, the studies just reviewed suggest that the direct influence of religious belief on the acquisition of literacy was weak at best.

Like Protestantism, urbanization appears to have been positively correlated with literacy during the early modern period (Houston 1985). But, as with Protestantism, this observed association may mask the influence of other contextual factors. Market towns and administrative centers possessed higher literacy rates than industrial areas in both England and France during the eighteenth and early nineteenth centuries (Sanderson 1972; Schofield 1968; Furet and Ozouf [1977] 1982). During this period a clear association between literacy and occupation in both rural and urban areas also was evident (Graff 1987). Thus, the positive correlations between urbanization and literacy observed for the early modern period may simply reflect the tendency for occupations that made use of literacy to have been more likely to cluster in towns during this period rather than any environmental influence of urbanization.

Literacy also has been associated with migration. In late nineteenth-century Russia, literacy rates and outmigration were positively correlated across regions. But did migration actually encourage literacy, or did it merely select those who had acquired literacy for other reasons? Here the evidence is mixed. While the pull of opportunity could encourage literacy among migrants, the push of poverty and misfortune also spurred migration of illiterates (Briggs 1978; Fitzpatrick 1986). Linguistic minority groups provide another example of how the erosion of traditional communities held ambiguous consequences for literacy. Groups whose native language differed from the prevailing language, or at least prevailing written language, were frequently especially resistant to acquiring literacy (Houston 1985). But assimilationist desires were present in some regions. In areas of Wales in the nineteenth century, for instance, Welsh-speaking parents were reported to have been more eager to send their children to school than English-speaking parents. A parliamentary commission attributed this eagerness to the desire of Welsh-speaking parents to have their children learn English in order to improve prospects for migration (*British Parliamentary Papers* 1870; Houston 1985).

Burgeoning amounts of printed material were another possible cultural influence on literacy. By the mid-nineteenth century inexpensive books, newspapers, and pamphlets aimed at working-class audiences were widespread throughout Europe (Altick 1957; Brooks 1985). Two issues must be addressed to evaluate the impact of the diffusion of literature intended for working-class markets. First, what proportion of the working class actually read such literature? Second, was the development of such literature primarily a cause of rising literacy, or did it simply in large part reflect widening literacy? In England and France, despite the visible presence of working-class literature, actual readership was rather restricted (Graff 1987). In Germany and Russia, publishers developed a working-class literature only after a solid market was evident (Fullerton 1977; Brooks 1985). But the English case suggests caution in attributing the development of popular literature to an expanding working-class readership. The Education Act of 1870, establishing compulsory schooling and state-operated schools, was followed by the spread of cheap daily newspapers aimed largely at the working classes. But working-class readership may have been large enough far earlier to support such newspapers (Perkin 1957; Williams 1966).

If cultural factors were not the driving forces behind the rise of literacy, they certainly reinforced the impact of economic and other social factors. As literacy became more widespread, society and culture developed further uses for literacy, thus reinforcing its benefits. The development of popular publishing provides one illustration. Only when working-class readership became sufficiently large did mass publications become profitable. The development of printed street signs provides another example. In London, the transition from pictorial to printed signs in the eighteenth century has been attributed to sufficient growth in literacy rates to justify such a transition (Larwood and Camden 1870; Heal 1947). In 1839, Rowland Hill managed to establish the penny post in England based on arguments that rising working-class literacy would increase the volume of mail and revenues stemming from lower postal fees (Vincent 1989).

During the initial rise of literacy between 1500 and 1800, it would seem by default that demand-side factors were important. Except in Sweden, Germany, and Scotland, government or elite efforts to promote literacy and primary schooling were neither extensive nor effective. But after 1800, it is difficult to point to dominant forces that would clearly have reached marginal groups in the late nineteenth century. Nevertheless, as literacy continued to spread—whether because of public policy or private demand—that by itself generated further demands for literacy.

DID PUBLIC ACTION INFLUENCE PRIVATE BEHAVIOR?

State-sponsored schooling slowly became the dominant means of providing basic education and literacy over the nineteenth century. Given the diversity of European societies, it is hardly surprising that the timing and character of such government provision varied considerably by region. Sweden and Prussia already had taken significant steps toward developing national educational systems by the end of the eighteenth century, as had Scotland to a lesser extent. Spain and Portugal, by the end of the nineteenth century, had made only nominal efforts at the national level to provide for popular education. By the end of the nineteenth century, the provision of schooling in France and Prussia was clearly centralized, while in England and Russia a mix of centralized guidance and local effort prevailed. In Italy and Greece schools were provided largely through local effort.

Responsibility for financing and administering elementary schools during the nineteenth century continued to rest with local authorities. Nevertheless, local efforts to provide schools were increasingly incorporated into centralized educational systems. Among the policy aims of these systems were (1) "filling in the gaps" (a phrase used by English reformers) in local provision to ensure that rural families and peripheral social classes were reached, (2) standardization of curricula, (3) government inspection of schools, (4) establishment of normal schools for teacher training and of national standards for teacher certification, (5) national laws requiring school attendance and restricting child labor, and (6) elimination of pupil fees to encourage school attendance.

By the century's end most European countries had passed compulsory schooling laws requiring attendance by all children. Many central states were now spending over 1 percent of national income on public education. And government schools were enrolling over 10 percent of their populations in publicly run elementary schools that did not charge tuition (U.S. Bureau of Education 1893).

Given the sheer scope of this effort, the development of public schooling has commonly been viewed as the major impetus to the surge in popular literacy over the nineteenth century. Yet the actual results of policy implementation may fall far short of intentions. Simply providing schools, even at no charge, did not guarantee that such schools were well attended or that children learned what the schools attempted to teach.

State educational policy was likely to have been ineffective in two situations. The first situation was where popular demand was weak. Public school provision in the presence of weak popular demand often led to half-empty public schools. And where popular demand for schooling was lacking, compulsory schooling laws were simply ignored for decades (see Chapter 3 in this volume). Local officials often were opposed to enforcement or were afraid of popular hostility if they did attempt to enforce such laws. Studies of England, Wales, Italy, Spain, Portugal, Greece, and Austria indicate that the impact of state educational policy was stifled by weak popular demand (*British Parliamentary Papers* 1877; Wardle 1971; Vinao Frago 1990).

The second situation in which public policy was ineffective was where state action was simply redundant. This occurred when government financing and compulsory schooling laws followed already widespread support for primary schooling and already high levels of literacy. In these situations newly founded public schools often displaced existing private schools. West (1975) has argued that this displacement was extensive in nineteenth-century England. In France and Germany, centrally financed school systems and compulsory schooling laws were not fully in place until the 1880s, well after literacy had spread to the majority of the population.

When Was State Action Effective?

In several circumstances, state action clearly was effective in boosting literacy and school enrollments beyond what private schools would have provided. One condition was the presence of pent-up popular demand. This occurred in some instances because of an initial shortage of schools. Here children rapidly filled up additional places in public schools. Public schools at times were overcrowded and had long waiting lists. In rural areas, poverty and sparse population density accounted for the private market's failure to supply instruction to meet slowly rising popular demand. In late nineteenth-century Russia, for example, peasants greeted new public schools with enthusiasm (Eklof 1986). Opposition of local elites to popular education at times prevented adequate facilities from being constructed in rural areas of Italy despite peasant demand, and new school places supplied by the state were rapidly filled (Briggs 1978; Bell 1979).

In more intermediate situations, public policy was effective in augmenting and improving an initial level of educational attainment. Specific policy aims in these situations were (1) incrementally providing new schools, (2) standardizing and raising the quality of instruction, (3) lowering or eliminating school fees, and (4) establishing compulsory schooling laws. Such policies were able to reach peripheral groups not already in school or literate. This is the traditional interpretation of the experience of Victorian England and much of France and Germany. But even though educational histories of these countries have commonly emphasized the impact of state policy, initially high levels of popular literacy and the incentives they created for peripheral groups to acquire literacy were likely to have reinforced the influence of state policy.

State policy also may have been effective when national literacy campaigns provided a major leadership role. These campaigns provided both incentives and means for acquiring literacy. Scandinavian countries mounted literacy campaigns in the seventeenth and eighteenth centuries. Here basic reading knowledge of church catechisms was commonly required to participate in church sacraments, including the act of marriage.[6] Informal instruction by the family was the basic way of transmitting literacy, supplemented with teaching and examination by the clergy.

An important determinant of the efficacy of state educational policy was the consonance between popular demand for literacy and the strength of the policy measures employed. This balance was influenced by the underlying distribution of power in society and by the extent of popular apathy toward literacy. In egalitarian, progressive societies, the risks were greatest that state educational policy would fall behind or be redundant of private demand. With an egalitarian distribution of power, educational policy set by the state or elites simply mirrored the educational preferences of society at large. A progressive working-class population with expectations of upward mobility would demand greater literacy. Here the net influence of public policy in accelerating the rise of literacy was slight.

However, in societies with more concentrated political authority yet retaining prospects for upward mobility, state action was more likely to be effective. Where sufficient popular demand for education was present, the state and elites could provide leadership in educational policy. Moderate inequality in the distribution of power may have generated elite support for popular education to keep the masses under control. England, France, and Germany generally conformed to these conditions during the eighteenth and nineteenth centuries.

Where the concentration of power was extreme and much of the population lived at subsistence levels with little hope of upward mobility, state policy alone rarely boosted literacy rates. Here popular apathy to education was high, and local elites resisted any attempt to expand mass schooling. Such conditions were present in nineteenth-century Spain and Portugal (Vinao Frago 1990).

An additional conclusion is that state policies were far more effective when supported by both popular demand and local elites. This helps to explain the effectiveness of Scandinavian literacy campaigns as early as the seventeenth century. These campaigns were reinforced by already existing church networks and by the powerful requirement of being literate to qualify for church sacraments. In France, Germany, and England, state financing of primary schooling was based upon already existing networks of schools with support by competing local elites. In Italy, Spain, and Portugal, where local elites were at best apathetic, it was more difficult to effectively implement national policies.

In sum, the various ways in which local demand for literacy and state supply of basic schooling interacted in Europe offer analogies with common views of the variations that occurred in European industrialization. Gerschenkron (1962) distinguishes between early industrializing areas and those areas regarded as economically backward. Early industrializing countries included Britain and Germany. Late industrializing countries included Russia, Italy, Spain, and Portugal (see also Cameron 1985). With the former group, the rise of literacy was a gradual process spanning several centuries. Here the incremental rise of literacy led to an interaction between economic and cultural demands and public supply, providing momentum in the diffusion of literacy. As these societies became more literate, more occasions for using literacy emerged. And rising literacy facilitated political support for policies aimed at promoting greater literacy and basic schooling.

In more economically backward areas of Europe, the spread of literacy came later but exhibited a more rapid pace, going from perhaps no more than a third of the society to an overwhelming majority in less than a century. The central state played a stronger initiating role and local elites a weaker role compared with the early industrializing nations. Popular demand may have surged exogenously as migration opportunities expanded, more market orientation developed, and land reform was undertaken.[7] Here diffusion of literacy proceeded with a rapidity that may have precluded effective interaction between public and private demands for literacy. Gerschenkron (1962) argues that an important force pushing rapid industrialization in backward economies was the backlog of new technology that could be borrowed from advanced economies. Analogously, the large gap in literacy rates between advanced and backward political economies likely contributed to both popular eagerness and official desperation in low literacy areas to close that gap.

NOTES

This chapter was written while I was a Spencer Fellow. The assistance of the Spencer Foundation and the National Academy of Education in making this fellowship possible is gratefully acknowledged.

1. See Graff (1987). In this chapter I will treat the ability to read and write as a yes-or-no category. In fact, the term *literacy* encompasses a wide range of abilities from being able to barely sound out individual letters to the writing of inspired poetry. For consideration of the ambiguities in measuring literacy, see Schofield (1968). There are two reasons for focusing on crude measures of literacy in this survey: (1) The marked changes in crude measures considered here are likely to reflect profound changes in the full range of literacy skills generally available. (2) My focus is on examining the causes rather than measuring or considering the consequences of rising literacy.

2. The etymology of the word *mumpsimus* offered by the *Oxford English Dictionary* suggests that during the Renaissance some priests also were illiterate.

3. This is not to say that civic efforts, whether by centralized state and church agencies or by local communities, were purely benevolent and disinterested. Numerous historians have argued that apparently "public" efforts to promote schooling were in fact aimed at promoting the well-being of particular interest groups. Such class interests included factory and mine owners seeking a more orderly and docile work force, or established church hierarchies seeking to prevent competing sects from converting their membership. However, such efforts are public in the sense that the interests involved are larger than those of a private individual, family, or immediate community. The distinction between public and private effort used here roughly corresponds to the distinction between corporate and private actors made by Craig (1981).

4. The effectiveness of the Swedish campaign in conveying true mastery of reading, and the extent to which it was actually conducted through informal instruction, has been questioned in Sandin (1988). Sandin suggests that some local church leaders found that the family alone could not be relied on to provide instruction. He reports that some church boards provided funds for building schools and hiring teachers instead of relying on informal instruction alone.

5. See Mitch (1991) for details. Phrases used in these advertisements varied. Some referred to education in a vague manner, such as "respectable and well educated," suggesting screening or credentialing functions of education. Others referred to very specific skills such as keeping books or being "able to write a clear hand" or "write quickly," asking applicants to apply in "their own hand," suggesting that literacy was directly demanded as a productive skill.

6. See U.S. Bureau of Education (1891). An alternative explanation for lower-class involvement in education in Sweden has been offered by Sandin (1988). Sandin argues that the lower classes in seventeenth- and eighteenth-century Stockholm sent their children to school primarily to obtain various types of charitable donations.

7. For an account of the growth of literacy in Spain along these lines, see Vinao Frago (1990). See Blaug (1970) on the influence of communism and rapid economic growth in eliminating illiteracy in the Soviet Union.

Building the Institution of Mass Schooling: Isomorphism in the Modern World

Francisco O. Ramirez and Marc J. Ventresca

Mass schooling is a global phenomenon. It is increasingly ideologically enshrined as a citizenship right, a state goal in national constitutions, and a dominating topic in policy discourse. Mass schooling continues its steady worldwide expansion despite many practical difficulties. There is evidence of a growing homogenization of what constitutes primary school subjects and how curricular time is distributed among these subjects (Benavot et al. 1991). The virtues and outcomes of mass schooling at individual and societal levels are celebrated within nation-states and throughout world organizations. A strong consensus has developed on the virtues and outcomes of mass schooling, with primary emphasis on productivity/economic growth and patriotism/political unity. Most importantly, schooling the masses is a nation-state project that is strongly validated at the level of world political culture, which defines basic education as a fundamental human right (Article 26 of the United Nations Declaration of Human Rights) and identifies primary schooling as the main delivery system for basic education.

Mass schooling is not only global in its reach but also highly institutionalized at the world level. An institution comprises "standardized activity sequences that have taken for granted rationales, that is, some common social 'account' of their existence and purpose" (Jepperson 1991, p. 145). Mass schooling is institutionalized to the extent that it is a fixture in a social environment and explicated as a functional element of that environment (Meyer and Rowan 1977). The social environment within which mass schooling is institutionalized consists of both the territorial nation-state and the wider world that validates mass schooling as a feature of nation-states and, more recently, as a direct feature of the world political culture itself. That is, mass schooling is celebrated not only for the benefits it confers on individuals and their national societies but also for its role in promoting a world society in which schooling for all would result in global understanding and world peace, provided that the right interests (the people) with the correct motives (emancipatory) shape schooling.

The institutional character of mass schooling is often overlooked or under-theorized in the sociological literature for three reasons. First, much of the literature is fearlessly ahistorical in character. Schools, pupils, curricula, educational ministries, national educational agendas—these are taken-for-granted realities. This truncated vision prevents us from directly reflecting on the origins of mass schooling and on the processes through which mass schooling survived the "liability of newness" as an organizational innovation and gained worldwide status as a highly legitimate entity. Second, much theory and research continues to be trapped within the framework of functionalism, both the social-order and class-reproduction variety. Either schools function to maintain the social order or they function to satisfy the interests of the dominant class. Even functionalists like Bowles and Gintis (1986), however, note that institutions do not merely reflect or enforce preexisting interests, but rather generate them. Third, the case study tradition in comparative education often results in explanations that favor the unique features of particular nations, eschewing a logic of similar causes for similar outcomes and favoring national renditions linked to the familiar functionalist story.

Within many policy-driven explanations of schooling, the individual and societal effects of schooling are conceptualized in technical terms. When the putative effects at one or another level fail to take place, intentional educational reforms make things work. The more critical reaction is to argue that schools fail to attain goals that were never seriously pursued since these goals were inconsistent with the interests of ill-motivated elites, bureaucrats, or reformers. Implicit in the heated debate on interests and motives is the assumption that mass schooling has transformative powers affecting all individuals and all societies. It is this cornerstone of educational common sense that the institutional theory of mass schooling seeks to scrutinize.

Assumptions regarding the efficacy of schooling are in fact of relatively modern provenance. Whether the masses were educable was widely debated during the nineteenth century (Müller et al. 1987). State involvement in mass schooling was suspect, not only among conservatives in Catholic France (Furet and Ozouf [1977] 1982) but also among liberals in Anglican England (Sommerville 1982). Education was not always thought of as the salvation of the nation. National leaders did not promise that "their" children would outscore the children of other countries in presumably comparable standardized tests. A world conference to promote schooling for all was unimaginable. The farther back in time we extend our frame of reference, the less mass schooling is evident as a general organizational phenomenon, or even as an isolated national aspiration. This is because mass schooling emerged as a nation-state project, and even in the West, nation-states came to be a dominant form of political organization beginning only in the late eighteenth century.

This chapter addresses the rise and institutionalization of mass schooling in two ways: first, we clarify the underlying premises of our theoretical perspective. Then we illustrate the viability of the institutionalist perspective by depicting three worldwide trends in the organizational development of mass schooling systems. These are the organizational expansion of (1) primary school enrollments, (2) legal mandates for compulsory schooling, and (3) national education ministries. We deal first with the origins of mass schooling and its ideological elaboration, then turn to the dynamics of educational institutionalization from the late nineteenth century to the present.

ORIGINS OF MASS SCHOOLING

We have addressed the origins and institutionalization of mass schooling in several papers that emphasize the transnational character of mass schooling as a nation-state project (Boli and Ramirez 1986; Ramirez and Boli 1987). Our focus on the transnational character of mass schooling involves three key points:

1. Mass schooling does not emerge and develop as a function of specific endogenous societal characteristics such as urbanization or industrialization, class structure, or the character of political or religious elites. Even plausible societal-level interpretations of its earlier rise become more difficult to maintain in the contemporary era. While conditions of political and educational decentralization may have given the United States an enrollment lead over its western European counterparts, after World War II enrollment growth is little affected by the nature of the organizational linkages between states and schools. While the presence of a Protestant national church may have earlier propelled some European countries in the direction of enacting compulsory schooling legislation, the latter today is too widespread to be explained in societal-level terms (Meyer and Hannan 1979).

2. Mass schooling developed and spread as an increasingly familiar set of general ideological and organizational arrangements. Over historical time and through diverse processes, features of modern schooling coalesced into one normative institutional model. This model is one that became privileged over traditional and alternative schooling arrangements, and it was increasingly linked to the ascendant nation-state. The model is not an abstraction, but rather comprises specific ideological and organizational components.

3. The ascendant nation-state form itself was fostered by a world political culture emerging from the conflicting dynamics of the world capitalist economy. The nation-state as a mode of political organization involves the formation of citizenship and the conferral of this status on individuals. Citizenship links individuals not merely to the state as a bureaucratic organization but, more importantly, to the "imagined community" that national states are expected to embody (Anderson 1983). Mass schooling becomes the central set of activities

through which the reciprocal links between individuals and nation-states are forged.

From an institutionalist perspective, what is striking about both nation-state formation and the establishment of mass schooling is the pervasiveness of ideological and organizational isomorphism. This takes place among an increasing number of entities that clearly vary with respect to both internal structural characteristics and historical developmental trajectories. Following DiMaggio and Powell (1983), one can imagine three different sources of this isomorphism: coercion, imitation, and adherence to normative standards. Colonies or defeated powers may end up with specific political and educational ideologies and organization because these were imposed upon them by the colonial or victorious power. This is often the preferred imagery when the point is the lack of fit between externally imposed forms and internal realities. Ideological and organizational isomorphism may also be brought about through mimetic processes. German, American, and (more recently) Japanese models of primary schooling are imitated to the extent that these countries are viewed as successes in the wider world. Nation-states and national mass schooling may look similar because their formats are derived from world models external to any particular nation-state. Exogenous rules of sovereignty legitimate the constitution of modern societies as nation-states (Giddens 1984); exogenous principles of human and national development legitimate national mass schooling.

Nation-states and national systems of mass schooling are clearly not identical in every respect. Much comparative research examines variations between nation-states and variations between national school systems. This research tradition has yielded many interesting findings but is silent on the growing ideological and organizational isomorphism in the world. We proceed from the premise that much of the observable political and educational standardization across varying geopolitical entities over time requires an explanation at a world level of analysis.

The institutionalist explanation we have set forth argues for the emergence of a world political culture that both fostered the nation-state mode of organizing collective action and social structure and triggered mass schooling as a means for constructing members of the new national societies. Mass schooling both presupposed the attainability of progress through purposeful action and the centrality of socialization in shaping individual will. With the discovery and triumph of childhood socialization theories, the stage was set for nation-state programs of mass schooling.

This was not an uncontested process. What was involved was a fundamental and long-term restructuring of the Western cultural framework, a reordering of public life around territorial nation-state and individual citizenship principles that would transform transnational masses into national citizens. There was nothing inevitable about this historical transformation, nor were the politically incorporative consequences of mass schooling anticipated or understood in uniform ways. This movement reconstructed varied forms of schooling under local and transnational religious authorities into nation-state programs of compulsory mass schooling.

Within the Western framework, calls for mass literacy are often attributed to the unplanned coupling of Gutenberg and Luther (Stinchcombe 1965). What the former made possible through the invention of the printing press, the latter transformed into a spiritual obligation by making the Bible the fulcrum of the Protestant challenge. The cultural impact of the Reformation was not restricted to the people who embraced the new faiths. The Counter-Reformation was compelled to fight the Reformation on its own terms, unevenly and often reluctantly, but nevertheless endorsing literacy and ultimately schooling. Much literacy preceded mass schooling in the West as well as elsewhere (see Chapter 2). Earlier calls for compulsory education in the West were directed at parents to educate their children rather than to create differentiated schools. Though the German towns received Luther's letter of 1524 urging them to establish compulsory schools (Stone 1969) and though the Council of Trent in 1563 placed the primary school within the sphere of the parish priest, differentiated schools for the masses did not emerge until the eighteenth century. Though highly religious in their curriculum, the schools that developed in numerous German states, in much of the Netherlands, in some Swiss cantons, in Scandinavia, and in the northeastern American colonies involved higher levels of organizational distinctiveness. Schooling the masses involved a move beyond familial boundaries and into what would be constituted as the public domain.

In the nineteenth century the parental obligation to educate children was transformed into the duty to place children in schools organized and regulated by public authorities. Compulsory school laws were passed and national educational ministries established. Schooling the masses became the business of the nation-state, symbolically affirming its authority over its children qua future citizens, against the claims of older religious authorities and alternative visions of social order. The ideological and organizational foundations of national programs of mass schooling were established in what has been called the century of nationalism and the idea of progress. This may be most evident in the centralized states of the Continent but also holds true in England, the United States (Tyack et al. 1987), and Latin America (Anderson 1983).

Class reification and the notion of a social order made up of unchanging strata constituted a major source of opposition to the mass schooling project. Among conservatives there was much concern and fear that the masses were receiving a form of schooling beyond their station in life. Consider the reaction of Taine to the introduction of compulsory free schooling in France:

[E]ducation prepares . . . the adult (peasant or laborer) not for his life as he will live it, but for another life less monotonous, less restricted, more cerebral. . . . His own [life] . . . will go on disgusting him for a long time, until his education, quite superficial, shall have completely evaporated . . . [into] empty phrases; in France, for a peasant or ordinary labourer, the sooner that day comes the better. (Furet and Ozouf [1977] 1982, p. 129)

Similar sentiments were expressed in Prussia and in England. But there were also optimistic observers who saw in the proliferation of schools "beacons of the future" (Donald 1985). As early as 1826, Baron Dubin had the audacity to imagine a schooling/national development connection in France. For our purposes the accuracy of his analysis is not the issue; what counts is that this early voice of optimism was amplified throughout the nineteenth and twentieth centuries. Across the Atlantic, the benefits of mass schooling were strongly proclaimed:

Practically all modern nations are now awake to the fact that education is the most potent means in the development of the essentials of nationality. Education is the means by which peoples of retarded cultures may be brought rapidly to the common level. Education is the means by which small or weak nations may become strong through their cultural strengths and achievements. . . . Education is the only means by which the world can be "made safe" for the national type of organization. (Monroe 1927, p. 4)

We see in these comments the crystallization of many of the ideological elements underlying national programs of mass schooling. Higher levels of primary enrollment were achieved earlier in the United States than anywhere in Europe. But the decentralized character of the union meant that the American state would historically be involved in mass schooling in a less direct and bureaucratic fashion. Among nineteenth-century liberals, enthusiasm for schooling was often tempered by a suspicion of the state intruding into civil society. In 1859 John Stuart Mill declared,

If the government would make up its mind to require for every child a good education, it might save itself the trouble of providing one. . . . That the whole or any large part of the education of the people should be in State hands, I go as far as any one in deprecating. . . . A general State education is a mere contrivance for moulding people to be exactly like one another. . . . An education established and controlled by the State should only exist, if it exist at all, as one of many competing experiments carried on for the purpose of example and stimulus, to keep the others up to a certain standard of excellence. (Mill, *On Liberty*, 1859, cited in Sommerville 1982, p. 193)

From the mid-nineteenth century onward, educational debates and reforms in one part of the world reverberated in other parts. Military, political, and economic setbacks were often followed by periods of intense revitalization that emphasized educational blueprints for the new and improved society. Some blueprints were imposed, and others were copied. Long before the development of Unesco and worldwide conferences as explicit organizational carriers of world models of education, international definitions of educational reality and norm setting were well under way. What educational statistics to collect and report, what constituted reasonable educational goals, who was to be schooled and under what authority—

these are but some of the agreed-upon normative standards that influenced entry into the Western world. These standards operate in nonhierarchical but nonetheless influential lateral fashion, providing the bases for structural conformity and organizational isomorphism.

DYNAMICS OF EDUCATIONAL INSTITUTIONALIZATION

Next we identify three crossnational trends over a long historical period that characterize the world model of national mass schooling systems: (1) mass primary enrollment ratios, understood not only as an aggregate of individual students but also as an organizational property of the schooling system, (2) legal rules that make schooling compulsory for all children within the national polity, and (3) centralized education policy authority.

Data Sources

Mass primary enrollment ratios. Much research and popular imagery sees educational enrollments as an outcome of rational supply and demand calculations; we propose instead to treat mass enrollment ratios as an organizational property of an education system and to examine trends in reported primary enrollments as an indicator of organizational expansion. Unesco sources provide standard compilations of school enrollments for the recent modern period, from 1950 to 1980 (Unesco 1972; 1978; 1983). Enrollment data for the earlier historical period of interest (1870–1940) come from a recent dataset reported by Benavot and Riddle (1988). We report on primary enrollment ratios, which are calculated by dividing reported gross enrollments by the standard primary school–age population.

Compulsory schooling rules. Compulsory schooling rules begin to appear in the early nineteenth century. Earlier religious and state initiatives directing compulsory education lacked the mass normative impetus to push all children into formal school institutions. The dates of legal compulsory rules, defined as national laws requiring all children to attend primary school, come from diverse sources, including Flora and Albers's historical compendium (1983), Unesco (1971), Garrido (1986), and Kurian (1988). For the passage date of compulsory schooling rules, we coded on the criteria of meaningful legislation (whether by royal decree, colonial mandate, constitutional provision, or national law) meant to apply throughout the polity and to all children for the period of primary schooling.

Central education policy authority. A third characteristic of the world model of mass schooling is centralized policy authority, in the form of organizational arrangements that consolidate authorization for school inspection, fiscal and budgetary matters, curricula and textbooks, teacher training, and related functions in some combination at the supra-local level. As an indicator of this tendency toward central, state control of mass education, we coded the founding dates of national ministries or bureaus of education. Data sources include the range of compendia already noted, augmented by a survey mailed to current ministries of education. As with dates of compulsory rule passage, we use the date of founding as an indicator of the process of codifying central authority; for both variables, the dates capture relative timing across country cases.

RESULTS

We now describe basic crossnational trends in the three organizational and legal components of the mass schooling model.

Primary Enrollments as Organizational Expansion

The existence of enrollment information for a country is itself related to the existence and organizational expansion of mass education. Countries with no primary enrollments to report—common throughout much of the world through the early twentieth century—rarely acknowledge the absence of such data, which is an important point for our argument. Our concern is with the presence of reported mass enrollments and the patterns of change in enrollment ratios over time between and among countries and world regions. For our purposes, "mass" schooling is less an absolute level of enrollments and more a qualitative organizational phenomenon implied in formalized schooling initiatives.

Table 3.1 reports mean primary enrollment ratios by region for the period 1870–1980. Many more countries report mass schooling enrollments, rising from less than 40 in 1870 to 115 countries by the 1930s; by the 1960s upwards of 150 countries were routinely reporting mass enrollments. These trend data show striking increases in the mean reported enrollment ratios across all categories of countries, even as substantially more cases begin to report. The mean primary enrollment ratio overall rose from slightly more than 30 percent in the late nineteenth century to about 60 percent in the post–World War II period, to over 90 percent in the recent period.[1]

For the first decades of the period, primary enrollments were reported predominantly by countries in western Europe and the Americas (both Anglo-settler colonies and independent states of Latin America). The West (western Europe and the settler colonies) enters this period with already high enrollment ratios. Latin American countries and the countries of eastern and southern Europe begin to report in greater numbers from the 1890s onward, and are next to show expanded and substantial enrollment ratios in the first decades of the twentieth century. From the 1920s onward, mean enrollment ratios in these regions rise, although analysis of shifts in standard deviations suggests that there is substantial heterogeneity within these country groupings. Other regions show relatively fewer countries reporting in this early period, as well as relatively low reported mean enrollment ratios. These are not expanded or mass education systems in structure, capacity, or practice.

Table 3.1
Mean Primary Enrollment Ratios, 1870–1980, by Region

	1870	1890	1910	1930	1950	1960	1970	1980
All countries	32.7	30.9	33.6	37.9	60.1	76.2	83.9	90.9
	(38)	(72)	(98)	(115)	(134)	(156)	(160)	(154)
Africa	16.6	10.2	13.1	15.2	26.7	47.1	53.9	72.9
	(2)	(5)	(17)	(24)	(43)	(46)	(43)	(42)
Middle East		5.6	9.5	15.3	38.3	63.7	75.6	91.1
	(0)	(2)	(8)	(11)	(14)	(17)	(18)	(18)
Asia	8.1	12.1	16.7	25.4	52.1	66.9	80.7	89.9
	(4)	(7)	(10)	(11)	(16)	(22)	(22)	(22)
Latin America	16.5	24.3	34.2	40.8	78.9	99.8	99.9	99.8
	(11)	(31)	(34)	(34)	(27)	(34)	(36)	(35)
Eastern Europe	16.9	21.1	39.4	46.8	88.1	99.9	99.9	99.6
	(3)	(5)	(6)	(8)	(8)	(9)	(9)	(9)
Western Europe	52.6	55.7	64.1	67.1	99.9	99.9	99.9	99.9
	(18)	(22)	(21)	(24)	(23)	(24)	(23)	(21)
Oceania			44.6	58.1	67.3	67.8	99.9	99.9
	(0)	(0)	(2)	(3)	(3)	(4)	(9)	(7)

Notes: Number of countries (*n*) appears below enrollment percentages.

Data for 1950–1980 are gross primary enrollment ratios. Changing definitions of primary enrollments and of the relevant age cohort during this period may result in enrollment ratios not being comparable to ratios at earlier time points. In addition, where ratios are estimated at greater than 100 percent, we report than as "99.9" since our concern is not with absolute levels.

Sources: Unesco *Statistical Yearbooks* (1972, 1978, 1983); Benavot and Riddle (1988).

The spread of mass education in the colonial context is reflected in the increasing numbers of countries reporting enrollments, and expanded enrollments, prior to the formal breakup of empires after the turn of the century. We see from Table 3.1 that slightly more countries in Africa, Asia, and the Middle East begin reporting enrollments by 1910. The number of countries reporting increases substantially in subsequent decades, with bursts of increase in the 1950s and 1960s among (postcolonial) African and Asian states and somewhat later among Oceania and Middle Eastern states.

Figure 3.1
Proportion of Countries Having Passed a Compulsory Schooling Rule, by Region and Decade, 1810–1990

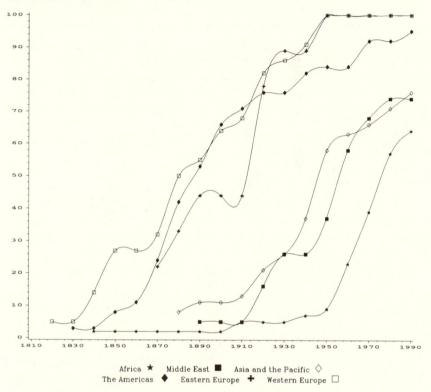

Africa ★   Middle East ■   Asia and the Pacific ◇
The Americas ◆   Eastern Europe ✚   Western Europe □

Table 3.1 presents the data in terms of geopolitical regions, but similar trends are manifest when the data are presented in terms of levels of economic development (measured in terms of standard indices), by dominant colonial power, or by a typology of linkage to the world polity (Benavot and Riddle 1988). Mean values do obscure variation in mean enrollment ratios among countries within each category. For the early period and prior to the large increases in the number of countries reporting mass enrollments, the standard deviation by region varies and, indeed, increases in several regions; it underscores the often quite substantial variation among reported enrollment levels.

Compulsory Schooling Rules

Figure 3.1 shows the cumulative proportion of countries that have passed compulsory schooling legislation, again by region and for a longer historical period of interest, 1810–1990. The figure shows the general prevalence of compulsory schooling legislation as a standard feature of modern mass schooling—by the late 1980s, over 80 percent of national education systems had at some point instituted compulsory rules. We emphasize the historical passage of such legislation *intending* universal inclusion in mass schooling as a legal component of a national system.[2]

Figure 3.1 shows that a steadily growing proportion of countries in Europe and the Americas adopted compulsory schooling over the period we discuss here. Education systems in well over 70 percent of these countries included a compulsory mandate by the 1920s, reaching upward of 95 percent by the 1970s. Countries in Africa, Asia, and the Middle East show somewhat slower and later patterns of adoption of compulsory rules, with rapid increases in the proportions that mandate compulsory schooling in the period 1950–1980. Overall, national compulsory rules are present in 65 to 75 percent of the education systems in these regions; nonetheless, national plans and reports to international agencies routinely discuss plans to institute compulsory schooling. More recently, such discussions tend to emphasize the "universalization" of schooling, explicitly noting the lack of "need" for compulsory rules in light of the universal character of enrollments (Garrido 1986).

Centralized Policy Authority—Ministries of Education

Figure 3.2 shows the cumulative proportion of countries that have established a central education authority for the long historical period from 1810 to 1990. This central authority is most commonly located within the national ministry or department of education.

The establishment of central (nation-state) authority for education now appears nearly ubiquitous. Central control over education policy and practice is a pervasive feature of mass schooling systems, appearing early among countries in nearly all regions of the world, and now present in over 90 percent of countries in all regions save western Europe. As we have discussed, the nineteenth-century construction of mass schooling systems in Europe often involved struggles between church and state, or, in more liberal polities such as England, struggles between local authorities and the expanding national state. The structure of central organizational control remains a contested issue in these cases, whereas for schooling systems established later and outside the European core, the notion of national and central authority and responsibility for education is simply taken for granted. Indeed, mass schooling is assumed to be an obligation of the modern state, central in purpose to the varied ameliorative and progressive ideologies that authorize state action in the modern context.

CONCLUSION

During the last two centuries, transnational masses have been transformed into discrete national citizenries. Mass schooling has been the modern alchemy

Figure 3.2
Proportion of Countries Having Established a Central Education Authority, by
Region and Decade, 1810–1990

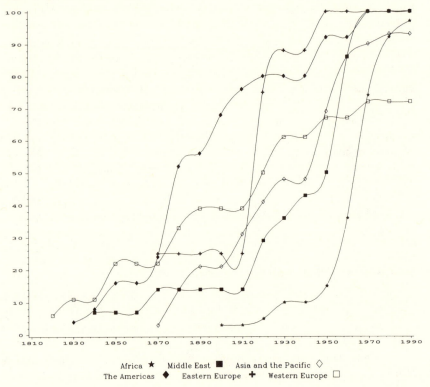

Africa ★   Middle East ■   Asia and the Pacific ◇
The Americas ◆   Eastern Europe ✚   Western Europe □

through which this transformation has taken place. Indeed, the connection between mass schooling and the nation-state has become a truism. We have attempted to illustrate steps in the institution-building process that has unfolded
across historical time and geopolitical space. We have argued that adherence to
world models of national mass schooling has yielded ideological and organizational isomorphism. Despite much variation in many endogenous characteristics of national societies, mass schooling has been globally institutionalized.

From the middle of the nineteenth century to the present, we find strikingly
similar regional trends resulting in expanded, mandated, and nationally authorized systems of mass schooling. Comparisons at any one point in time do show
some cross-regional differences and within-region heterogeneity. Much policy
talk focuses solely on these differences, neglecting the extent to which schooling
the masses has become both a fixture in a densely woven global environment
of nation-states and an agreed-upon recipe for individual amelioration and national progress.

As we approach the twenty-first century, one cannot but wonder whether the institutionalization of mass schooling as a central nation-state project will be further intensified. The economic and political benefits of mass schooling enjoy worldwide currency in theories of human capital and political democracy. Will an increasingly competitive world environment lead to an even greater national preoccupation with ensuring that the next generation gains the educational edge? Alternatively, amidst growing ideological and organizational isomorphism, will a worldwide community come to be imagined, transforming national citizens into world citizens? The latter seems unlikely and, to some, dangerous—just as the expansion of mass schooling appeared to many a nineteenth-century observer.

NOTES

The research reported here was supported in part by funds from the National Science Foundation (Grant SES–8420232) and by funds from the Stanford Center for the Study of Families, Children, and Youth.

1. In a related analysis, Benavot and Riddle (1988) report on two sets of constant cases, thirty-three cases for the period 1870–1940, and sixty-six cases for the period 1940–1980, observing that the "longitudinal trends for these two groups of countries indicate a steeper rise in the mean primary enrollment [ratio] than is evident" where all cases are included as they become available.

2. Implementation of the compulsory mandate in educational practice has more varied determinants and realization; in individual country cases, compulsory rules may lapse in practice, though formal rescission is uncommon.

Institutions, Citizenship, and Schooling in Sweden

John Boli

An underlying assumption of this book is that by the nineteenth century mass schooling had become a social imperative. Schooling was considered a functional necessity, a rational and indispensable means of achieving individual goals. The technical-functionalist argument emphasizes schooling's capacity to equip children with skills and knowledge useful in adult life; schooling is supposed to make modernization possible. Under class-imposition theories, schooling imbues lower-class children with values, attitudes, and beliefs that legitimate elites' superiority and privilege. The status-competition model differs in that it downplays the substantive effects of schooling. The mere fact of having completed a given level of schooling "certifies" children as endowed with "cultural capital" that they can invest to improve their social standing, regardless of how they have performed as students (Collins 1979; Archer 1979).

Yet none of these "rationalist" perspectives addresses the fundamental question: Why did schooling become socially imperative for the transmission of skills, the legitimation of elite rule, or the acquisition of cultural capital? The institutional perspective developed in Chapter 3 takes this question as its central concern. The argument is that profound and mutually reinforcing changes in the symbolic and organizational framework of society produced a broadly institutionalized conception, or model, of society that made mass schooling seem both necessary and desirable to all sorts of social groups. In this Chapter I flesh out this argument, using the Swedish case as an example.[1]

The chapter contains four sections. The first section develops the institutional argument by introducing a broad concept of *citizenship* as the fulcrum by which to gain leverage on the problem of schooling's origins. Citizenship is analyzed as being intimately related to childhood socialization, implying that changes in conceptions of citizenship were crucial for the emergence of mass schooling. The second section discusses the development of religious, economic, and political citizenship in Swedish society during the period 1700–1850. Here I attempt to show how religious, economic, and political change involved processes of reciprocal reinforcement between symbolic and organizational structures, leading to the institutionalization of the new model of society in which mass schooling was seen as an imperative. The third section describes two phases in the development of Swedish mass schooling: a social movement phase of decentralized school construction, followed by a nationalization phase in which a universal state-directed system was established. The fourth section argues that the technical-functional, class-imposition, and status competition perspectives are not consistent with the Swedish experience. The institutional perspective, I believe, provides a more plausible explanatory framework.

CITIZENSHIP, CHILD SOCIALIZATION, AND THE NEW MODEL OF SOCIETY

Most discussions treat citizenship as a purely political construct. The broader concept of citizenship used here refers to the rules specifying how elemental social entities are related to social collectivities, or polities. Citizenship rules identify the social entities that are members of the polity, that is, authorized participants in polity-wide activities. They also specify the content of such participation—the "rights" and "duties" of citizen members.

This general conception of citizenship entails a similarly broad concept of polity. If a polity is any organized community that is socially bounded, we can speak meaningfully of not only political but also religious and economic polities.[2] Rules of citizenship can be identified for any type of polity. For example, citizenship rules in Christian religious polities may stipulate that (1) only people can be citizens (nothing else has a soul), (2) citizens must adhere to a given set of doctrines, and (3) citizens have the duty to observe certain prescriptions as well as the right to participate in rituals and, perhaps, in religious administration. Similarly, economic citizenship rules specify the social units authorized to engage in various economic activities—production, taxation, consumption, and so on. Political citizenship rules specify the social units authorized to engage in the administration of state and local government authority structures.

The importance of citizenship for the origins of mass schooling lies in the fact that the nature and content of childhood socialization is closely linked to the nature of the citizenship rules tying societal members to the larger polity. To see how this works, consider the character of citizenship and childhood socialization in Sweden before the nineteenth century.

To begin with, religious citizenship was the major form of membership in a society-wide collectivity, for the Church was the most authoritative and penetrative societal organization. But religious citizenship was ambiguous. On the one hand, it was entirely egalitarian. Every individual had a soul and was supposed to seek spiritual salvation in direct relation to God. On the other hand, religious citizenship was differentiated. Parishioners were subject to the authority of the clergy, who upheld the "pure evangelical faith" of Lutheranism. Most parishioners were excluded from participation in Church governance.

In the economic realm, citizenship was less universal and more highly differentiated (Carlsson 1961). Only burghers were permitted to engage in trade and artisanry. Peasants were obliged to engage in agriculture and were excluded from burgher activities. The nobility and clergy were hardly economic citizens at all because they lived off rents and state salaries. Economic citizenship was also corporate rather than individualist. Families, households, villages, and manors were the main economic units, though taxes and rents were often assessed against individuals.

Political citizenship also was differentiated. During absolutist periods only the monarch was a formally authorized political actor, though informal authorization was granted to the nobility and segments of the burghers (Carlsson 1961). In other periods, larger segments of the population enjoyed political citizenship through representation in the Riksdag (parliament). The Riksdag was composed of four estates: the nobility, comprising all heads of noble families; the burghers, made up of master craftsmen, merchants, and town magistrates; the clergy, including parish priests and higher clerics; and the peasants, comprising landholding peasants and peasants leasing crown land. All other social strata (landless peasants, rural artisans, etc.) were not political actors.

Each type of citizenship can be related to childhood socialization. Since religious citizenship was primary, the most morally charged dimension of socialization was the religious. Parents were expected to transmit religious precepts and norms to their children, and the clergy conducted periodic examinations of parishioners' religious knowledge and ability to read the Scripture (Johansson 1981). This practice made education compulsory for the entire population. Schooling, however, was quite rare, involving only a small percentage of children (Sandström 1978).

In accordance with the nature of eighteenth-century citizenship, childhood socialization was differentiated, inegalitarian, practical, and closely linked to adult roles and activities. Only in the religious dimension was there a more universalistic, egalitarian, and diffuse form of socialization—in line with the universalistic, egalitarian, and diffuse character of religious citizenship. The purposes of this religious "education" were twofold: to ensure that children conformed to the Lutheran mold; and, more optimistically, to transform children into pious individuals who would help create a righteous society (Ullmann 1966).

During the period 1700–1850, economic and political citizenship was restructured along universal, egalitarian, individualistic lines. The principle that every child—male or female, noble or peasant—was to be transformed into a religious, economic, and political citizen, on a basically equal footing with other citizens, won the institutional high ground. This dramatic conceptual change reflected and reinforced the restructuring of economics and politics around the universal egalitarian individual.[3] At the same time, the principle that the national polity was the primary social collectivity—and that citizenship was therefore primarily national rather than familial, local, or occupational—was strongly institutionalized. This development took organizational form with the expansion of the state and the elaboration of multiple links between the state and the individual.

These two lines of change—the rise of the individual as the primary social unit and the rise of the national polity as the primary collectivity—constituted the core of the new model of society. A third crucial change was a fundamental shift in the assumed purposes of social activity. In place of the salvation of the soul and the glorification of God, the new purposes became the development of the individual and the glorification of humanity, that is, the pursuit of progress (Dumont 1965; Nisbet 1980). Individuals were supposed to seek both private gain and the public good: The former meant personal wealth, happiness, and cultivation; the later meant national wealth, justice, and prestige.

As we shall see, this model of society made the construction of a formal, universal, egalitarian school system not only sensible but essential. Mass schooling came to be seen as the only way to generate technically competent, economically rational, politically astute citizens whose self-interested pursuit of personal development would also promote national development. It is to the emergence of this model in Sweden that I now turn.

THE NEW MODEL OF SOCIETY AND THE MASS SCHOOLING IMPERATIVE

The changes to be analyzed in this section were similar in kind and mutually reinforcing. Individuals became the elementary units of society, replacing more collective entities. The individual became a universal, egalitarian construct such that each person was seen as a potential citizen authorized to participate fully in the polity. The polity assumed a secular character under the rational tutelage of the expanding state, which displaced the Church as the dominant authority structure. In every dimension of change, schooling came to be seen as necessary for "progressive" development.

Religious Transformations

For members of the traditional Lutheran polity, citizen participation was largely passive, involving church attendance, household devotions, the singing of hymns, and so on. Citizenship was ritually conferred through baptism and renewed through communion. Passive citizens were subject to the jurisdiction of higher authority (the clergy); they were not a locus of authority in their own

right. The Lutheran creed existed independently of the individual and was maintained by the Church as an unalterable institutional complex.

From the late seventeenth century, however, numerous religious sects and
heretical movements boiled up in Sweden (Gustafsson 1973). They marked the
formation of a new religious individual, the dissenting citizen, who appropriated
the word of God to himself. This more active citizen emerged not only in the
recurrent Pietist waves that swept through the upper strata in the eighteenth
century but also in the lower-class fundamentalist movements of the early 1800s.
In these movements the individual sought salvation autonomously, without the
guidance of the clergy. The rejection of Church authority is perhaps best illustrated by the many unauthorized catechisms published in the eighteenth and
nineteenth centuries. Luther's *Little Catechism* was not the final statement; every
individual could find a path to the Lord.

As autonomous religious individualism gathered strength, the Church was
gradually "spiritualized," particularly after 1800. The distinction between the
sacred and the profane was sharpened: Religious rituals were to be conducted
solely in church, church buildings were no longer to be used for parish council
meetings, graveyards were closed to grazing animals (Åberg 1979). Hundreds
of small, familiar wooden churches were replaced by huge stone bastions, turning
parishioners into awed spectators rather than supplicating participants. The
Church gradually withdrew from local life, concentrating on spiritual matters
alone.

But religious citizenship did not die in the nineteenth century. On the contrary,
it became more devout and fervent, but in a form more consonant with the new
institutional purposes of rational exchange and progress. The doctrine of neology
emerged as a theological accommodation to rationalism and utilitarianism, and
the Church became a major promoter of the temperance movements, thereby
conjoining a secular concern (the salvation of the body) to its main spiritual
mission (the salvation of the soul).

As religious citizenship became more activist, schooling became a more central
religious concern. The first attempt to institute mass schooling occurred in the
1760s when Riksdag Pietists generated resolutions urging priests to arrange for
the instruction of children whose parents shirked their religious responsibilities.
In succeeding decades, religious educational associations emerged both within
and outside the Church to combat immorality at all levels of society. Church
resistance to mass schooling was offered mainly by highly placed clerics, who
feared that schooling would be more secular than religious.

Yet the Church hierarchy undermined its own position by promoting universal
literacy and maintaining obligatory education through the household examination
system. The lower clergy was more favorable toward schooling. Parish priests
often promoted the founding of parish schools in the period 1800–1840, and
many favored both secular and religious training. They sought pious but competent religious citizens who would contribute to spiritual progress through the
construction of a righteous, orderly society.

Economic Transformations

In the economic realm of pre-nineteenth-century Sweden, the individual was largely absent from institutional and organizational structures. The guilds, manufacturing and mining concerns, and the several peasant strata were all conceived as corporate participants in the economic polity. Discussions of economic policy reified these corporate entities, while economic policies were administered on a corporate basis. Hence, the first efforts to promote agricultural rationalization were limited to wholesale changes in corporate "privileges": Farmstead subdivision was freed up (1747) and peasants were given the right to sell grain (1775–1780). The activity of the individual peasant was not the object of public policy.

Economic citizenship also was highly differentiated. Corporate groups were seen as performing specific functions in society: the production of basic necessities (the peasantry), trade and handicraft production (the burghers), military protection and the maintenance of civilization (the nobility). Peasant economic membership in the polity was limited to the rents and taxes they paid to the nobility, clergy, and state. Individuals in these upper reaches of society were relatively inactive economic citizens because they were consumers much more than producers.

Between roughly 1750 and 1850, economic citizenship was radically universalized. Four lines of development are central. First, virtually all of the regulatory apparatus reifying corporate entities and restricting individual economic choice was dismantled (Carlsson 1956). Peasants gained control over incidental resources on their land (forests, fish, game animals), the right to trade, and the right to purchase noble lands. Peasant ownership rights and economic "freedom" thus became entirely equivalent to those of burghers and nobles. After 1800, town monopolies on trade were abolished, the mineral and timber industries deregulated, and the guilds abolished. Hence, burgher activities were opened to all. This piecemeal process of redefining all individuals as equivalently authorized economic citizens culminated in an 1864 regulation affirming complete economic freedom in all domains.

Second, corporate local collectivities were replaced by rationalized, individualistic extensions of the state. The Land Consolidation Reforms initiated after 1803 resulted in the consolidation of each peasant's multiple and widely scattered land holdings into one or a few large plots. The peasant villages were "shattered" (Åberg 1979) when peasants who were accorded holdings distant from the villages were required to relocate on their new farmsteads. Village unity was undermined; so too were collective agricultural activities.

Simultaneously, local government was reorganized and tied to the state. The traditional parish meeting that had formerly been charged with diffuse responsibilities, many of them religious, took on a more formal and secular character under close state supervision. New local structures (the Church council, parish board, and poor relief board) were established with differentiated, specific responsibilities (Johansson 1937). These reforms were in effect by mid-century.

Third, production for household consumption gave way to market production. A major factor in this shift was the differentiation of the peasantry. Large landholders became firmly embedded in markets and accumulated capital to expand their holdings; small landholders were squeezed into untenable positions. Rapid population growth meant that adequate holdings were unavailable to many children of small landholders. A large rural proletariat emerged, laboring for wages that increasingly were paid in cash rather than kind. Meanwhile, the rationalization of agricultural production methods, a process in which the state played an ever-expanding role, made Sweden a sizeable net exporter of grain by the 1820s (Sundbärg 1907). This development tied the economically advancing peasantry into price-competitive world markets, further boosting the rationalization of agricultural methods and individual producers.

Fourth, the exchange economy was fully monetarized as a national entity (Johansson 1937). State salaries were paid increasingly in cash; tax payments to the state and nobility shifted from produce to cash; the clergy's salaries were monetarized. Exchange so thoroughly penetrated the economy that by the 1840s integrated national markets had developed for all major agricultural products.

The individualization of economic citizenship indicated by the establishment of an entirely ''liberal'' exchange-oriented economy led to policies that focused on individuals, not just corporate groups. A good example is the rural-economy associations established in the period 1810–1820. The state organized local bodies to promote improvements in the methods used by each individual producer, whereas previous reforms had focused on the juridical condition of landholders as a group. The new programs were clearly predicated on the view that the individual was the unit of participation (citizenship) in the economic polity.

The emerging exchange economy based on technical change and individualistic organization strongly affected debates about schooling. As early as 1746, Jacob Faggot, head of the Land Survey Office, argued that schooling was needed to break the hold of traditional methods on the peasantry. His was one of many eighteenth-century voices arguing that schooling should be not only cultivating but useful (Löfberg 1949). But Faggot was exceptional in his call for *universal* schooling. Most proponents of utilitarian education held a more elitist view of schooling.

It was only toward the end of the eighteenth century that schooling for the entire population became a major concern. By that time, however, strict utilitarianism had given way to a more diffuse concern for what came to be called individual and citizen education (Sjöstrand 1961). This term referred to education that would endow individuals with diffuse capabilities and attitudes suitable to the new society that was taking shape. It included religious training, to be sure, but also literacy, numeracy, knowledge of the sciences, and Swedish geography and history—secular subjects that were seen as prerequisites for meaningful participation in the national polity.

Political Transformations

The spiritualization of the Church and expansion of the state led to the primacy of political over religious citizenship. As this shift occurred, political citizenship was redefined. In the older conception, citizenship was largely corporate, an attribute of families, guilds, estates, and the like (Ullmann 1966). The new conception was far more individualistic, linked as it was to the theory that progress was a central purpose of society.

Progress was seen as having two basic components: rising technical productivity and the expansion of monetarized exchange. The new form of polity was thus inherently "economic," though economic growth was sought not simply for its own sake but because it made broader social and cultural progress possible. In this framework it became obvious that political citizenship depended on economic citizenship: Those who were active in the pursuit of progress should be authorized to direct the societal project. Economic criteria thus became the basis of voter eligibility. And because economic citizenship had been thoroughly individualized, political citizenship followed suit.

We therefore find a shift in the formal criteria for political participation in the nineteenth century. At the local level, until the mid-eighteenth century all adults were expected to participate in village and parish council meetings (Johansson 1937). By the early nineteenth century participation was linked to landowners, a practice officially confirmed by the 1817 Riksdag. By 1843, however, land ownership was replaced by exchange activity as the criterion for political citizenship: Parish council participation required payment of a minimum amount of taxes, and a graduated voting scale was introduced (Åberg 1979). Eligibility to vote for Riksdag delegates evolved in the same direction.

The transformation of political citizenship toward a universal, individualistic model had clear implications for schooling. The term *individual and citizen education* is indicative. Policymakers were explicitly concerned with how tradition-bound peasants could be transformed into proper, productive individuals and citizens; hence, Swedish geography and history were part of virtually every proposal for mass schooling. Everyone was to learn what the nation was and where its roots lay, not least to ensure loyalty to the national polity.

But citizenship involved more than mere subordination. As publisher Gustaf Silverstolpe put it, schooling should teach the peasant "to know his duties *and his rights* as subject and citizen" (quoted in Aquilonius 1942, p. 32; emphasis added). The peasant was to be activated, not simply indoctrinated, if progress and national success were to be achieved.

Perhaps the clearest political effects on the schooling debate emerged among advocates of military conscription (Malström 1813). They favored universal schooling for a number of purposes: to instill loyalty to the national polity, to teach children the discipline required of good soldiers and civilians, to lower social tensions by putting all children through a common schooling experience. In these writings we are continually confronted by the dual nature of mass schooling. Schooling was to mold children in desired directions, but it was also to activate them to function well in society.

Summary

Between 1750 and 1850, citizenship in Sweden was restructured along universalistic, egalitarian, activist lines. Religious citizenship was transformed from a model of acquiescent acceptance into a model of self-authorized moral striving. Economic citizenship was generalized to include all individuals participating unrestrictedly in the rationalizing national market. Political citizenship came to depend on participation in the market completely apart from all "ascriptive" membership criteria, with its most egalitarian feature being compulsory military service. The institutional redefinitions emerged in tandem with organizational structures reflecting and reinforcing them: dissenting and reforming movements, temperance associations, the exchange economy, the citizen army, and differentiated political bodies supervised by the central state.

The egalitarian universalization of citizenship was both cause and consequence of the expansion of the state in the coalescing national polity. The polity was being reconceptualized as a unified social project oriented toward collective progress and success through the action of capable, committed citizens. It became evident, however, that these capable, committed individuals were not born; they had to be made. In other words, children had to be taken out of traditional socialization milieus (the home and family) and trained within a formal, distinct, disciplined structure. In the new model of the individual and polity, only schooling could produce the kind of citizens who were to build the progressive society. At a time when less than 5 percent of Swedish children attended school and over 75 percent of the population was engaged in agriculture, a broad public consensus had emerged around the necessity of mass schooling.

SWEDISH MASS SCHOOLING: TWO STEPS IN INSTITUTION BUILDING

The development of Swedish mass schooling occurred in two phases. The first, when schooling was a grass-roots social movement, lasted from roughly 1800 to 1840. The second, when the state entered the schooling arena and spurred the grass-roots movement from a trot to a run, occupied the next forty years.

During the first phase, the number of permanent rural primary schools (*folkskolor*) expanded from roughly 200 to 1,000, with a similar expansion of ambulatory schools (Torpson 1888). By 1840 over 20 percent of school-age children were attending school, a huge proportion by historical standards. Some of these new schools were founded by noblemen or wealthy burghers; the great majority (62 percent), however, were founded by "the parishes themselves,'' that is, the parish councils (Paulsson 1866). State involvement was minimal.

Schooling in the first phase, then, was initiated at the local level and was neither demanded nor funded by the state. It is significant that this school-building boom went virtually unmentioned in the prolonged schooling debate conducted between 1809 and 1840. It typified a Tocquevillian associational model of modern social organization, with individuals at the local level making collective decisions to build modern institutions on a voluntary, self-directed basis. As such, it had much in common with the early phase of mass schooling in many other Western countries (Craig 1981).

The public debate that mostly ignored the rapid expansion of schooling taking place in the countryside assumed familiar proportions (Aquilonius 1942). "Conservatives," especially the upper clergy, a portion of the nobility, and the guild-based burghers, favored schooling only for the poor (whose parents were seen as incapable of providing adequate socialization) and only for religious purposes. "Liberals," particularly peasant Riksdag delegates, merchant and professional burghers, and the lower nobility, favored an all-encompassing system that would teach both religious and secular subjects. By the 1830s little opposition to schooling remained, not least because the schooling projects underway in countries like Denmark, the United States, and Prussia were seen as evidence of Sweden's backwardness. The debate then began to focus on the content of the curriculum and how the schools would be financed rather than the desirability of a universal system per se.

The final result of the debate, the 1842 Statute on Common Schools, was prompted by a severe economic and political crisis in the late 1830s (just as "crises of national opportunity" prompted state action on schooling in other countries: Ramirez and Boli 1987). Marking the beginning of the second phase, the statute stipulated that every parish must establish a school and institute an ambitiously broad curriculum. Teacher-training seminaries were to be opened in every diocese seat, state subsidies were to be paid to poor parishes, and poor children were to be exempt from school fees. Within five years, over 500 additional schools had been built and nearly 2,800 teachers were at work. By 1859 there were over 4,200 teachers, by 1880 more than 10,000. School enrollments expanded proportionately, from about 52 percent of the school-age population in 1847 to 65 percent in 1859 and 86 percent in 1880 (Schelin 1978).[4]

As the system expanded, so did the state's regulatory and supervisory role. A school inspection system was established; standards for the school day, year, and sequence of instruction were instituted; and the proportion of teachers certified by the state approached unity. At the practical level, daily attendance rose steadily and the proportion of the stipulated curriculum actually taught to all children increased remarkably. Hence, by 1880 the institutional model of a universal school system socializing children in a standard program conducted by certified experts under the watchful guidance of the state had been largely realized.

THEORIES OF MASS SCHOOLING AND
THE SWEDISH EXPERIENCE

The Swedish experience does not accord well with any of the three rationalistic theories of mass schooling. The technical-functionalist argument links mass schooling to urbanization and industrialization, which are supposed to make a new form of social solidarity (Durkheim) or the transmission of new skills and values (Parsons) functionally mandatory. Yet as late as 1880, when the common school system was fully in place, only 15 percent of the population lived in urban areas and only 17 percent of the labor force was employed in industry or handicraft production (Isling 1980).

The abstract, "useless" nature of the curriculum undermines the class-imposition argument. If elites imposed schooling to create productive but slavish workers, as Bowles and Gintis (1976) maintain, they certainly chose an oddly intellectual curriculum with which to accomplish that task.[5] It has been argued instead that the "hidden" curriculum—the discipline, respect for authority, and subservience to elites that is "built in" to school structures—is the real key to elite dominance through schooling. This fallback position begs a crucial question: Why would the Swedish elites have relied solely on the hidden curriculum for their purposes of control? Why did the manifest curriculum exclude useful knowledge, emphasizing instead such esoterica as Bible history, geometry, and nature study? Introducing lower-class children to abstract knowledge previously reserved to the elites was bound to give these children an inflated sense of self— so inflated that they would even dare to raise claims against the elites who had imposed schooling on them.

A second major difficulty for the class-imposition argument is that the common schools were so thoroughly egalitarian. Isling (1980) argues that the primary target of the Statute on Common Schools was the rural proletariat, which was seen as criminal, morally depraved, and rebellious. Yet the statute made education obligatory for all children, not just the proletariat, and in fact school attendance was positively correlated with social status—proletarian children attended less than the landed, who attended less than burgher children. Furthermore, there was little differentiation within the schools. All children were supposed to study the same impractical curriculum.[6]

The status competition theory of mass schooling also is contradicted by the egalitarian nature of the schools. During the grass-roots phase, one might be tempted to interpret the schooling movement as status striving by freeholding peasants and elite urban groups. But the freeholders did not found schools for their own children alone; the parish schools were open to all, and children from poor families were especially encouraged to attend by being exempted from school fees. In addition, many upper-strata children (probably more than half, by the 1860s) attended common schools right alongside peasant and proletarian children. Evidence directly counter to the status/competition argument is provided by Gerger and Hoppe (1980) in their study of Locknevi parish in the period

1830–1880. They show that school attendance made little difference in children's adult status: Children usually inherited their social position from their parents. Furthermore, Agrell (1977) found in a study of populous southern Sweden that parishes with more rationalized and productive agricultural operations were only slightly more likely to found schools than other parishes.

Another problem with the status competition argument is that, in the first phase, it is difficult to identify any particular status group that was consistently in favor of, or opposed to, mass schooling. During the 1830s peasant freeholders were among the strongest advocates of schooling, but when it appeared that the burden of funding the schools would come to rest primarily on their shoulders, they backed off. In 1838, such prominent conservatives as historian E. G. Geijer and archbishop Johan Wallin suddenly abandoned their opposition to mass schooling and converted to the liberal line. On the other hand, in the final vote in 1841 all four of the Estates supported the Statute on Common Schools. The only vociferous opposition came from elite noblemen and clerics (exactly contrary to the class-imposition argument). By 1840, nearly everyone was ready to jump on the schooling bandwagon that was steamrolling through the countryside.

A more general problem applying to all three arguments is the fact that the objects and subjects of schooling were children. Nowhere in the Swedish debate do we find proposals for the schooling of adults, neither for functionalist purposes nor for social control nor for status attainment, even though the Church had always included adults as much as children. The reason children were singled out for attention, I believe, is to be found in the same theory of the individual that led to schooling becoming a major social concern in the first place. Children had to be the focus of schooling because individual identity was assumed to be relatively fixed and resistant to change after childhood. Because children were coming to be seen as the potential creators of progress and perfection, they were the "hope of the future" with the potential of transcending the limitations imposed by stubbornly immutable adulthood.

In general, the problem these theories share is their lack of attention to the institutional meaning of mass schooling. Some elite individuals certainly hoped that schooling would help control the lower strata, just as some debaters hoped that schooling would teach skills needed in a rationalizing economy and some activists hoped that schooling would increase the social prominence of their status groups. But the reason all such individuals turned to mass schooling—universal, egalitarian, impractical but deliberate socialization conducted outside the home—was that they were all inspired by the same institutional imperative. The entire population of children had to be transformed symbolically in accordance with a highly idealized vision of the pious, productive, disciplined citizen, and only formal socialization could convert these brutish little beasties into the "right" kind of participants in the national polity. A generalized faith in schooling—a faith never known before because never before had the cause of national progress through individual competence and striving become so dominant—pushed all sectors of society toward mass schooling.

That this faith rested more on hope than reality becomes clear when we consider the actual operations of nineteenth-century schools. Children attended sporadically and for only one or two years, all told (Johansson 1981). Teachers were often barely literate themselves, and the monitorial method that was obligatory until 1864 compounded teacher inadequacies by having poorly educated older students take charge of younger pupils. School attenders were only marginally more knowledgeable about religious doctrine than non-attenders, despite the fact that they came from more literate and affluent families.

For rational purposes, no matter how envisioned, nineteenth-century schools were thus wholly inadequate. For ritual purposes, however—and this is how we must, in the end, conceptualize mass schooling—the schools did a splendid job. Rough, unformed children were enrolled at the age of seven; capable, informed, devout citizens emerged at the age of fourteen—by definition. There was no evidence that schooling in fact produced better citizens than the home, the church, or the workplace. Rather, it was widely assumed that schooling could and should do so. This assumption was never evaluated. It was an article of faith.

CONCLUDING REMARKS:
SWEDEN IN WESTERN CIVILIZATION

A case study can be misleading because it suggests that schooling developments are the result of "indigenous" processes. In the nineteenth century this was largely true of the politics of mass schooling, as Archer (1979) has demonstrated at such length in her work on other European cases. But political analysis fails to come to grips with the underlying conceptual and organizational processes that place issues like mass schooling on the political agenda. Clearly, the Swedish schooling experience was not a product of local historical and cultural processes alone. Rather, schooling happened in Sweden because it happened in Western civilization. The same can be said of any other Euro-American country in this period: Schooling happened there because it happened elsewhere.

What I mean by this is less cryptic than it appears. Mass schooling was one of the consequences of the transformation of Western civilization from, in Parsons's terms, the ascriptive, particularistic, affective, and collectivist structures of medieval society to the achievement-oriented, universalistic, impersonal, and individualistic structures of modernity. This transformation involved an entire civilizational complex, and its precipitates included both the national polities that scholars tend to reify as "independent" units of analysis and the concept of the individual we take so much for granted as the basis of social organization.

From this perspective, explaining the origins of mass schooling in Sweden is an impossible enterprise. We need to understand the origins of mass schooling in Western civilization as a whole. But this project takes us straightaway into the central problems that Western intellectuals have been grappling with throughout the modern period. Why the transformation from medieval to modern society? Why the individual, the national polity, the state? Why the exchange economy, the technical system, representative democracy? For obvious reasons, I have not addressed these questions here. I hope I have shown that once the transformation process was well under way, mass schooling emerged as a logical, even necessary, consequence. So necessary, indeed, that we can hardly imagine modern society functioning without it.

NOTES

1. This chapter draws heavily on my book *New Citizens for a New Society* (1989), which treats these issues more fully and contains more detailed references.

2. Religious, economic, and political polities are usually not coextensive. Consider contemporary Sweden. The *political* polity is the "community" organized by the Swedish state: a defined territory, a given population, and so on. The primary *religious* polity is the community organized by the state Church, but it does not include Muslim or Orthodox confessors who are nonetheless members of the political polity. The *economic* polity can be defined as the unit encompassing all individuals and legal entities that must pay Swedish taxes. Some of these are neither religious nor political citizens.

3. The conceptual foundations of this restructuring were, of course, not Swedish but European in origin, and they appear to have been laid well before the Enlightenment (Hazard 1964; Dumont 1965). During the eighteenth and nineteenth centuries, much of this "modern" conceptual scheme was realized in social organization, though never to more than a partial extent.

4. In 1880 about 5 percent of school-age children were enrolled in private schools or state-run academic schools, 7 percent were in upper-level primary schools, and 7 percent were receiving "home education." Only 2 percent were accounted as receiving no formal education at all.

5. Another class-imposition argument has it that the Church imposed schooling to regain its control over the population. Apart from the fact that the Church was rapidly losing social power throughout the nineteenth century, this argument does not square with the secular nature of most of the curriculum nor with the fact that most of the upper clergy were staunch opponents of mass schooling.

6. A minimal course was defined for poor children, consisting of the catechism, reading, writing, and arithmetic—implying that the schools demanded least, not most, of the "unruly poor." The main form of differentiation at this time was constituted by the (now defunct) "parallel systems" of urban academic and private schools, which enrolled mostly upper-strata children.

5

Western versus Islamic Schooling: Conflict and Accommodation in Nigeria

William R. Morgan and J. Michael Armer

In Third World nations with roots in traditional civilizations, the process of educational expansion began centuries before Western colonial influence. Contemporary education in these countries, most of which are now struggling with issues of Western dependency, static economies, and ethnic rivalry, must deal with competing Western and non-Western forms of schooling. Understanding the transformation of educational institutions in such societies requires an examination of both the dynamics of Western school expansion and the viability of traditional forms of education.

So far this book has emphasized North American or European settings. Authors have assumed that family demand for Western schooling has become institutionalized, the central state responds with greater school supply, and modern ideals regarding child socialization proceed unchallenged. This chapter drops these basic assumptions.

We examine the ongoing process of educational expansion within one region of the multiethnic state of Nigeria. We begin by describing the northern Nigerian context and by providing an overview of Islamic and Western educational developments leading up to the Universal Primary Education program advanced by the central government in 1976. We then show how implementation of this initiative was shaped in the absence of strong centralized state authority by two traditional institutions—the patriarchal extended family system and Islamic clerics working within their pervasive, religious institution. The influence of these traditional forces on local demand for education is detailed in terms of school developments involving mutual accommodation between Islamic and Western schools. This results in a dual educational system in which educational choices for children are made primarily by parents. Finally, we discuss the strengths and weaknesses for the larger society of this particular resolution of the conflict between modern and traditional non-Western educational systems in the Third World.

NIGERIAN EDUCATIONAL DEVELOPMENT

School expansion across Nigeria's eastern, western, and northern regions was uneven during the British colonial era (1900–1960). In the more populous northern region, powerful theocracies known as emirates reigned prior to the imposition of British rule. These emirates were governed by the British on the principle of indirect rule, whereby colonial officers delegated day-to-day authority to traditional native rulers (emirs). It was in Britain's interest to support these Islamic rulers in their efforts to preserve traditional authority and to minimize disruptive Western influences. They supported native Islamic authorities by discouraging the development of Christian missionary schools that had become prevalent in the south. Thus, at the time of independence in 1960, Islamic areas in the north had the strongest unbroken cultural tradition but also the lowest level of Western-schooled human capital.

By 1964 it was estimated that only 11 percent of age-eligible children in the northern region were enrolled in primary schooling (Eastmond 1964). The universal educational experience in the region remained traditional Qur'anic instruction interpersed with occupational apprenticeship training—the same pattern that had existed since the fifteenth century. Small numbers of youth receiving Western schooling continued to come from the traditional ruling elite, those formerly charged with administering colonial policy and now controlling the independent government.

The major political unit in northern Nigeria has been the state of Kano, the largest in Nigeria and the cultural center for the Hausa-Fulani people. Contemporary Kano State and its capital city evolved from Kano Emirate and several surrounding emirates. Its modern statehood was granted in 1967, whereas Kano Emirate's first Islamic ruler took office in 1463. Within Birnin Kano, the part of the capital city that is the original Muslim quarters and bounded by thirteen miles of protective mud walls, the traditional badge of citizenship remains espousal of Islamic religious values, as demonstrated by recitation of the Qur'an during daily public prayers and other ritual observances. Such observances at once demonstrate one's sacred self-worth and communal loyalty.

In southern Nigeria, where predominant religious observances included forms of animism and ancestor worship, Islamic cultural influence in precolonial times was much weaker. Resistance to Christian missionaries was minimal; mission schools quickly proliferated. By 1913 in the south, 35,712 primary schools, mostly mission-based, had already been established (compared to 1,131 in the larger and more populated north). Upon independence many of these mission schools became government-supported and provided the core for a Western-like educational system.

Numerous educational plans were prepared to promote the goal of an equally modern school structure for the north. The most important was the Ashby Commission Report, prepared in 1960 by a group of Nigerian scholars and Western advisors. A central chapter in the report was authored by Frederick Harbison, a prominent founder of human capital theory and manpower planning (Harbison and Myers 1964). This scheme called for a large increase in secondary, technical, and postsecondary school enrollments, in order to fulfill the estimated manpower requirements linked to anticipated industrial growth. By contrast, Samuel Bowles's later plan (1968) emphasized the greater economic efficiency of an increase in primary education, with no immediate increase in secondary education and a decrease in more expensive technical education. The underlying rationale was a projected high net social return from an increase in primary-educated workers, and much lower returns for workers receiving expensive secondary and technical education.

While both these plans contributed valuable ideas to the knowledge base used in the educational development of the north, the final impetus to major action was apparently a demand-driven political act. In response to a question from a young girl during an official visit to the north in 1974, military ruler General Gowon announced before a group of journalists that he would implement universal primary education within two years (Arnold 1977). Education would become freely available to all six-year-old children, though not yet compulsory, and parents would be strongly encouraged to send their sons and daughters to school. This new national commitment was aimed primarily at the north, since the southern areas already had implemented similar plans by 1960 (Abernethy 1969). In 1975 the four northern states, containing over one-half of Nigeria's population, still had only 15 percent of the nation's total primary school enrollment (Arnold 1977). Such a political promise seemed credible due to the plans that had already been developed, the centralized political authority of a military government, and most important, the country's new petroleum wealth.

Neither General Gowon nor these technical plans addressed what would happen to the traditional Qur'anic system. Much political authority in the north came from communal solidarity rooted in the common religious heritage of Islam. Destruction of the traditional education system could weaken this source of political strength. Thus, the possibility existed that the goal of northern economic development could in fact be impeded by overly rapid achievement of regional parity in modern schooling.

In view of the continuing political strength of northern traditional elites and the absence of strong federal direction of local education policy, the implementation of universal schooling in the north has been greatly influenced by local demand. The key local actors have been representatives of the two primary preservationist institutions of northern society: the Hausa-Fulani extended family and Islamic clerics (*mallams*). In the following section we examine these two institutions and their impact on the emerging educational system.

LOCAL INSTITUTIONS

The Hausa-Fulani Extended Family

Most young persons in northern Nigeria are reared in a patrilineal, patrilocal extended family. Needless to say, this differs substantially from the bilateral kinship, nuclear family that is the normative arrangement in Western societies. At issue is whether or not such a difference affects how the institution of the family operates to shape demand for schooling and influence the size and character of the formal educational system. In considering these issues we have drawn primarily on our field observations, interviews of government officials, and two sample surveys of young men in Birnin Kano conducted in 1965 and 1979 (Morgan and Armer 1988), buttressed by the anthropological work of Fortes (1978) and Goody (1982).

Most noticeable to Western observers is the greater strength of the residential family unit. The presence of many children and interrelated adults in relatively close quarters creates the potential for more frequent and complex interaction, requiring the exercise of elaborate avoidance rituals, social space rules, speaking rules, and related customs. The traditional Hausa-Fulani compound is headed by a senior male with two or more wives, each co-wife and her children sleeping in a separate dwelling unit. One or more of the male head's junior brothers and their co-wives also may have quarters within this compound. Typically the family compound contains a grandparent generation as well, and barring health considerations, the senior male is usually the titular and often the actual head of the compound.

Child-rearing and socialization tasks of parenthood are not confined to the natural parents but rather are distributed across kin on a wide range of caring and fostering roles. There is an enormous moral and emotional investment in progeny. Childlessness, for example, is regarded as a more stigmatizing social problem for a couple than marital discord. In a patrilineal system the husband owns the children, but not the wife, who can fall back to her own kin network. In Hausa-Fulani society polgyny and wife seclusion, or purdah, are normal practices. Among the young men in our Birnin Kano surveys, 63 percent reported having fathers with two or more wives in 1965, and 61 percent in 1979.

This patrilineal parental authority was further magnified when set against the traditional absence of any state authority over family matters. This situation is very different from Western Europe, where state intervention in marriage, reproduction, and socialization of children dates back to the fifteenth century. In Hausa-Fulani society, as in most of West Africa, the idea of citizenship with individual rights and responsibilities within a modern polity is still a novel concept. The practice is still to consider an individual's rights and responsibilities to be vested in, and emergent from, a particular segment of society defined by kinship and descent rules.

Nevertheless, there has been a steady increase in popular acceptance of the state education system for males. The proportion of young men in Birnin Kano who received encouragement from their family to attend Western school increased from 58 percent in 1965 to 71 percent in 1979. Fathers were identified as the most important source of influence by over two-thirds of the young men surveyed, the remainder selecting other male relatives as most important.

Schooling and Family Status

A primary reason why Hausa-Fulani fathers increasingly have embraced Western education for their male children relates to their patrilineal role obligation to preserve the family lineage. Survival of the lineage depends on the economic viability of their progeny. Patrilineages and their associated neighborhoods in Birnin Kano and other cities of northern Nigeria tended to specialize in a particular trade or occupation. Sons as a rule would inherit their lineage's occupations through long apprenticeship training. The elaborate social exchange network of patron-client relations also made it possible for sons to be placed for apprenticeship in new occupations.

Since Nigerian independence in 1960 the largest new occupational sector has been government employment. Placing one's child in a Western bureaucratic-style school has been viewed as an apprenticeship in modern government employment. A son's success in schooling, as certified by the level of examinations passed, determined the level at which he could be expected to work in government, holding direct implications for the future prosperity of the lineage. Such an apprenticeship experience was deemed less important for daughters, however, as the continuing practice of wife seclusion made it more pragmatic to continue to provide them apprenticeship training directly within the female-run household economy.

A second reason why Hausa-Fulani fathers have stopped viewing Western schooling as an unwelcome state intervention has to do with their long-held practice of giving over their children to the local *mallam* for Islamic training. It was generally understood that besides teaching Islam, the *mallam* functioned as the principal extra-familial link with the larger society, a natural bridge between the patrilineal authority of the extended family and the patron-client relationship that were the foundation of all Hausa-Fulani adult institutions. Nowadays, however, the skills and knowledge learned and the certification received in the Western school increasingly have become accepted as prerequisites for a position in the state bureaucracy. Patron-client relations do indeed continue to operate in this new employment setting, but without the legitimation and sponsorship once provided by *mallams*. Paradoxically, despite the *mallam*'s diminishing placement role, an important source of cultural validation for this new schooling lies in the development of curriculum options that provide for continuing exposure to *mallams* and their Islamic values. Their presence in the emerging modern school system has helped families transfer the sacred trust the *mallams* once exclusively enjoyed to the more secular setting of the modern school classroom.

The *Mallams*

Islamic education for centuries provided the main calling for a large segment of the adult male population of northern Nigeria. As late as the 1960s, religious instruction was the third most common occupational activity, after farming and trading. Our survey data indicated that in 1965 one of every eight adult males residing in Birnin Kano identified himself as a *mallam*. By 1979, after the push for universal primary education, the introduction of television, and numerous other major social and technological changes, this proportion had dropped to a still sizeable one in twenty-five.

The actual title of *mallam*, however, traditionally has conferred an honored status in the northern Nigerian stratification system more than it has denoted a specific occupational role. A *mallam* was a learned man, one who had achieved knowledge of the Qur'an, and in varying degrees, the Hadith and religious commentaries. What he did with that knowledge and status varied greatly. *Mallams* with more advanced training tended to specialize either in Islamic legal doctrine or Sufi mysticism, thus focusing on either worldly or spiritual affairs. Beyond this division, their role activities were quite diffuse. The traditional mix of role activities within the *mallam* class is one factor that has permitted them to adapt to changing social conditions and still maintain their social prominence. Respondents in our two Kano surveys assigned prestige scores to a set of sixteen modern and traditional occupational positions. In 1965 *mallams* were ranked fourth, after government and military leaders, doctors, and lawyers. In 1979, despite their shrinking numbers, *mallams* ranked third in prestige, just ahead of lawyers (Table 5.1).

The most common role activity of *mallams* had been as Qur'anic schoolmaster to young children. This involved daily or twice daily sessions at or just outside their residence, leading their pupils through prescribed stages of recitation, memorization, and copying of Qur'anic verses. This routine continued for however many years were needed to reach the required level of mastery. Other *mallams* offered instruction and discussion for advanced students and adults, usually based on the books of commentaries on the Qur'an.

A few particularly important *mallams* held special salaried titles as Imam and served as advisors to the emir and other ruling officials. The popular expectation was that these *mallams* would use their religious knowledge, both in private counsel and in public criticism, to check any abuses of power by the ruling class. Given the absence of an Islamic priesthood, *mallams* also led prayers during the principal life-cycle rituals—naming ceremonies for the newborn, marriage services, Qur'anic graduation ceremonies, and funerals. For these various activities

Table 5.1
Prestige Ratings of Selected Occupations, 1965 and 1979 Surveys of Kano Young Men

Occupation		Prestige Rating	
		1965	1979
1.	Government Officials	1.47	1.82
2.	Doctors	1.92	1.94
3.	Lawyers	2.03	2.30
4.	Mallams	2.40	2.24
5.	Office Clerks	2.77	2.89
6.	Primary School Teachers	2.80	2.79
7.	Store Clerks	2.81	3.14
8.	Market Traders	3.12	2.30*
9.	Factory Workers	3.29	2.89*
10.	Building Contractors	3.34	2.49*
11.	Policemen	3.39	3.31
12.	Tailors	3.46	3.35
13.	Farm Owners	3.54	2.68*
14.	Butchers	3.95	3.73
15.	Leatherworkers	4.10	3.92
16.	Praise-singers/ drummers	4.26	4.37
Mean rating, all occupants		3.04	2.89
Sample size		591	632

Note: Ratings were positions on a "status hill," having scale values from 1 to 5. *Indicates shift of 0.5 or more on the 5-point scale.

mallams received alms either in the form of monetary payments or ceremonially prescribed amounts of food or clothing. Increasingly, those *mallams* with political influence are men whose knowledge base and place of work are centered primarily in the new modern institutions of higher education. A firm and public Islamic identity affirms their communal value structure, but it is the modern federal university linkage that is becoming vital in addressing the national issues facing Kano State. Instead of serving as a check on the power of the emir, these new *mallams* must be able to intercede with the representatives of the federal (whether military or civilian) government. Modern educational credentials and expertise, as signified in holding a university academic title, provide the necessary legitimation for participation in "blue-ribbon" commissions whose influence is wielded in the form of "white paper" policy recommendations. Such formalism, despite the new genre of rational empiricism, represents an important continuity with traditional *mallams'* practice of invoking the revealed wisdom of Islamic legal doctrine in their earlier intercessions before the emir.

THE EMERGING DUAL EDUCATION SYSTEM

Primary Education

The most important role change has occurred for *mallams* who serve as Qur'anic teachers. In the typical primary school this traditional *mallam* was transformed into a subject-matter specialist, offering a daily period of instruction to each student in Islamic Religious Knowledge, commonly referred to as IRK. This new classroom teaching format required fewer *mallams*, since over the course of the school day a single *mallam* could reach many more children than by the traditional tutorial approach.

IRK class was positioned between the modern subjects of math, English, Hausa (the prevalent language of northern Nigeria), science, and social studies. By itself the class does not provide anything more than the rudiments of the Islamic training that most parents seek for their children. What it does provide is sacred legitimation for an otherwise secular curriculum.

Most primary school students also attend a daily session of Qur'anic school, held usually in late afternoon or early evening. These Qur'anic schools either take place at the residence of the *mallam* and follow the traditional group recitation–tutorial format, or else are held in the newer, Islamiya schools where *mallams* teach in regular classrooms. Some of these Islamiya schools actually occupy the same buildings as the modern primary schools, their classes being scheduled after regular classes.

Some fathers responded to the government appeal that they enroll their children in primary school by sending them exclusively to an Islamiya school. These particular Islamiya schools offer morning instruction in the modern subjects parallel to the regular primary schools, but with a relatively stronger emphasis on Islamic and Arabic training. In 1979 an estimated one of every three students in state-sponsored schools at the primary level in Birnin Kano attended an Islamiya school, with one of every six attending there exclusively. The total enrollment in the thirty-one modern schools was 29,814, compared with 11,381 students in the eighteen state-supported Islamiya schools, of whom about half attended there exclusively and the other half also attended a modern primary school. The appeal of the Islamiya schools has continued during the 1980s, and by 1987 seven more of the state-sponsored schools had been established in Birnin Kano, making a total of twenty-five. This does not include the unknown number of Islamiya schools that exist without government recognition or support.

Local authorities give mixed reports as to the instructional adequacy of the Islamiya schools. In contrast to traditional Qur'anic schools, however, these schools have the incentive of state financial support subject to the condition that a fixed portion of their staff meet the minimum standards for modern primary-level instruction, which involves the completion of a primary education or its equivalent. Out of a total of 263 teachers in the state-sponsored Islamiya schools in 1979, 60 percent qualified for state salaries. These 158 teachers included 41

Table 5.2
Comparison of Educational Backgrounds of Islamiya Primary School Teachers with and without Government Funding, Birnin Kano, 1979

Education Received	Teachers Funded	Unfunded
Secondary School	4%	6%
Primary School	41%	12%
Higher Islamic Studies	19%	34%
Islamic Training	20%	47%
Unreported	16% (100%)	1% (100%)
Total	158	105

Source: Kano State Ministry of Education.

Table 5.3
Proportion of Male and Female Students in Western and Islamiya Primary Schools, Birnin Kano, 1979

Students	Primary School Western	Islamiya
Male	74%	46%
Female	26% (100%)	54% (100%)
Total	29,814	11,381

Source: Kano State Ministry of Education.

percent who had a modern primary education and 4 percent with modern secondary education, the remaining half having Islamic training only. For the 105 without state salaries, only 18 percent had completed any modern schooling (Table 5.2).

One indication that fathers consider Islamiya schools to be culturally safer than the Western school alternative is the higher proportion of female youth who attend them. In 1979 girls constituted only 26 percent of the total Western primary school enrollment in Birnin Kano. This was the same percentage as ten years earlier, when 27 percent were girls. In the Islamiya schools, however, girls represented 54 percent of the enrollment. Paradoxically, in this Islamic society the availability of the more conservative Islamiya schools offers a new opportunity for young women (Table 5.3).

Another traditional accommodation in this expansion of Western education in

Birnin Kano is that for the most part it took place in already existing school sites. Even with a 328 percent enrollment jump in ten years (from 6,968 to 29,814), all but four of the thirty-one modern primary schools antedated the 1976 universal primary education edict. During the colonial era, five schools were established prior to World War II and five more afterwards. Within a year of national independence another fifteen had been established, consistent with the political and social demand nature of Nigeria's educational planning. Why few new schools have been built in Birnin Kano in the recent period has to do primarily with the shortage of building space in this ancient city and the need to expend available building funds in the less developed rural areas. Nevertheless, keeping in mind that many adults continue to perceive modern education as a negative Western cultural influence, containing the enrollment expansion within familiar school settings also serves to facilitate community acceptance.

In summary, this developing dual primary school system offers Kano fathers two main educational options for their children. They can attend a Western primary school that includes the standard subject of IRK with supplemental religious instruction at a traditional Qur'anic or Islamiya school. Alternatively, they can attend an Islamiya school exclusively. Whether or not these modern and traditional alternatives will eventually comprise an integrated school system remains to be seen.

Secondary Education

Primary school leavers seeking to enter a state-supported secondary institution must pass the state common entrance examination and then a screening interview at each institution considering the applicant. The overall size of the demand for secondary education can be gauged from the number of secondary school entrance examination candidates and subsequent actual enrollments. In 1968, 6,800 primary school leavers in all of Kano State took the examination. Of these, 2,900 received interviews (meaning that they had passed the written examination), but less than 900 were admitted. These numbers jumped to 23,300 examinees in 1979, of whom 13,000 were interviewed and 10,800 admitted. The candidates that year from Birnin Kano numbered 2,100.

One indicator of how much of this demand was for *traditional* secondary education is the number of students who took the optional test of IRK that was offered as part of the entrance examination. Whereas all candidates had to take exams in Hausa, English, and mathematics, only those interested in attending the Islamic Studies institutions took the IRK test. In 1979, 400 students out of a total of 2,100 candidates from Birnin Kano took the IRK test. This number approximates the one in six proportion of secondary students currently enrolled in local traditional institutions. As of 1978, twelve modern secondary schools operated in the Kano metropolitan area, enrolling a total of 6,300 students, and three Islamic secondary schools enrolled another 1,400 students.

Within these two sectors students were distinguished according to the course of study being pursued. In the modern sector 2,300 students in the five secondary grammar schools were working toward West African Examination Council certification, a prerequisite for modern postsecondary schooling. Another 2,150 youth in three teacher-training colleges were seeking terminal degree teaching licenses, and the 1,850 youth in four technical institutes were working toward various specific vocational licenses. At the Islamic institutions, 850 youth sought teaching licenses and 550 were pursuing Higher Muslim Studies certificates.

The clear preference for Western education at the secondary level reflects the increasingly prevalent belief among young men and their families in the importance of modern education credentials for successful occupational placement and economic well-being. Yet dwindling petroleum revenues over the past decade have placed severe constraints on the ability of the crowded government bureaucracies to offer positions to hopeful youth. In the future, successful job placement will depend upon more rapid development and indigenization of corporate industrial production, agriculture, and services. Such development is, of course, the substance of sustained economic growth. In the meantime, demand for Western postprimary education can be expected to continue to grow faster than the economy can absorb its graduates. As in other societies, the dominant response of individual youths to this modern job shortage has been not to lose interest in schooling but rather to pursue higher education credentials in order to compete more effectively for scarce positions. Despite the shrinking economy of the 1980s, secondary school enrollment in Kano State increased more than fourfold.

CONCLUSIONS

Dual Equal Educational Opportunity

The introduction of universally available Western schooling so far has done little to diminish the continuing importance of Islamic training in Birnin Kano. In the absence of a compulsory education law, Islamic education remains more universal than standard Western primary education. The change is that religious instruction has become more efficient, entailing fewer hours of instruction and fewer *mallams*. The other key change is the increased recognition that this form of education is in fact religious. Each new teaching position for a *mallam* signifies a more exclusively religious definition of his teaching role. Thus, in the context of the modern primary school, *mallams* are the teachers in charge of the religious curricular component. In the larger context of the total primary educational facilities for Kano youth, they become the providers of after-school Islamic instruction. And finally, for a substantial minority of youth, the *mallam*-headed Islamiya school signifies a viable religious alternative to the secular Western primary school.

Continued reverence in northern Nigeria for Islamic cultural tradition can be expected to perpetuate the demand for advanced Islamic training. The magnitude of social demand ultimately will depend on the creativity of this society in defining new and appropriate occupational roles for the *mallams*. Even in the absence of such creativity, however, increasingly nationalistic and non-Western implications of an Islamic cultural identity can be expected to help attract youth to this more traditional form of education.

A dual education system as described in this case study is only one of several possible resolutions to how new nation-states can expand Western education to their less developed, culturally diverse regions. This resolution was a form of demand-driven, joint optimization that was totally unanticipated by the earnest educational planning specialists. We have argued that the two key northern Nigerian institutions of the patrilineal extended family system and the religious clerics have been responsible for shaping this particular institutional outcome.

This outcome has a number of strengths, but it also has some glaring weaknesses that may eventually require more direct state intervention. In particular, the present system as described here gives short shrift to the education of women. In new nations having a different configuration of key local institutions, the comparable demand-driven resolution might be quite different. Alternatively, in the presence of a strong federal establishment with vigorous centralized planning, the impact of these demand pressures, whatever their institutional composition, could be considerably diminished.

The overall strength of the dual systems outcome can be understood with respect to the two forms of equal educational opportunity they unwittingly work to optimize. First, from the standpoint of development, there is the belief that all regions of the country and/or ethnic groupings have equal rights to share in the economic, social, and intellectual benefits of a modern education. If exogenous influences such as prior colonial policy are responsible for creating a preexisting condition of inequality, then it is right and fair to allocate national resources in a remedial manner. This first interpretation of educational equality is consistent with the view of education as serving the goal of balanced modernization and economic growth.

A second goal recognizes the continuing importance of education in its role as the transmitter of tradition, representing the cumulative historical experience and symbolic forms that define the unique cultural identities of a people (Shils 1981). From this perspective each distinct region or ethnic group believes it has an equal right to have its local culture and heritage preserved, and at the same time to have it legitimated more widely across society as part of the new national identity.

In addition to their symbolic importance, these local ethnic traditions often represent a way of life that until recently may have existed intact for generations. This fact alone gives value to tradition, however oppressive and inferior in quality that life-style may have been. Its local proponents therefore will value educational institutions that can transmit this tradition to future generations. From the standpoint of nation building, this second goal for equal opportunity via schooling permits a channeled expression of the primordial sentiments and ethnic identities that are at once so volatile and energizing in new nations (Geertz 1963). These sentiments properly harnessed can supply much of the necessary individual and collective mobilization for a nation's development. Of course, they also can make the task of nation building more difficult insofar as they help to perpetuate ethnic rivalry and conflict.

Counterforces to Western Schooling

While social demand for modern schooling may be pervasive in much of the world, the present study illustrates resistance and counterforces that operate in many societies. In Nigeria we have seen a combination of cultural resistance and structural accommodation with Western education. The potential conflict between Islamic schooling and modern Western schooling is defused by modifying both systems in ways that allow each to meet educational demands of the population and educational needs of the society, as perceived by both political and religious leaders, while simultaneously preserving Islamic and cultural values of the society. Rather than imposing an alien system, the colonial policy of indirect rule gave local authorities room to limit Western school expansion, especially Christian mission schooling, and eventually to develop curricular modifications that are compatible with traditional institutions. Religious instruction in Islam was incorporated in Western schools, and modern Islamiya schools were developed with expanded curricula and classroom organization to produce a broader range of skills and knowledge.

This dual educational structure is only one possible way new nations can expand Western education while preserving traditional systems. The strength of these parallel school institutions lies in their contribution to (1) the equalization of modern educational opportunity in a country where colonial policy and other influences led to an imbalance in educational resources, and (2) the preservation of unique cultural identities of pluralistic groups within Nigerian society.

6

Legitimating the State's Involvement in Early Childhood Programs

Sorca O'Connor

Remarkable changes in family structure and labor force participation are shifting the care and education of very young children to formal organizations. The number of children between the ages of three and five who now attend an organized preschool of some kind has risen dramatically since 1965 (Figure 6.1). This shift is empirically linked to increases in women's labor participation, particularly among those employed in manufacturing and service sectors of industrialized nations (O'Connor 1988).

Yet despite rising workforce participation, state provision of preschool supply lags behind rapidly climbing local demand. At the same time, many parents still rely on kin and less formal networks. State actors may desire to incorporate young children into the mass schooling institution, but first a government must establish its own legitimacy as a credible player. Only then can the state effectively raise the supply of preschool organizations and broaden expressed demand.

In this chapter I sketch out the organization of early childhood programs at the national level and contrast them with the organization of primary schooling. I emphasize the point that rationales for the incorporation of children into systems of mass education, advanced by political actors, are not sufficient to respond to existing local demand. The legitimacy of mass schooling systems is contrasted with the still stigmatized and disorganized activity of daycare providers. To understand these contrasting levels of institution building, I utilize a framework that delineates the conditions under which the state can incorporate young children and its own loosely knit programs into the formal mass schooling institution.

Figure 6.1
Preschool Enrollment Rates by Geographical Region, 1965–1980

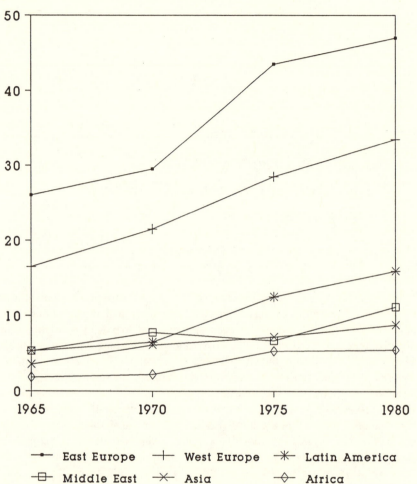

Source: O'Connor (1988).

THE STATE'S AUTHORITY OVER YOUNG CHILDREN

A good deal of debate persists over the role played by the state in relation to its citizens and the degree of its autonomy (Skocpol and Amenta 1986; Bowles and Gintis 1986). There is general agreement that the state is not powerless as a bounded organization and that states do construct policies that constrain or enhance choices related to economic action or social services. Clearly, influence is exercised by interest groups, experts, social reformers, and career civil servants in shaping certain policies. However, state actors and their government agencies often exhibit a fair amount of independence from other corporate actors and individuals.

State interest in preschool children is relatively recent, but the school has long been the state's socialization agent for children above a certain age. As state authority grows in nations, children are increasingly regarded as "citizens" and are rationally and uniformly socialized by the state with the intention of advancing technical competence and promoting economic development (Boli-Bennett and Meyer 1978). At the individual level, schools help teach obedience to impersonal authority, punctuality, and categorical conformity (Parsons 1959; Dreeben 1968). At an institutional level, mass schooling has influenced economic development, served as an occupational sorting mechanism, and unified otherwise disparate populations around national symbols and culture (Berg 1971; Meyer and Hannan 1979). What is most interesting is that the state holds such popular support to encircle children and their primary schools—a level of institutional authority not yet reached in relation to very young children.

Some researchers suggest that the state-organized educational system "takes the place of the family and other informal socialization systems in the modern world" (Ramirez and Boli 1987). Yet this interpretation fails to take into account mothers' child-rearing activities vis-à-vis the school. In fact, schools have assumed responsibility for certain tasks while explicitly refusing to take on others. Mass schooling limits itself to certain child-rearing functions by being available to families only for certain hours, by excluding very young children, and by defining various "caring" and custodial functions as falling outside the domain of education. In most countries the greatest proportion of care and education for children below the compulsory schooling age continues to come from less organized sectors: neighborhood childminders, parents, and relatives. Child care, of course, is carried out by women and is traditionally attached to the domestic sphere. Shifts in responsibility in this arena from the informal private sector to governments need economic or social justification.

The State Struggles for Legitimacy

The entrance of the state into the area of early childhood can be justified on two distinct grounds. (1) Human and cultural theories argue that children who are "deprived" during their early years will be unable to make up the deficit later (Selowsky 1976; Committee for Economic Development 1987). (2) Economies increasingly depend upon the labor force participation of women (Ward 1985). Which political justifications are employed depends on whether states regard education as an investment or a consumption good (Craig 1981). Investing in young children with an eye to their future citizenship may be more acceptable than offering a service to mothers as consumers whose need is for someone else to take responsibility for their children while they work.

Early education programs that respond to alarms from economic observers about the need to develop a higher achieving and more competitive work force clearly follow the investment rationale. As a result, many nations have incorporated preprimary schools into existing educational institutions. Such arrangements take early ''education'' out of the home; yet responsibility for children continues to be divided between the school and home. The school provides skills and social training, while most nurturing activities and physical care still occur in the home. This arrangement permits an early and direct link between the state and the child. Yet the needs of working women are not entirely responded to by the state. Not only do preschool programs operate for an insufficient amount of time, but also ''education'' is typically defined in terms of cognitive and citizenship skills, not in terms of close physical and affective care.

Social scientists still characterize the functions of the school and family vis-à-vis the child as being in opposition to each other (Dreeben 1968). To successfully absorb activities identified with the home, educational institutions must either dilute their own definition to include nurturance or shortchange children in their need for both education and nurture. Educational rationales for preschools afford high levels of legitimacy but lead to organizations that fall far short of providing child services now demanded by many parents (Myrdal and Klein 1968; Tilly and Scott 1978).

Under what conditions can state actors legitimately take charge of the education and care of young children? As states in the modern world gradually accept responsibility for a wide range of tasks once provided by families, several patterns have become evident. Researchers have suggested four prerequisite conditions that make state action credible. First, institutional differentiation of an activity depends on an adequate and legitimate definition of the activity. Second, organization of the activity must be clearly distinguished from organized activities of other institutions (Ramirez and Rubinson 1979). Third, authority over the social activity must be concentrated in a single decision-making agency in order for the state's bid for authority to be valid. Finally, for the state to command authority over social activities previously labeled as local or private concerns, they must be reclassified to embody national purposes that come legitimately under state jurisdiction. I will address each necessary condition in turn, recognizing that social ideologies and cultural reproduction often mitigate against state incorporation of early childhood programs.

Defining the Preschool Institution

Preschool, kindergarten, day nursery, nursery school, day care, daycare center, crèche, and children's center are all designations that suggest distinctions based on historical and organizational antecedents. In a study of twelve countries, Stone (1972) found that most preschool organizations were founded either in the eighteenth or nineteenth century as refuges for children who had been deprived of parental care. Custodial ''charters'' or educational ''charters'' have followed the descendants of these early preschools into the late twentieth century, with educational settings carrying greater status and legitimacy than custodial settings.

Organizational structures established a century and a half ago are astonishingly resistant to change. As a result, personnel in custodial programs whose goal is the health or welfare of the child often have no training in education, even though many children attend such programs for a full day. Teachers prepared to educate young children most often work in places called "schools" with programs lasting for a few hours each day (although sometimes for fewer than five days each week).

Custodial and educational rationales parallel consumption and investment goals. Modern nations, endorsing this constructed dichotomy, rely on educational definitions to define and justify their public programs. A content analysis of information from *The International Encyclopedia of Education* (1985) reveals that of eighty-eight countries mentioning preschool systems, "education" was listed more often than any other goal. Programs are far more often labeled "nursery school" or "kindergarten" than "day care," and most countries name ministries or departments of education as the responsible agency. In a survey of sixty-seven countries, 52 percent of preschool systems were in ministries of "education and related activities," 25 percent were in public health ministries, 12 percent in social health ministries, and 11 percent in others including labor, population, culture, and youth agencies (Mialaret 1976).

Among the stated goals for early childhood programs, developmental and educational goals appeared most often, while the goal of "looking after the children or helping mother" was relegated to fourth place (Mialaret 1976). Taken together, these data suggest that preschool-age children are formally served most often by agencies that are defined as educational. Educational rationales are important to parents who hope to place their children in preschools that will coach them for primary school academic routines, especially in light of widespread school failure (Bettelheim and Takanishi 1976).

Most descriptions of preschools used for academic preparation echo historical rationales for other levels of schooling centering on the child's individual development. Other commonly accepted schooling goals focus on political and ideological intentions to promote democracy, loyalty, and citizenship—providing broader rationales for state involvement (Goodnow and Burns 1984). The dual purposes of the modern state—building nations through the eradication of local collectivities while providing individuals with the means for personal development—are commonly articulated in government descriptions of preschool programs. These descriptions fail to incorporate, and indeed are antithetical to, definitions that place the familial facets of preschool services at the center.

Institutional Distinctiveness of the Preschool

The public interest in children below the age of compulsory schooling is still being elaborated, but signs point to extension of the educational model to accommodate demand for services for young children. State involvement in the lives of school-age children is legitimated by reference to the state's obligation to the child itself as a citizen, not as a member of its family. School marks the beginning of the child's right to education and to equal entitlements available to citizens. If very young children's needs are redefined as education, then the state can legitimate its intrusion into this area with reference to technical-functional goals and nation building.

Those who promote the insertion of early childhood programs into educational systems circumvent the issue of the state's intrusion into the heretofore sacrosanct province of the family. When the intrusion is veiled in educational garb, early childhood becomes a proper domain of the state. But a comprehensive definition of "preschool activity" must include some functions of both institutional partners in child rearing: the school and the family. This complicates efforts to distinguish preschool from either one of them, particularly in Western industrialized societies where the dichotomy between school and family is deeply entrenched. Preschool programs either fill in for disadvantaged families or prepare children for formal schooling, but rarely do they address both functions.

Concentration of State Action

The range of state agencies sponsoring preschool programs is "clear proof that in most countries pre-school education has not yet found its place and achieved stability" (Mialaret 1976). As a result of continued intra-state conflict over definitions and purposes, programs fostering very similar activities often are housed in an array of competing agencies. Fragmentation also results from territorial disputes among agencies and resistance from a range of private groups and individuals who have ideological or pecuniary interests in controlling programs. In India, for example, there are at least seventeen different government departments dealing with some aspect of child care. According to one report, field activities overlap, administrative costs rise, and programs often fall short of policy (Khalakdina 1979). In France, where ministries of health, welfare, and education all share programs for young children, "the compartmentalizing which exists among the different agencies dealing with child care is a permanent source of difficulties and of dissent" (David and Lezine 1976). In Israel, services for young children have been initiated in different time periods in the interest of child welfare, as education for all children, or as support for women to work; existing rivalries and tensions among ministries are one of the primary problems blocking development of quality day care (Jaffe 1982).

The high degree of privatization in the field supports widely held beliefs that child rearing is the exclusive responsibility of private families or their chosen agents—further evidence of the state's low level of incorporation. Despite a worldwide trend toward greater state responsibility and spending between 1965 and 1980 (O'Connor 1988), the level of privatization and decentralization in the United States, for example, has increased strikingly over the past several years as the political climate has taken on a decidedly conservative tone. In the Unesco report (Mialaret 1976), of thirty-eight countries responding to a question about jurisdiction, sixteen mentioned only private preschools, fourteen mentioned both public and private, and eight mentioned only public schools. Territorial battles, constituencies with competing needs, powerful economic interests, cultural and local norms all converge to impede the organization of state-sponsored and universal early childhood programs.

Reclassification of Women's Familial Work

An underlying theme in the debate over state responsibility for the care and education of young children revolves around accepted cultural norms that place women in the primary role of raising children in family settings. Women's participation in the labor force, while often poorly paid and monotonous, does offer a measure of economic autonomy and has influenced their reproductive and socialization behavior. The relationship between labor force participation and fertility has been firmly established, although the direction of causality is difficult to sort out (World Health Organization 1980).

A strong relationship also is observed between women's labor force participation and early childhood programs. My earlier empirical analysis shows that increases in female labor force participation in service and industrial sectors are followed over time by increases in preschool enrollment rates (for detailed findings, see O'Connor 1988). Two points stem from this historical influence of labor force participation. First, it tends to be associated with parents' rising preference and expressed demand for daycare and preschool services. But the state is only one organized provider, located in an institutional landscape still dominated by private provision. Second, as the state struggles to act in a more legitimate role, it continues to rely on tried and true educational rationales in legislating programs rather than reclassifying women's caretaking functions as an appropriate concern of the state. Historically, states have justified involvement in the provision of caretaking as distinct from education only in reference to maternal deficiency among the poor.

The ideology of the deficient mother calls into question the primacy of women's right to uninterrupted economic activity over her duty to rear children. Women's work outside the home is consistently considered problematic vis-à-vis children. Researchers from several European nations have documented widespread resistance to reclassifying the care of young children as a responsibility of the state.[1] Cultural norms concerning women's ties to children are complemented by norms that exclude men from close parenting. Swedish men seldom take advantage of the state's liberal paternity leave policy; blue-collar workers in the United States refuse certain child rearing tasks; kibbutz men in Israel recoil at the idea of working in the children's house (Boocock 1977). In the United States, the assumption that mothers should have primary responsibility for raising children has kept child care "underground, chaotic and disreputable," according to Grubb and Lazerson (1988).

State authorization of adequate and universally available early child care and education would further free women from domestic activity, enabling them to pursue achievement-oriented lives, theoretically leaving them no more burdened by the presence of children than their male counterparts. The compulsory provision of child care services would promote women's fuller realization as adult political and economic actors and move them closer to equality with men in the eyes of employers. Assisted by such new social rights (Mann 1987), women could be viewed as workers, managers, and professionals rather than as potential or actual mothers. Even women whose market work is in day care, though unfairly compensated, are free agents in choosing that work, are paid for it, and are free from expectations that accompany a biological connection to the child.

Analytically it is important to distinguish between child rearing as women's work and child rearing as work belonging to the family sphere. Even where child rearing is performed in a public or collective setting, it is done almost exclusively by women. In countries where state responsibility for children is greater, as in Eastern Europe and Scandinavia, the care of young children continues to be identified as women's work even though it often takes place outside the family (Jancar 1981). Systems in both East and West that make it possible for women to become economic actors have had little effect on women's roles in the family; this, in turn, constrains their economic or professional achievements. In most countries preschool teachers and care providers are women with low pay and low status.

Child rearing has been classified not only as women's work but also as family work. It may be reclassified as non-family work even as it continues to be women's work. Reclassifying child rearing as men's work would not necessarily lead to state responsibility, although it would likely have profound effects on both gender relations and child socialization (Chodorow 1980). To place women in as unburdened a situation as men (with respect to children) would require a dual reclassification, making children a public responsibility and revising the gender division of labor within the home.

The family's sexual division of labor, in which women have assumed primary responsibility for the care of children, can be understood as a function of cultural patterns that predate modern state and economic institutions. However, the tenacity of such patterns can be attributed to mutually reinforcing practices in various institutional sectors. Practices in the family and in the economy mirror one another and spuriously justify the continued inhibition of women's freedom to practice certain adult privileges. In this context, the family and the economy mutually reinforce the inequitable division of child rearing labor and discrimination against women employees (Bowles and Gintis 1986). Since most women earn significantly lower wages than men (due to discrimination or the prevalence of gender-defined employment categories), it is unprofitable for adults living in heterosexual pairs to assign the male to child rearing tasks.

Over the last century, in most industrialized countries liberal theory and practice have fueled the expansion of rights for citizens. But political and economic agents of that expansion have proceeded without recognizing the cultural baggage of constraints on women resulting from familial habits that fall outside the purview of legitimate political activity. As a result, women are left out without a political explanation for their exclusion and share in the mystification induced by "rights language" that clouds the cultural component of political dictums.

In the march toward extending citizenship rights, schools focus on extending the direct state-individual relationship downward in age as they offer programs to younger and younger children. What educational systems and the state ignore is the necessity for a "functional right," to use Bendix's term (1964), in the form of wider services for children to accommodate women's full-time work and to make possible their exercise of already granted economic and political rights. The state, through the temporal and curricular organization of the school, continues to depend on the traditional other half of the child rearing enterprise: the female parent in the family. Women's familial care of children may be the linchpin in a system that applies rationalistic and bureaucratic principles to economic and political spheres but maintains a separate sphere for the family within which such principles are not applied.

Alternative State Policies

In the late twentieth century, it is possible to envision alternative systems that neither continue to hold individual women solely responsible for child rearing nor encourage the bureaucratization of child rearing. Domestic routines and workplaces could be restructured to enable male and female parents to participate equally in child rearing: Parental leaves for both parents, shorter working hours, on-site child care facilities, and other "child-friendly" benefits would all facilitate such a shift. National and local governments could cooperate in offering neighborhood-based child care and education centers.

Given the expected impact of such proposed modifications, it has been in the interest of both the corporate world and most individual men to maintain existing cultural conditions that constrain women. Women continue to be relegated to subordinate positions, working sporadically, receiving lower wages, and serving as a reserve pool of labor for times of economic and political emergency. It is interesting that during such times, states have reclassified women's childbearing functions and have provided elaborate programs for children.

CONCLUSION

The preschool does not fit easily into modern educational systems because individual and private demands require a model that departs from the citizenship-building and skills-acquisition model favored by the state for children. This explains why studies of the expansion of preschools show more effect from endogenous factors (such as labor force participation of women) than is the case for expansion at other levels of schooling (Meyer et al. 1979; O'Connor 1988). Because the formal education of children has long been regarded as a legitimate interest of the state, policymakers seize this ready-made legitimacy. This leads to legislation that creates education-like programs for young children despite the lack of fit between such programs and parents' demand for full-day child care services. At the same time, day care programs sponsored by a variety of state agencies and private concerns expand in an uneven, unregulated marketplace of providers. States are hindered in institutionalizing custodial programs for young children because of traditional characterizations of daycare programs as "necessary evils," simply marginal programs for marginal families.

Although barriers to the institutionalization of early childhood programs can be isolated analytically, it is important to consider connections among them. States are reluctant to define universal, *non*-educational child care as a primary responsibility, limiting their role in the lives of children to the formal educational system. Daycare provision is fragmented at the national level, as welfare, health, and labor departments share the domain with an army of proprietary and nonprofit organizations. States that intend to institutionalize child care (broadly defined) that is truly complementary to parents' full-time work schedules must await the reclassification of child care from its status as women's family work to an activity over which the state can assume legitimate authority. In progressive societies where explicit links are made between gender equality and the provision of child care services, the state attempts to construct comprehensive programs that eschew the distinction between care and education (Kärre et al. 1973). This model, which acknowledges working parents' need for full-day supervision for their children, also considers the child's individual needs for the appropriate development of social and cognitive skills.

Since the tie between women and children continues to characterize the ideology of many nations, resistance to change in women's roles is among the greatest barriers to the institutionalization of early childhood programs. Therefore, changes in attitudes toward women's roles constitute an important research topic for those interested in expanding child care systems. By the same token, discussions about women's legal and economic equality must fully consider women's traditional responsibility for children as problematic and search for designs by which that responsibility can be shared by other individuals and institutions.

NOTES

Related versions of this chapter have appeared in *Sociology of Education* and the *American Journal of Education*.

1. Several reports refer to the appropriate roles of women, their duty to raise children, their close ties with the child, and their paid labor (e.g., Khalakdina 1979).

When Does School Expansion Influence Economic Change?

Specifying the Effects of Education on National Economic Growth

Richard Rubinson and Bruce Fuller

Does education increase national economic growth? Most people assume, as does the recent U.S. publication, *National Goals for Education*, that "education is at the heart of national economic strength and the key to international economic competitiveness" (U.S. Department of Education 1990, p. 2). But showing the contributions of education to economic growth has been difficult, more like hunting for elusive effects than finding easy evidence for the conventional wisdom. A large gap now exists between the common assumption that education increases national economic growth and social science skepticism that education necessarily matters. This chapter reviews the current state of theory and research on this issue.

Over the last twenty years, research findings on the effects of education on economic growth have changed considerably. Initially there was an optimistic camp, led by human capital economists, which assumed that more schooling invariably increased economic growth; the major problem was simply to accurately measure the size of this effect. Later there emerged a rather cynical tendency, led by sociologists, which questioned the existence of any economic benefits of education. This tendency saw schooling as a form of either class reproduction or status competition. Rather than accept either view, we will argue that a more useful, although perhaps more prosaic, answer to the question can be developed by reframing the issue in three ways: (1) by changing the methods used, (2) by altering how the questions are posed, and (3) by rethinking the way in which the major theoretical models are used.

CHANGING METHODS: FROM STUDIES OF INDIVIDUALS
TO STUDIES OF NATIONS

What methods should we use to find the effects of education on national economic growth? Certainly, individuals, national governments, and international organizations take it for granted that education increases economic growth. The reasoning seems simple: We know that people with more years of schooling have higher-status jobs and higher wages than do people with fewer years of schooling. We then reason that if more people get more schooling, they will all have better jobs with higher wages and the economy will expand.

This conclusion, however, is not necessarily valid. Its logic reflects a "cross-sectional illusion" or an "aggregation fallacy" (Boudon 1974; Meyer and Hannan 1979) that assumes that wages paid to workers with different amounts of schooling reflect differences in their economic productivity, and that these wages aggregate up to increases in national output. As people receive more education, there will be more productive jobs with higher wages and the economy will grow. This argument is the basis of the human capital theory of education (Schultz 1961; Becker 1964). Its intuitive appeal notwithstanding, the theory is seriously flawed by the assumption that increased schooling in itself causes a more productive job to be created, rather than simply determining which person will fill a job that already exists.[1]

There is another way to explain why workers with more schooling have higher-status jobs and higher wages. Education may either increase or certify people's job capabilities, so that people with more schooling are assumed to make better employees. Then people with more schooling become the first to receive the higher-status, better-paying jobs that already exist; those with less schooling receive the lower-status and lower-paying jobs that are left. Education then simply allocates people within a fixed distribution of jobs; it does not create more productive jobs and thus has no necessary effect on economic growth. This argument forms the basis of the allocation, or credentialing, theory of education (Thurow 1974; Collins 1979).

To the degree that allocation processes occur, more schooling may only reflect greater educational requirements for access to the same jobs, and the inference of increased economic growth is a cross-sectional illusion. Note, however, that this reasoning does not imply that education necessarily fails to increase economic growth—only that we cannot answer this question by looking at the relationship between schooling and occupation among *individuals*. To look for the national economic effects of education, we need evidence from the proper level of aggregation: *national* level studies of the effects of education on economic growth.[2]

CHANGING THE QUESTION POSED: FROM ABSOLUTE
RELATIONSHIPS TO CONDITIONAL EFFECTS

Although many empirical studies conducted at the national level have found some economic effects of education, these results have not been as strong, uniform, or consistent as might be expected from human capital theory. A typical reaction has been to dismiss both the claim that education increases economic growth and human capital theory itself, and then switch to a class reproduction or status conflict theory. A more useful reaction may be to change the way we view these studies.

A problem common to all three theories is that their manner of formulation implies the existence of an absolute relationship: Each theory expects that education does or does not increase economic growth. None of the theories can easily account for the inconsistent pattern of effects found in the empirical research. The analysis by Aaron Benavot in Chapter 8 is typical. His results, like those of most crossnational and single country studies, do find some effects of education on economic growth. But what stands out is that these effects are often not very large compared to other influences on economic growth; they are not uniform across different levels of schooling; and they are not consistent across time periods. The seemingly random pattern to these effects is what has led some researchers to conclude that education has no effects on economic growth.

Rather than jumping to this conclusion, we might assume the effects are indeed variable as the research shows, but also valid. We can then ask a much more theoretical question, "Under what *conditions* does education affect economic growth?" We might explain these seemingly random effects as resulting from a set of underlying processes in which education affects economic growth but only under certain conditions. The theoretical puzzle is to specify those conditions.

RETHINKING THEORY: FROM UNIVERSAL THEORIES TO SOCIAL PROCESSES

Our new strategy means recasting what are now formulated as universal theories into what are better understood as distinct social processes: a class reproduction process, a status competition process, and a human capital process. We will then argue that the effects of education on economic growth are a function of when (historically) and where (situationally) these processes operate. We should expect that the effects of education are not uniform but variable, depending upon which processes are operating and the salience of each process. This strategy also allows us to conceptualize these theories not as competing but as operative under different institutional conditions.

Class Reproduction Theory

The basic point of class reproduction theory has been that education's primary function is class reproduction and that the process of class reproduction obstructs any contributions of schooling to economic output (Bowles and Gintis 1976; Carnoy and Levin 1985). Reformulating the theory makes it possible to retain its insight while making the relationship variable: *To the extent that schooling is organized to reproduce the class structure, its contribution to economic growth will be weakened.* Reproducing the class structure, in this context, refers to systems that are organizationally structured into different class streams. France, with its separate working-class and middle-class schools, is a classic case.

School systems structured to reproduce class divisions may weaken the economic effects of education in three ways: through the content of the curriculum, through restriction of enrollments, and through linkage to the civil service. First, in upper- and middle-class schools, the curriculum typically reflects high culture as opposed to technical, scientific, or vocational training; it is a curriculum built around class-relevant cultural capital instead of economically relevant skills. Second, in both upper-class and working-class schools, regulations determining the size of school enrollments reflect class reproduction pressures rather than labor market demands. Third, the tight coupling of schools for the middle class to the civil service means that their students are less likely to be allocated to jobs in economic enterprises. Thus, when schooling is organized to reproduce the class structure, the effects of education on economic growth should be weaker.

Status Conflict

Status conflict theory can be reformulated in a similar way. Collins's theory (1979) argues that education makes no economic contribution because the primary function of schooling is as a currency for buying one's place in the job queue. This mechanism engenders a nefarious game in which each group acquires more schooling to move ahead of its competition, engendering a spiral of educational expansion. Since school expansion is driven by each group's demand for the greater job status that education can buy, rather than by labor force demands, there should be no economic effects of increased schooling.

Not all educational systems are organized in a way that fosters this kind of status competition process. But we can recast the theory by turning the basic insight into a proposition about the relationship between variables: *To the extent that the expansion of schooling reflects status competition, the economic benefits of schooling will be weakened.* Educational systems in which status competition processes are salient tend to be those in which the supply of schooling is not restricted by political regulations. These systems tend to be mass systems, rather than elite or class-structured systems. The United States is the classic case of such a system.

Educational systems with a high degree of status competition may weaken the effects of education on economic growth in two ways. First, the expansion of schooling responds more to the competition over status than to any corresponding demand from the labor market. Second, the pressures in such systems lead to a focus on increased promotion through grade levels and a corresponding weakening of both the quality of education and the content of the curriculum.

Human Capital Theory

Human capital theory errs in the opposite direction from the two theories we have just discussed by assuming that schools necessarily create skills and that these skills are automatically transformed into increased economic output. Lacking any meaningful concept of social structure, human capital theory does not question if schooling actually creates economic skills among students or if the economy can utilize these skills.[3]

Three conditions are necessary for the human capital process to operate. First, education must create the kind of skills required by the economy. Second, the economy must be able to absorb the skills created by schooling. Third, there must be a close coupling between the educational and economic systems so that the people with the appropriate skills are allocated to jobs that can utilize those skills. These conditions may not necessarily occur: For example, both class and status processes can prevent schooling from creating the necessary skills, and a given economic structure may contain some sectors unable to make use of these skills. So we need to formulate human capital theory as a variable proposition: *The human capital process increases economic output to the extent that education creates the kinds of skills and knowledge that can be utilized by the economy.*

A BASELINE MODEL OF SCHOOLING AND ECONOMIC GROWTH

We argue that the conditions under which education contributes to economic growth are a function of the extent to which each of these three processes is operating. Since these processes are dependent on the organization of education and the economy, we expect that education's effects will be neither uniform nor consistent, but highly variable by country, level of schooling, and time period. We now review a number of studies to see if we can explain the variety of their findings using the theoretical formulation just presented.

For comparability, each study we review is a quantitative time-series study of a single country that analyzes the effects of education on economic output using an aggregate production function model. Such a model estimates the effects of schooling on economic output, controlling for the inputs of capital and labor. We expect these school effects to be only partial or marginal, and not of the same magnitude as the effects of political regulations, industrial policies, international competition, or resource factors. The aggregate production function method allows these other factors to be controlled, showing the marginal contribution of education.

To match this theoretical formulation with the research, a useful device is to outline a baseline model of education that would contribute perfectly to economic growth. We can then look at the research and ask two questions: (1) Do these characteristics contribute to economic growth? (2) Are the effects of these characteristics weakened by the presence of class and status processes, and are they strengthened by the presence of the human capital process? Such an ideal educational system would have the following characteristics:

1. There are exactly the right number of students enrolled in each level of schooling, neither too many nor too few, to meet the requirements of the labor market. So we need to consider how these social processes affect the supply of schooling.

2. Students actually learn what they are taught, and there is high uniformity in learning across all students. So we need to consider how these social processes affect the quality of schooling.

3. The content of what is taught is relevant only to the requirements of the economy. So we have to consider how these social processes affect the curriculum.

4. The outputs of education are allocated to corresponding positions in the economy. So we have to consider how schooling is related to such characteristics of the economy as industrial policy and its periodization.

5. Finally, the economy is linked to education through a set of signals that tell the schools what the needs of the economy are so that the process can continue. So we must consider feedback mechanisms.

THE EFFECTS OF THE SUPPLY OF SCHOOLING

We first look at economic effects stemming from the supply of schooling, usually measured as enrollments, on economic growth. We ask two questions: (1) Do greater enrollments increase economic growth? (2) Is this effect of enrollments limited to the degree to which status competition and class reproduction processes are salient?

The United States and Status Competition, 1890–1970

A study of the United States from 1890 to 1970 by Walters and Rubinson (1983) found that primary school enrollments contributed to economic output in the period 1900–1928 but had no effects in the period 1933–1969. Secondary school enrollments made no contribution to economic output during the earlier period but had significant effects during the later period. Tertiary enrollments had no effects during either period.

This study shows the typical pattern: The effects of school enrollments on economic growth are not consistent; they vary by level of education and by time period. This pattern can be explained by our theoretical formulation, which argues that the effects of educational expansion on economic growth will be weakened when the process of status competition is salient.

A complementary study of the United States during this same period (Rubinson and Ralph 1984) found that the expansion of primary and secondary enrollments from 1890–1970 was driven by the dynamics of both status competition and technical change, as measured by total factor productivity. During the period 1900–1928, primary school enrollments increased due to the demands of technical change and status competition; secondary school enrollments increased due to status competition with no effects of technical change. But during the period 1933–1970, the pattern of effects was opposite. Primary school enrollments increased due to status competition with no effects of technical change; secondary school enrollments increased due to both technical change and status competition.

Taken together, these two studies show that the growth in enrollments increased economic output to the extent that the growth reflected the demands of technical change, while the effects of enrollments on economic output were weakened to the extent that enrollment growth reflected status competition. The initial expansion of each level of schooling was driven by the mechanism of status competition and showed no effects on increasing economic output, but the later expansion was driven by the demands of technical change and did increase economic output. These findings from the United States imply that (1) *greater enrollments do increase economic output*, but (2) *this effect is weaker to the extent that the increase in enrollments reflects the pressures of status competition* and (3) *this effect is stronger to the extent that the increase in enrollments reflects technical demands of the economy.* These findings also suggest that (4) *the size of enrollments may need to reach a certain threshold before they increase economic output, since the effects on economic growth took place when both primary and secondary education were becoming mass institutions.* This may explain the lack of effect of enrollments in tertiary education during this period.

France and the Effects of Class Reproduction, 1825–1975

A detailed study of the effects of secondary schooling on economic growth in France also found that the effects of enrollments varied by type of schooling and by period. In the period 1825–1875, secondary school enrollments had no effect on economic output. But in the subsequent period, 1875–1938, secondary enrollments did have substantial effects on output, but only for enrollments in working-class, not middle-class, schools. These same differential effects also continued throughout the later period, 1950–1975 (Hage et al. 1988).

These findings further refine our hypothesis that the effects of enrollments on economic output are weakened by a system of class reproduction by specifying the exact location in the educational system where the effects occur. These findings imply that (5) *a system of class reproduction weakens the effects of enrollments on economic output because there is no effect in the middle-class stream, while increasing enrollments in the working-class stream have sustained effects on increasing economic output.* These findings may reflect a threshold effect of size, as we saw in the United States, since enrollments in the French elite middle-class schools were relatively small, while enrollments in the mass working-class schools were large. But the differential effects may also reflect the divergence between the classical curriculum of the middle-class schools and the modern curriculum of the working-class schools.

Germany and the Effects of Class Reproduction, 1850–1975

A study of the effects of secondary and higher education in Germany (Garnier and Hage 1990) shows similar effects. From 1850 to 1928 secondary enrollments had a large effect on economic output, but this effect was located in the mass secondary stream only, not in the lower or upper elite secondary streams. From 1950 to 1975 these effects of mass secondary schooling disappear, but during this same period there are large effects of university, higher technical, and lower elite secondary enrollments, corresponding to significant growth in each of these levels of schooling. The findings again suggest that a structure of class reproduction limits the effects of education on economic output because it limits the size of the elite streams, although we still have to consider the confounding effect of the differential curriculum in the mass and elite streams.

THE EFFECTS OF THE QUALITY OF SCHOOLING

We now turn to studies that analyze the effects of the quality, rather than the quantity, of schooling on economic growth. Again, we ask two questions: (1) Does the quality of schooling matter for economic growth? (2) Is the effect of quality limited by the extent to which status competition and class reproduction processes are present? We expect that quality does matter, since higher quality implies more learning of what is taught in schools and greater uniformity of that learning across students. But we also note that the degree of quality is often correlated with class-structured systems, with higher quality being a characteristic of the upper or elite streams. This suggests the necessity of analyzing quality only within a particular stream of a system.

Mexico, 1888–1940

A study of Mexico in the period 1888–1940 measured school quality in several ways: literacy rates, newspaper circulation, the percentage of students passing the first grade examination, and the proportion of students in private primary schools (Fuller et al. 1986). The analyses, which examined both the quality and quantity of schooling, found the effects of quality on economic growth to be more consistent than the effects of quantity as measured by school enrollments. Literacy levels significantly influenced economic production levels in earlier (1888–1900) and later (1927–1940) periods, as did the quality of formal schools. These effects of quality were stronger on economic output in the manufacturing than in the agricultural sector. Although school quality is not easy to measure, the general conclusion from this and other studies we will review is that (6) *school quality does have important effects on increasing national economic growth.*

France, 1875–1975

The study of France reviewed earlier also analyzed the effects of school quality as measured by the student/teacher ratio and by educational expenditures per student. From 1885 to 1938, the quality of working-class schooling had a significant effect on economic output, in addition to the significant effect of the expansion of working-class enrollments. But there was no effect of the quality of middle class schooling. However, from 1950 to 1975, the quality of working-class schooling had no effect, even though there was still a significant effect of working-class enrollments. The quality of tertiary schooling had a negative effect in this period (Hage et al. 1988).

The findings from France reinforce those from Mexico that quality contributes to increased economic growth. They also suggest that the effects of quality, like the effects of enrollments, are mediated by the presence of a system of class reproduction. In particular, (7) *the effects of quality are dependent on the size of enrollments*. Quality had a positive effect only in the large working-class stream; it had no effect in the much smaller middle-class stream. The negative effect of quality at the very small tertiary level suggests further that a small enrollment of high quality may actually have negative effects on economic growth.

Germany, 1850–1975

The study of Germany reviewed earlier also analyzed the effects of quality as measured by educational expenditures per pupil. During the period 1850–1928, although enrollments in the mass secondary stream increased economic growth, the quality of schooling in this stream had no effect. Quality did have a positive effect in the lower elite secondary stream, a negative effect in the upper elite secondary stream, and no effect in higher education. From 1950 to 1975, quality had strong effects on increasing economic growth in both the university and higher technical streams, the two streams that were tightly coupled to the economy.

These results further support the idea that the quality of schooling matters for economic growth but that the effects are confined to specific locations in a system of class reproduction. In particular, this study modifies the idea that quality matters in the mass rather than the elite stream in such a system. For it suggests that (8) *high quality in a small elite stream may increase economic growth if the stream is tightly coupled to the economy (as in the German higher technical and university streams) but may reduce economic growth if the stream is not coupled to the economy (as in the German upper elite secondary and French university streams)*.

THE EFFECTS OF CURRICULUM

The studies of France and Germany are the only two studies that analyze the effects of curriculum on economic growth. Again we ask: (1) Does the content of the curriculum affect economic growth? (2) Are the effects of curriculum mediated by class and status processes?

Both of these studies suggest that the content of the curriculum does matter, although in each study it is hard to separate the effects of curriculum from other characteristics of schooling. In France, the effects of working-class secondary schooling on economic growth coincided with the introduction of the modern curriculum for this stream; the classical curriculum was maintained in the middle-class schools, which showed no effects on economic growth. And in Germany, the largest effects on economic growth occurred in the higher technical and university streams from 1950 to 1975, the period when the curriculum became very scientifically based. These results imply that (9) *a modern, scientifically based curriculum increases economic growth, while a classical curriculum does not.*

THE EFFECTS OF ECONOMIC STRUCTURE: SPECIFYING THE HUMAN CAPITAL PROCESS

While many studies have analyzed how characteristics of educational systems condition the effect of schooling on growth, few studies have analyzed how characteristics of the economy affect this relationship. Human capital theory implicitly assumes that any economy can utilize the skills produced from schooling to increase economic growth. Although sociological theories of schooling have rejected human capital theory, it is more useful to see the theory as underspecified in the sense that it fails to consider the structure of the economy and its coupling to the educational system as necessary conditions for the operation of the human capital process. Like school systems, economies are organized by political rules and regulations, and there is no reason to assume that economic structures will necessarily be congruent with school structures. To understand how the human capital model operates, we need to analyze the economic conditions under which the quantity and quality of skills and knowledge created by education are actually utilized.

More specifically, we need to ask whether research has supported the basic idea that education can contribute to economic growth only to the degree to which the outputs of schooling are congruent with the requirements of the economy.[4] We then ask: Do the effects of schooling on economic growth depend on the correspondence between levels of schooling and the structure of the economy? The one economic dimension that has been studied is variation by economic sector.

Korea, 1955–1985

A study of South Korea from 1955 to 1985 found that primary school enrollments had positive effects on total economic output, but the effects were specific to the manufacturing and mining sectors, not the agricultural or service sectors. Secondary school enrollments had no general effect on total economic output but had positive effects on output in the agricultural sector and negative effects in the manufacturing and service sectors. Tertiary education had no general effects on total output, but it had positive effects on agricultural output, no effects on manufacturing output, and negative effects on service sector output (Jeong 1988).

This complicated pattern, however, can be explained by the correspondence between levels of schooling and the structure of the economy, when we take account of the economic policies of the Korean state. Korean industrial development has rested on the comparative advantage of labor-intensive industries using low-skilled, low-wage labor. The traditional exports of textiles, footwear, clothes, and plywood did not require advanced technology or skills. In the 1970s, when the focus of economic growth shifted from light to heavy and chemical industries, the policy of industrial growth based on industries demanding a low level of skills and technology did not significantly change (Kwack 1986). This industrial policy explains the positive effect of primary, lower-skill education on manufacturing and mining, and the negative effect of secondary, or higher-skill, education.

Why the opposite pattern for agriculture? For thirty years Korea emphasized increasing agricultural output as a national policy for self-sufficiency in food, especially grains. To make food available to low-wage industrial workers, government policy underpriced farm products, even below production costs. Farmers were discouraged and many left for urban areas. These factors placed a premium on raising agricultural productivity, and the changing consumption patterns that came with rising living standards forced farmers to diversify. These pressures created a demand for advanced agricultural techniques, improved seeds, fertilizers, and irrigation systems. So the agricultural sector required personnel with the higher-level skills and knowledge that secondary schooling creates, while the manufacturing sector required the lower-level skills of primary schooling. This same reasoning explains why tertiary education in Korea had positive effects on agricultural but not manufacturing output, since the tertiary level was the location of agricultural research and development (Jeong 1988).

As human capital theory expects, these findings can be explained by the particular kinds of skill levels demanded by economic activities. But it is necessary to specify the economic structure in order to see precisely how the human capital process is operating, with the realization that the character of the economy is politically rather than technologically determined.

Taiwan, 1951–1985

A study of Taiwan from 1951 to 1985 found that primary and lower secondary school enrollments increased economic growth, with the effects of primary schooling being larger; but higher secondary and tertiary schooling had no effects on economic growth (Armer and Rubinson 1988). How may these findings be explained in terms of the particularities of Taiwan's economic policy?

Taiwan's economy has been organized around labor-intensive techniques in the manufacturing and assembly export industries, as well as in agriculture. Here the contribution of schooling to the economy would be expected to lie in the spread of basic educational skills to the mass of the population. In fact, when we look at the characteristics of Taiwan schooling during this period, we see that it developed a mass system at the primary and lower secondary (junior high) levels, but a rather restricted elite system at the higher secondary (senior high) and tertiary levels. We find that the economic effects of schooling occur in the expansion of these two mass levels of schooling and not the more advanced levels.

Mexico, 1888–1940

The study of Mexico reviewed earlier also analyzed the effects of primary education by economic sector (Fuller et al. 1986). Distinguishing between quality and quantity, this study found over the period 1888–1940 that educational quality increased output in manufacturing but not in agriculture. The pattern can be explained by the correspondence between levels of schooling and the different skill levels required by these economic sectors. During this period Mexican agriculture saw little technological innovation and required very low skill levels, while manufacturing required some literacy and basic skills.

Germany, 1850–1975

Finally, the study of Germany also finds that the effects of education on economic growth are stronger where schooling is closely coupled to the demands of the economy. From 1850 to 1928, enrollments in higher technical education (*hochschulen*), but not university education, increased economic output. This was because the *hochschulen* were linked to jobs in industry and commerce, while the university was linked to jobs in civil service and university employment. From 1950 to 1975, enrollments and quality in the *hochschulen* continued to have positive effects, as they did for university enrollments during this period. Again, this pattern is explained in terms of the increasing demand for the higher-level skills found in the *hochschulen* and university levels.

All of these studies show that (10) *the effects of education on economic growth are a function of the correspondence between levels of schooling and characteristics of the economy.*

THE EFFECTS OF FEEDBACK PROCESSES

The last component in our baseline model of a system that maximizes the effects of education on economic growth is a set of feedback processes in which the economy provides signals of its requirements to the educational system. For only if there is a set of such feedback processes is it possible to reproduce the conditions under which school increases economic output (for review, see Figure 1.2). Although there is no explicit research in this area, we can posit two ideal kinds of mechanisms, a market mechanism and a bureaucratic mechanism. We suspect that neither one nor the other is necessarily more effective; rather, we can specify the kinds of problems that each mechanism entails.

The ideal market mechanism is a system in which the wages attached to particular kinds of jobs act as incentive mechanisms to students and families about what and how much education is required. The market mechanism seems to have two kinds of problems. The first is that even if this feedback mechanism correctly signals students about economic demands, student demands cannot directly affect the structure of schooling. These demands must be channeled into the political process and transformed into the political decisions that determine the size and shape of schooling. We know from the present experience of the United States, which most closely approaches a market system, that effective political change in education is not guaranteed, since the variety of organizational interests around schooling itself are not necessarily congruent with the interests of the economy. What is required is an institutional analysis of the kinds of organizational structures that are more or less sensitive to transmitting this feedback process.

The second problem with a market mechanism is one we have discussed previously. The more an educational system is organized as a market, the more likely there is to be a status competition process that drives enrollments, producing a situation in which expansion becomes much greater than any demand from the economy. The dilemma for a market system, then, is how to ensure feedback from the economy yet at the same time control the status competition process.

The ideal bureaucratic mechanism is one in which a central state organization, linked to both the economy and the educational system, directly regulates the supply of schooling, curriculum, and quality in accord with economic requirements. But such a centralized mechanism would also be subject to two kinds of problems. First, bureaucratic mechanisms are prone to credentialing. In such situations the state is a significant employer, and state employment is typically based on bureaucratic credentialism, which tends to weaken the economic basis of change in schooling, as in France and Mexico. The middle-class track, with explicit ties to the civil service and formal credentialism, is the track that makes the weakest contribution to economic output.

The second problem in a centralized bureaucratic system is the constant tendency for class politics to intrude into educational decisions. If the state has control over schooling, class interests are more likely to be entrusted to the bureaucratic mechanisms that control schooling. And to the extent that schooling comes to reflect class interests, the less schooling will tend to reflect economic demands. So the dilemma for a centralized bureaucratic structure is how to insulate its political decision making from the state's own interests in credentialism and from the politics of class interests.

An even greater impediment to effective feedback mechanisms may lie in the same institutional processes that John Meyer analyzes in Chapter 14. These processes are increasingly important in determining the structures of schooling in most countries. Congruence between education and economy requires mechanisms to structure schooling in relation to the particular demands of the national economy. Much of the research on the factors that shape schooling, however, reveals that education seems to develop in terms of a standard, uniform model based on a worldwide picture of what national systems of education should look like. Studies show that national educational systems increase their enrollments (Meyer et al. 1991) and develop very similar curricula (Benavot et al. 1991) rather independent of the particular characteristics of their national educational and economic systems. Education as an institution is inextricably linked to the modern nation-state because it is the major way in which citizenship is defined. The shape of education comes to be driven by processes unrelated to national economic conditions. The characteristics of schooling that we have analyzed— its supply, quality, and curriculum—are becoming shaped by these processes. As a result, the possibility for effective feedback from the economy to the educational system is often blocked by political processes that correspond more to these nation-state models than economic pressures. In considering the ways in which educational systems might be designed to contribute effectively to economic growth, it is not sufficient to understand which structures of schooling to design and support. At the same time, one must consider how to overcome those processes shaping national school policy that are linked to worldwide political pressures rather than the particular imperatives of national economies.

NOTES

1. Individual-level rate of return studies are thoroughly reviewed in Psacharopoulos (1989). He partially addresses the problem of using wage rates as proxies for individual productivity by reviewing the literature on directly measured variation in agricultural productivity of small farmers, then relating this variation to their schooling levels. For a sharp critique of conventional human capital models, see Knight and Sabot (1987), who argue that under most labor structures wages do not reflect the marginal product of labor.

2. Denison's (1964) growth-accounting model uses aggregate, not individual-level, data to test for human capital effects. But this research uses school attainment levels as weights to determine labor quality among occupational groups. Workers with more schooling and higher occupational status are assumed to be more productive, an assumption that has received little empirical substantiation. Jorgenson's more recent work (1984)

improves on the Denison model by constructing aggregate production functions, but the same assumption is made to calculate labor quality.

3. Political agencies often exogenously influence the array of skills and jobs present in the economic structure. Government employment comprises the bulk of the wage-sector jobs in many developing countries. Government licensing requirements shape the level and form of schooling demanded, even when these demands fail to reflect actual requisite skills for some occupations. Evidence from Mexico suggests that penetration of the central government into secondary towns and rural areas stimulates semi-skilled and unskilled white-collar employment, which may not be directly connected to greater and less expensive production of goods and services (Fuller et al. 1990).

4. Again, the economy's requirements may include labor demands that are unrelated to the more productive provision of goods and services (see note 3, this chapter).

8

Educational Expansion and Economic Growth in the Modern World, 1913–1985

Aaron Benavot

Debate over the causes and conditions of economic growth in the Third World has shifted dramatically over the past three decades. Arguments rooted in modernization and human capital perspectives, dominating social science discourse in the 1960s and early 1970s, have been sharply attacked and partially supplanted by neo-Marxist conceptualizations based on dependency and world-system theories. At the same time, ideas about the impact of education on economic development have undergone serious revision. Once upon a time, education was invariably viewed as an important contributing factor to economic growth in the human capital and modernization models (Denison 1964; Inkeles and Smith 1974). Yet the underlying models supporting this view have been called into question by neo-Marxist scholars (Amin 1975; Irizarry 1981; Carnoy 1982) and by theorists advancing reformulations of the relationship between education and society (Meyer 1977). To some observers, we have moved from an "age of optimism" to an "age of skepticism" concerning the impact of education on national development (Weiler 1978).

In Chapter 7, Richard Rubinson and Bruce Fuller reviewed this theoretical debate, focusing on schooling's economic effects under varying institutional conditions within nations. The present chapter instead looks at crossnational economic effects of school expansion. Here I raise the level of analysis to the worldwide political economy. Is empirical support sufficient, especially from a crossnational vantage point, to refute earlier models and arguments that alleged positive contributions from education? Is the economic impact of educational expansion perhaps more conditional than previously assumed? Is it conditioned by broad global economic cycles, so that the effects of education on economic growth change from one historical period to the next? Is the education-economic development affected by a nation's position in the world economy or other related transnational linkages? Here I make a start in answering these questions, examining the long-term impact of each level of school expansion (primary, secondary, tertiary) on economic growth in four historical periods (spanning the years 1913 to 1985).

MODELING EDUCATION'S EFFECT ON ECONOMIC GROWTH

Human Capital and Modernization Traditions

Although scholars and reformers have long advanced the thesis that the spread of education contributes to economic growth (e.g., Marshall 1890), the introduction of human capital theory by U.S. economists following the Sputnik crisis gave substantial legitimacy and scientific justification to this idea (Schultz 1961). A major component of human capital theory asserts that education augments skill levels and cognitive knowledge of future workers, thus contributing to a more efficient and productive use of labor. More educated workers, whose marginal product is of greater value, help to increase aggregate rates of national productivity in a wide range of enterprises. This process is not limited to wage labor in industrial, manufacturing, or service sectors. In the agricultural sector, higher school attainment by young farmers boosts their efficiency in organizing crop production and applying new farming techniques (Lockheed et al. 1980).

Critics argue that the human capital model makes unrealistic and overly rationalistic assumptions about how wages (the neoclassical indicator of productivity) are determined in labor market structures (e.g., Thurow 1974). Workers with more schooling may earn higher wages, but institutional characteristics also determine income structures. Governments often set artificially high minimum wages and inflate the wages paid to employees working in key manufacturing and export-oriented enterprises. Unions engage in negotiations to enhance wages irrespective of actual productivity differences. Certain classes of workers— women and minorities, for example—experience income discrimination despite their comparable and sometimes higher productivity. Indeed, promotion and pay scales of many workers are tied to highly structured "internal" and "split" labor markets. In the Third World, salary scales in the public sector may be determined not by productivity concerns but by reference to international pay scales or to salaries previously paid to expatriates (Thompson 1981).

Critics of human capital models see productivity as an attribute not of workers but of jobs (Thurow 1974). Jobs in certain sectors—public services, information technology, mining, for example—are defined as high-wage, high-productivity jobs and and workers line up for them. Skills necessary for performing these jobs are learned through a combination of informal and formal training at the workplace. Employers use school credentials to screen and sort job applicants in terms of their long-term trainability (Arrow 1973). Ongoing educational expansion forces graduates, especially in a competitive job market, to attain higher and higher levels of schooling just to maintain their position in the line of applicants. This process of educational inflation (or credentialism) leads to lower private rates of return, as the number of un- or underemployed graduates rises.

Modernization theorists, while sympathetic to many of the arguments advanced in the human capital model, stress the transformative role of education on individuals' values and behavior. According to this perspective, schools are one of several important forums (along with factories and mass media) in which an individual's ties to past communities and "traditional" value systems (viewed as obstacles to modernization) are fundamentally altered. Apart from teaching literacy and new skills, the education process inculcates "modern" attitudes and personality traits (diligence, rational calculation, punctuality, an achievement orientation) in young people. Schools also promote faith in meritocratic rules of status attainment and mobility, displacing ascriptive forms (Inkeles and Smith 1974). The diffusion of "modern" attitudes and values from urban centers to the "backward" hinterlands is to set the stage for societal modernization and economic development.

Critical Viewpoints

These central assertions of the modernization perspective have come under sharp criticism (e.g., Portes 1976; Delacroix and Ragin 1978). Critics claim that the perspective is ethnocentric because it assumes that all countries would pass through a series of inevitable stages to eventually emulate the West; its conceptions of both traditional and modern society are constructed ideal-types without historical basis; it ignores instances of traditional values legitimating rapid social and economic change (Japan); and it discounts the critical impact of international economic and political linkages on socioeconomic development. The issue is not whether modern institutions inculcate a syndrome of psychosocial modernity: Most would agree that education has a pronounced impact on an actor's personality and social behavior. The issue is whether modern individuals constitute a modern society. Individual motivations can undergo fundamental change without altering basic patterns of economic production and distribution.

Critics also stress the tensions accompanying rapid educational expansion and slow-growing wage employment. A surplus of educated graduates, unable to find employment at an appropriate level and unwilling to work in lower-status jobs, may hamper economic growth. A rising surplus of unemployed graduates can fuel levels of disaffection and political dissent, constraining national economic growth (Hanf et al. 1975).

Emergence of the *dependencia* school and the world-system perspective in the 1970s further undermined models that posit strong economic effects from school expansion. Consider key arguments advanced by dependency and world-system scholars: (1) The global capitalist economy is a wholistic system characterized by structural inequalities both between and within nation-states; (2) Economies of Third World nations have been systematically exploited and underdeveloped in earlier historical periods and now constitute a peripheral component of the global system, continuing to supply raw materials and cheap labor to the industrial centers; (3) The expropriation of profit and surplus value by core nations and multinational corporations depended upon the complicity and power of national elites who often were educated in Western school systems; and (4) By seeking to maximize returns to foreign investments and by setting national priorities according to foreign standards, the actions of the national bourgeoisie have intensified internal inequalities, reinforced dependency of Third World nations, and retarded long-term economic development (Frank 1967; Cardoso 1972; Wallerstein 1974).

Rather than highlighting international school expansion and institutional change as influencing economic growth, these arguments emphasize a new set of factors that are referred to as external, or ''systemic.'' These include a nation's structural position in the world economy, composition of trade flows, dependence on primary product exports, state strength, the degree of foreign investment, and the presence of multinational corporations (Bornschier and Chase-Dunn 1985).

Recently, several scholars have integrated ideas from neo-Marxist and reproduction theories of education to argue that education affects the development process in a number of negative ways (Amin 1975; Carnoy 1982). First, neocolonial education of Third World leaders trained them to be acceptable intermediaries between colonizer and colonized without prodding them to fundamentally question this relationship. Instead of helping to ''liberate'' their country from dependency, elites maintained the educational systems created by colonial administrations and churches. Second, education reproduced and reinforced the class structure of peripheral nations, simply legitimating the power of local agrarian or capitalist elites to control the working class and rural peasants. Imported school models simply persuaded subordinate classes to believe that by sending their children to school, they could advance their own position. Third, in terms of economic growth, schooling enhanced the profitability of metropolitan capital in peripheral nations (by solidifying the position of local elites) and strengthened ties of dependency and exploitation. Some economic growth took place, but the fruits of that growth went primarily to foreign investors and local elites. Since education primarily aids national elites in accumulating power and privilege, its short-term impact on economic growth might be positive. But its long-term impact is at best weak, at worst quite negative. School expansion cannot fundamentally alter the historical underdevelopment and peripheral position of Third World nations in the world economy. Nor can it wash away the impact of the exploitative economic and political relations earlier formed between core and peripheral areas.

SURVEY OF EMPIRICAL RESEARCH

Most empirical work, until recently, was grounded in the human capital model and painted a glowing picture of education's contribution to economic growth (see Psacharopoulos 1989). My review will be brief, given the analysis already presented in Chapter 7. Beginning with the work of Schultz (1961) and Denison (1964), economists followed two major approaches in measuring the impact of education: the rate of return approach and the growth accounting approach. The former compared either individuals' costs of going to school with future expected income (the private rate of return), or the social cost of financing schooling with benefits of completing specific educational levels (the social rate of return). The growth accounting approach decomposed long-term trends in national productivity levels into three factors of production: land, labor, and capital. By measuring change in total factor inputs (mostly labor and capital) and comparing this to change in aggregate output, economists inferred that additional factors such as education or technological innovation increased the quality of labor and capital.

With respect to Third World countries, however, the evidence was generally less reliable and more dependent upon these questionable assumptions. The most extensive comparative data base consisted of cross-sectional estimates of the social rate of return in developing nations (see Psacharopoulos 1989). Primarily drawn from urban wage earners in the formal sector, average social rates of return demonstrated that investments in human capital compare well with—and even exceed—investments in physical capital. They tend to vary by educational level (highest for primary schooling and lowest for tertiary education) and by level of development (higher in low-income countries and lower in middle- or high-income countries). This work assumes that the wage variation consistently reflects individual variation in productivity.

To avoid this latter and highly controversial assumption, a supplemental line of research examined the impact of education on actual agricultural productivity in several developing countries (Lockheed et al. 1980). It concluded that, on average, four years of schooling increases productivity of individual farmers by about 7.4 percent after other factors—fertilizer, new crop varieties, and road provisions—were taken into account. Productivity increases were lower in "non-modernizing" societies (where traditional farming methods are in use) and higher in "modernizing" countries. These upbeat findings supported the claim that investment in primary schooling is the most efficient (and equitable) mechanism for economic growth.

The main problem with the human capital research tradition is that it attempts to draw national-level inferences from estimates of returns to education at the individual level. Data at both individual and aggregate levels are necessary; inferences based solely on the former are invalid and/or misleading because they mix levels of analysis (Bidwell and Kasarda 1980). Strong correlations between individual schooling and wages would be observed even if schools were simply sorting high-status youth into high-status jobs—but no national gains in productivity would necessarily result.

Inconsistent educational effects have been reported among comparative studies that examine variation across nations in their levels of school expansion and economic growth. Earlier studies of this type using correlational or cross-sectional regression techniques did find positive effects, but this work was beset with sampling, measurement, and modeling errors.[1] Such correlational analyses are deficient, mainly in their inability to inform us about the direction of causation. High enrollment rates may be a prerequisite of economic growth, or they may indicate that educational expansion is a luxury that wealthier nations can afford but is unrelated to economic development.[2] These studies also lacked controls for earlier levels of development, population change, and capital formation, all of which are known to affect economic growth.

More recent studies using longitudinal data and more sophisticated models arrived at more varied conclusions. These studies underscore the importance of conditionalizing the argument that all forms of education contribute to economic growth. Meyer and Hannan (1979), for example, found that secondary education and, to a lesser extent, primary education had positive effects on economic growth during the period 1950–1970. But tertiary education had a weak and usually negative effect on measures of economic change over time. Based on a larger sample and a panel analysis over twenty-five years (1960–1985), Benavot (1989) found that primary education had the strongest and most consistent positive effect on economic growth. The impact of secondary education was positive but less consistent, and the impact of tertiary education was found to be negative and significant. Other studies of economic growth, while focusing on the impact of nonschool factors, have also found that secondary education (Delacroix and Ragin 1978; Jaffee 1985) or primary education (Wheeler 1980; Hicks 1980) hold positive effects.

Despite differences in methodology, we can draw several tentative conclusions from this still growing empirical literature. First, mass education seems to have the greatest positive effect on economic growth, especially in countries where its cost is low relative to elite forms of schooling. Second, education at the tertiary level is an expensive form of schooling with lower economic returns and weak, often negative effects on economic growth. Third, the accumulating evidence suggests that the effects of mass education vary by historical period.

These findings, however instructive, clearly demand further specification and elaboration. In particular, we need to better specify the economic and institutional conditions under which mass and elite education affects economic growth. We need to determine whether the strength of primary, secondary, and tertiary school effects may change over time. And since most studies conducted to date are limited to the post–World War II period, we need to see whether the economic effects of mass education also appear in periods prior to 1945.

THE ECONOMIC IMPACT OF MASS SCHOOLING, 1913–1985

Next I report on the longitudinal influence of mass schooling on nation-level economic output across four different periods spanning the time frame 1913–1985. In addition to typical controls on economic inputs, I focus on the possible economic effects stemming from a nation's degree of economic dependence, state strength, and position in the world economy (that is, political-economic conditions that may lessen or mediate the discrete influence of schooling). My analysis follows the panel regression approach of previous crossnational studies. This involves regressing the outcome variable (economic output) on a set of explanatory variables, controlling for an earlier measured level of the dependent variable (Meyer and Hannan 1979). Analyses are drawn from a large sample of developed and less-developed countries; the number of cases studied in each period varies from 28 to 106 depending on data availability and historical period. This analysis disaggregates the direct effects of primary, secondary, and tertiary education within four historical periods: 1913–1929, 1930–1950, 1955–1970, and 1970–1985. The first and third periods were times of relatively robust world economic growth and expansion (Maddison 1982); the second and fourth periods witnessed stagnation and contraction in the world economy. In the second set of analyses, I focus on the possible confounding impacts of economic dependence, state strength, and world-system integration (restricted to the later two historical periods due to data limitations).

Two indicators of economic output are employed in this study: gross national product (GNP) per capita in the 1913–1929, 1955–1970, and 1970–1985 panels, and total energy consumption (ENERG) per capita in the 1930–1950 panel.[3] Total energy consumption per capita, the indicator of economic development used in the 1930–1950 panel, refers to the consumption of all commercial forms of primary energy. This is an excellent indicator of a country's level of industrialization, one that has been centrally collected by international agencies according to standardized and consistent definitions since 1930. Both measures of economic development are logged in order to adjust for their skewed distribution.

Educational data used in the post–World War II panel analyses are enrollment ratios coded from the 1970 and 1976 editions of Unesco's statistical yearbook. Educational data for the prewar panels come from several sources (see Benavot and Riddle 1988; Banks 1971; Mitchell 1983; Flora and Alber 1983). Primary enrollment data are standardized by the school-age population of children age five to fourteen, while secondary and tertiary data are standardized by total population figures. In addition to the lagged dependent variable, we include two other control variables: an indicator of population growth (either population change between time t and $t - 1$ or the total fertility rate at $t - 1$) and a dummy variable for countries that are major mining or oil exporters (those deriving over 20 percent of their GDP from mineral and oil exports). We control for population change because it is generally believed that rapid population growth has an adverse effect on economic growth. The mineral-extraction dummy variable is included because past crossnational studies (e.g., Meyer and Hannan 1979) have shown that much of their apparent growth is due to price fluctuations in oil and mineral commodities.

Empirical Findings in Four Historical Periods

Next I report on the effects of school expansion among different nations within the four twentieth-century periods. Due to fluctuations in the sample of countries included in each panel, I also estimate educational effects for two sets of constant cases. Means, standard deviations, and correlations for all dependent and independent variables are reported in Table 8.1. In examining these correlation matrices, we note that the auto-correlation between the dependent variable and lagged dependent variable in each historical period is high (ranging from .94 to .98). Since it is assumed that the economic infrastructure of each country and the antecedent forces shaping this infrastructure are generally stable from one period to the next, these high auto-correlations are not surprising.[4] Correlations between each dependent variable and measures of educational expansion are also strong. Some correlations exceed .80, increasing the likelihood that multicollinearity will affect the analyses. Multicollinearity does not bias estimated regression coefficients but can inflate their standard errors. The stability of the educational effects estimated in the models presented subsequently suggests, however, that multicollinearity is not a pronounced problem.

Table 8.2 reports the effects of primary, secondary and tertiary school enrollments on economic growth with appropriate controls for population growth and—in the latter two panels—mining and oil exports. The sample size varies from 28 in the earliest panel to 106 in the latest panel. Control variables included in the equations are generally in the expected direction and are usually significant. Rapid population growth has a negative effect on economic development in three of the four periods, but it is significant only in the period 1955–1970. As expected, countries with high levels of oil and mining exports tend to grow at a faster rate than other countries.

The main results from Table 8.2 can be summarized as follows: First, primary and secondary education both have consistently positive effects on economic growth in each of the four historical panels, although levels of significance vary. Second, educational effects are weakest in the most recent historical period, 1970–1985. Third, tertiary education tends to have negative effects, although marginal significance is reached only in the period 1955–1970. Based on these findings, our first impression is that insofar as education has contributed to economic growth in the twentieth century, this is mainly a consequence of the expansion of primary and secondary schooling.

To what degree is this conclusion influenced by the changing sample of countries analyzed in each panel? To answer this question, Table 8.3 reports parallel

Table 8.1
Correlations among Major Variables by Historical Period

Historical Panel: 1913-1929 (n = 28 countries)

Variable Name	1	2	3	4	5	6
1. Log GNP per capita 1929	.98	.81	.28	.58	-.07	
2. Log GNP per capita 1913		.80	.22	.56	-.05	
3. Primary Enrollment Ratio 1910			.24	.59	-.15	
4. Secondary Enrollments per capita 1910				.22	.22	
5. Tertiary Enrollments per capita 1910					-.01	
6. Population Change (1930/1910)						
Mean	2.71	2.65	53.3	.60	.10	1.26
Standard Deviation	.35	.33	25.0	.45	.08	.39

Historical Panel: 1970-1985 (n = 106 countries)

Variable Name	1	2	3	4	5	6	7
1. Log GNP per capita 1985	.94	.67	.82	.70	-.77	-.04	
2. Log GNP per capita 1970		.68	.87	.77	-.80	-.04	
3. Primary Enrollment Ratio 1970			.65	.50	-.62	.02	
4. Secondary Enrollments per capita 1970				.79	-.89	-.14	
5. Tertiary Enrollments per capita 1970					-.69	-.20	
6. Average Fertility Rate 1970-1975						.17	
7. Dummy Variable for Mining/Oil Exporters							
Mean	2.96	2.86	76.4	31.5	6.3	5.03	.14
Standard Deviation	.60	.52	27.8	26.9	8.0	1.86	.35

analyses based on two sets of constant cases.[5] In the first instance we track educational effects over time for 46 of the 51 countries included in the 1929–1950 panel. We find that the pattern of educational effects for this group of countries is almost identical to that reported in Table 8.2, with the exception of a weaker impact of primary education in the latter two panels. This is most likely due to the greater proportion of developed countries in this subsample that have reached the ceiling of universal primary schooling. In the second instance we isolate a constant sample of 77 countries with complete information in the latter two historical panels (Equations 4 and 5). Once again we find the same basic patterns as in Table 8.2. In the period 1955–1970, primary and secondary education have positive and significant effects and tertiary education has a negative

Table 8.2
Effects of Education on Economic Growth in Four Historical Periods (unstandardized regression coefficients; standard error in parentheses)

Historical Panel	Dependent Variable: Economic Development at Time 2			
	1913-1929[a]	1929-1950[b]	1955-1970[c]	1970-1985[c]
School Variables Time 1[d]				
Primary Education	.0013* (.0008)	.0035* (.0021)	.0014* (.0009)	.0006 (.0010)
Secondary Education	.049* (.027)	.021 (.054)	.005*** (.002)	.0002 (.0020)
Tertiary Education	.004 (.18)	-.12 (.34)	-.014* (.008)	-.0032 (.0042)
Control Variables Time 1				
Economic Development	.94*** (.06)	.73*** (.08)	.73*** (.06)	.99*** (.09)
Population Change	-.02 (.03)	.19 (.15)		
Fertility Rate			-.06*** (.01)	-.030 (.023)
Mining/Oil Exporters			.10** (.05)	.14** (.06)
Adjusted R^2	.97	.90	.93	.89
Constant Term	.13	.47	1.02	.18
Number of Cases	28	51	81	106

*** < .01   ** < .05   * < .10

Notes:
a. Economic Development is measured as log of GNP per capita in constant 1960 dollars.
b. Economic Development is measured as log of total energy consumption per capita.
c. Economic Development is measured as log of GNP per capita in constant 1980 dollars.
d. In the latter two panels, levels of educational expansion are measured by gross enrollment ratios. In the earlier two panels, however, gross enrollment ratios are unavailable and two alternative measures are employed. At the primary level, "unadjusted" enrollment ratios (primary enrollments/5–14 school-age population) are used; at the secondary and tertiary levels, enrollments are standardized by total population. For exact sources, see text.

Table 8.3

Effects of Education on Economic Growth in Two Sets of Constant Cases
(unstandardized regression coefficients; standard error in parentheses)

	Dependent Variable: Economic Development at Time 2				
Historical Panel	1929-1950[a]	1955-1970[b]	1970-1985[b]	1955-1970[b]	1970-1985[b]
School Variables Time 1					
Primary Education	.0038** (.0019)	.0010 (.0013)	-.002 (.002)	.0019** (.009)	.0010 (.0012)
Secondary Education	n/a[c]	.006*** (.002)	.0012 (.0025)	.0056*** (.0019)	.0028 (.0020)
Tertiary Education	-.10 (.24)	-.019** (.008)	-.002 (.004)	-.014* (.008)	-.0024 (.0039)
Control Variables Time 1					
Economic Development	.80*** (.07)	.78*** (.09)	.98*** (.10)	.72*** (.06)	.89*** (.09)
Population Change	.23* (.13)				
Fertility Rate		-.05*** (.02)	-.03 (.03)	-.06*** (.02)	-.016 (.024)
Mining/Oil Exporters		-.01 (.06)	.24*** (.07)	.09* (.06)	.15** (.07)
Adjusted R^2	.933	.925	.929	.929	.919
Constant Term	.20	.91	.35	1.02	.32
Number of Cases	46	46	46	77	77

*** < .01   ** < .05   * < .10

Notes:

a. Economic Development is measured as log of total energy consumption per capita.

b. Economic Development is measured as log of GNP per capita in constant 1980 dollars.

c. Secondary education per capita in 1930 is excluded in order to increase the constant sample size and also because it is nonsignificant when included. See notes to Table 8.2.

effect. In the period 1970–1985, all school enrollment effects are in the expected direction but are considerably weaker and statistically insignificant.

These findings suggest that it is necessary to formulate more specific conditions under which economic effects of school expansion will be observed. For example, the economic impact of different educational levels varies: Elite education— exemplified by the expansion of university enrollments—has had little impact on the economies of most nations in the world. Yet mass education—exemplified by primary and secondary education—is found to yield considerable economic benefits. This finding supports, at least in part, many of the critics of the human capital and modernization perspectives who maintain that pronounced economic inequities in less-developed nations are reproduced and exacerbated by expansion of elite forms of schooling. Second, the strength of this pattern of educational effects appears to vary by historical period and depends largely on the health of the world economy. During periods of relative boom in the world economy (1913–1929 and 1955–1970), the expansion of mass education had a more pronounced positive impact on economic growth. However, in periods of world economic contraction or stagnation (1929–1950 and 1970–1985), the benefits of primary and secondary education weakened considerably.

These findings also raise questions concerning the generalizations advanced in earlier crossnational studies (Meyer and Hannan 1979; Hicks 1980). These studies concluded that primary or secondary education had strong effects on economic growth, effects that were assumed to be historically invariant. We found that the economic impact of primary and secondary education declined over the recent period.[6] We also found that secondary education had only weak effects in the period 1929–1950. On the other hand, I corroborate earlier studies that reported a weak or negative impact of higher education on economic growth (e.g., Meyer and Hannan 1979).

I next explore whether this pattern of school expansion effects is altered significantly when controls for linkages to, and influences of, the world economy and political institutions are added to the basic model.

World-System Forces, Education, and Economic Growth, 1955–1985

At the same time that economic development is being driven by processes internal to the nation-state (e.g., educational expansion, population growth, mineral extraction), additional causal processes originating outside the nation also may be operating. Drawing from arguments advanced by dependency and world-system theorists, I expand my basic model to examine whether global forces significantly alter the economic impact of education. This exercise also is aimed at more clearly specifying conditions under which schooling effects will more likely be observed.

The empirical literature stemming from the world-system and dependency perspectives continues to grow (see Rubinson and Holtzman 1981). Several general findings have received considerable empirical support. First, economic dependence slows economic growth. Foreign investment and international aid have negative long-term effects on economic growth, while the effect of trade dependence varies with the type of commodity exported (Bornschier and Chase-Dunn 1985). Second, the negative effects of economic dependence vary according to a country's structural position in the world economy. Effects tend to be stronger for countries in the semi-periphery and weaker for countries in the "poorer" periphery. Third, economic dependence has negative effects on state strength and state power; these, in turn, have been shown to facilitate economic growth in both industrialized and Third World countries (Gobalet and Diamond 1979; Hage et al. 1988). Fourth, the degree of incorporation and integration in the world system (as measured by the volume of trade or number of international memberships) appears to have direct positive effects on economic growth as well as indirect effects through state strength and state centralization (Jaffee 1985).

In light of these findings, we must include certain variables in order to check whether the basic model tested previously is misspecified, yielding a spurious relationship between education and economic growth. The analysis reported subsequently examines whether the effects of education fluctuate when appropriate controls for world-system pressures and state strength are included.

The expanded model examines the effects of primary, secondary, and tertiary education when controlling for the lagged dependent variable (per capita GNP), the total fertility rate, the mineral-extraction dichotomous variable, and one indicator from each of four categories of world-system factors: (1) economic dependence, (2) state strength, measured in terms of government revenue as a percentage of GNP and the number of cabinet ministers, (3) world-system integration in terms of trade volume, and (4) structural position in the world economy based on a nation's status as weak, strong, or semi-periphery. These typical world-systems measures are reviewed in Bornschier and Chase-Dunn (1985).

The top half of Table 8.4 reports results for the period 1955–1970; the second half reports on the period 1970–1985. Findings for the 1955–1970 panel reveal substantial consistency in educational effects when measures of economic dependence, state strength, world-system position, and integration are controlled. The positive and significant effect of secondary education is stable among the equations. Both the size and significance levels of primary enrollment effects fluctuate, but overall they are consistently positive. Tertiary education has a consistently negative impact on economic growth in this period.

The bottom portion of Table 8.4 reports the same series of analyses for the later period (1970–1985). Once again a consistent picture emerges: Primary and secondary education show weak, usually positive effects on economic growth; tertiary education also has a weak, though consistently negative, effect. Size and significance of these educational effects fluctuate, due to changing sample sizes. Even for equations in which measurement error and multicollinearity are potential problems—for example, when export commodity concentration and

Table 8.4
The Effects of Education on Economic Development Controlling for World Systems Factors (unstandardized coefficients and *t*-statistics reported)

Equation Number	World System Measure	Effect of Measure	Primary Education	Secondary Education	Tertiary Education
Dependent Variable: Log GNP per capita, 1955-1970					
1	(without Controls)		.0014*	.0054***	-.014*
2	Export Dependence	.002***	.0006	.0047***	-.013*
3	Export Commodity Concentration	-.002**	.0016*	.0048**	-.014**
4	(Log) Average Debits on Investment Incurred	.032	.0008	.0048**	-.015*
5	Government Revenue as % of GDP	.006*	.0010	.0045**	-.013*
6	Number of Cabinet Ministers	.003	.0007	.0048***	-.014*
7	Institutional Integration Index	.016	.0003	.0050***	-.015*
8	Trade as % of GNP	.10***	.0006	.0047***	-.012*
9	World System Position				
	Weak periphery	-.07	.0021**	.0037**	-.011
	Strong Periphery	-.11*			
	Semi-periphery	-.13**			
Dependent Variable: Log GNP per capita, 1970-1985					
10	(without Controls)		.0006	.0002	-.0032
11	Export Commodity Concentration	-.003***	.0006	.0003	-.0043
12	Export Dependence	.002**	.0005	-.0001	-.0006*
13	(Log) Average Debits on Investment Incurred	.035	-.0014	.0017	-.0052
14	Multinational Penetration Index	-.0010	.0008	.0002	-.0040
15	Government Revenue as % of GNP	.002	.0013	-.0002	-.0034
16	Number of Cabinet Ministers	.004	.0005	.0020	-.0025
17	Trade as % of GNP	.08	.0006	-.0001	-.0015
18	Institutional Integration	-.03*	-.0005	.0030	-.0028
19	World System Position				
	Weak periphery	-.03	.0004	-.0001	-.0032
	Strong periphery	.003			
	Semi-periphery	.01			

*p < .10   ** p < .05   *** p < .01

government revenue are included—the effects of education are consistent. Once again this adds a measure of confidence to the findings reported earlier.

In sum, inclusion of these world systems measures did not appreciably alter the pattern of educational effects reported earlier. We have found no evidence that the relationships discussed earlier lack foundation because they are based on incomplete models. On the contrary, after controlling for world economic forces and relational features of nation-states known to affect the process of economic growth, the effects of education remain remarkably robust.

Table 8.4 (continued)

Lagged Dependent Variable	Total Fertility rate at T_1	Oil/Mining Countries	Adjusted R^2	Constant	N	Number (LDCs)
.73***-	.06***	.10**	.93	1.02	81	(60)
.83***	-.05***	.04	.94	.75	81	(60)
.71***	-.04***	.08*	.93	1.09	78	(58)
.77***	-.06***	-.02	.93	.92	55	(34)
.72***	-.05***	-.04	.93	.97	60	(39)
.83***	-.05***	-.04	.94	.62	55	(34)
.86***	-.05***	-.04	.94	.62	57	(36)
.82***	-.05***	.04	.94	.76	81	(60)
.74***	-.05***	.11**	.93	.99	81	(60)
.99***	-.03	.14**	.89	.18	106	(85)
.98***	-.01	.17***	.89	.29	104	(85)
1.00***	-.03	.13**	.90	.12	96	(78)
1.00***	-.03	.17***	.89	.19	84	(64)
1.07***	-.02	.21***	.91	-.04	86	(69)
1.00***	-.03	.13**	.90	.11	105	(85)
.94***	-.02	.22***	.91	.18	91	(71)
1.03***	-.03	.14**	.90	.06	95	(78)
.98***	-.03	.20***	.90	.34	89	(69)
1.01***	-.03	.14**	.89	.20	106	(86)

CONCLUSIONS

Most scholars (and virtually all policymakers) continue to view the economic benefits of educational expansion through the prism of individual-level changes. Schools—even those with few instructional resources and inexperienced teachers—are thought to be rather efficacious agents of socialization, fundamentally altering the attitudinal and behavioral make-up of children in ways that promote social and economic change. Once transformed, young educated individuals take their new skills, values, and attitudes into the adult world and behave in ways that create more ''things'' of greater economic and social value for themselves, their families, their firms, and their society. The argument entails an essential causal chain: More schooling means more young persons exposed to education, which means more productive workers, which means (in the aggregate) a more productive economy. Education contributes to economic growth because schooling transforms individuals so that they eventually enlarge the nation's economic pie.

The findings reported in this chapter should prod scholars and policymakers alike to reexamine this widely accepted view. First, all levels of education are not created equal: Some have clearly contributed to national economic growth, while others have not. The former category includes primary education throughout most of the twentieth century and secondary education in periods of global economic expansion; the latter category includes higher education in all periods.

Second, adherence to a model that hopes to exclusively observe the economic effects of education at the individual level must be questioned. Education most certainly changes central aspects of young people's lives, but at the same time it embodies a powerful social agency with direct institutional effects on the structure of society and the economy (Meyer, Chapter 14, this volume). School expansion, when viewed through an institutional prism, may extend membership rights and duties to formerly excluded segments of the population (women, ethnic minorities, nonpropertied classes); it may create and sustain new professions and occupations; it may foster a shared national faith in ''national culture'' among heterogeneous ethnic and racial groups; and it may erode traditional mechanisms (familial ties, apprenticeship, seniority) for allocating and promoting workers in the workplace. This study, explicitly designed to explore aggregate-level or institutional effects of education on economic growth, found that different levels of educational expansion had significant, yet contradictory, effects on the economy. In particular, elite education, when organized in institutions of higher learning, had a weak and usually negative impact on economic development. One reason for the negative impact of elite education may be that its economic impact on the individual and institutional levels is mixed: While higher educational attainment may be a boon for individuals, its institutional impact on the economy may be quite negative. While much income and economic value is generated by highly educated individuals, the formation and proliferation of programs certifying elites and their bodies of knowledge in less-developed countries may have deleterious consequences—emigration of the educated, highly consumptive behavior patterns, large government subsidies for the less-productive public sector—that act to retard the rate of economic growth.

By contrast, the consistent impact of mass education may be due to the conjunction of positive effects for both individuals and society. Individuals definitely have access to greater economic rewards by completing more schooling, and educated farmers may even produce more agricultural surplus for the market. But mass school expansion also transforms macroeconomic structures: rationalizing household work and creating wage-sector jobs; helping to extend the state and its services into formerly isolated economic regions; expanding cash transactions among those in the agricultural sector; redefining the economic value of children among parents; and pushing people to migrate into urban areas, perhaps into more "productive" industrial and service jobs (for evidence, see Fuller et al. 1990).

The most provocative finding to emerge from this study concerns the possible declining economic impact of mass education in contemporary times. The effects of education on economic growth apparently have weakened in the recent period (1970–1985). Dependency and world-system theorists would argue that this has occurred because the impact of educational expansion has been overshadowed by more important global economic processes: the persistent concentration of export commodities in the Third World, the long-term negative impact of foreign investment, and growing foreign debt. Yet the findings reported in Table 8.4 lend little support to such a claim. Others would argue that the weakening of school expansion effects is ironically due to education's unprecedented growth around the world and to contradictory consequences of this expansion. More schooling has meant greater emphasis on the inflationary pursuit of credentials and diplomas rather than the ability to master and apply knowledge productively. It also means increasing use by employers of education as a means of screening and sorting prospective employees. Thus, in a world of leveling economic opportunities, education increasingly serves to reproduce rather than reduce the unequal distribution of income in many nations.

Finally, these findings highlight the interaction between the relative health of the global economy and schooling's influence on growth. In times of global prosperity, mass education has held greater effect on national economic growth; in times of economic contraction, mass education appears to play a quite limited, even contradictory, role in the production and accumulation of wealth. The fact that educational effects are conditioned by global economic forces obliges us to question those who claim—indeed, celebrate—universal economic effects from the expansion of schooling.

NOTES

An earlier version of this chapter was presented at the annual meeting of the American Sociological Association, Chicago, 1987. I would like to gratefully acknowledge the comments and suggestions of Bruce Fuller, John Meyer, Francisco Ramirez, and Richard Rubinson.

1. The earliest and best-known study within this approach was conducted by Harbison and Myers (1964), in which they demonstrated that an index of "human resources" based on an average of secondary and tertiary enrollment ratios was positively correlated with per capita income for some seventy-five countries. The authors estimated a .89 correlation between their index and GNP per capita. By dividing sampled countries into four income groups, they also found that the correlation between the two variables progressively increased from the low-income group to the high-income countries. Their conclusion:

The effect of education on economic growth varies by development level. Primary and secondary education are most beneficial for less developed countries; tertiary education, especially in more technical fields, is best suited for developed countries. Associations between variables, however, tell us little about the direction of causation.

2. There is no reason to assume a priori that a stronger causal link exists between economic development and education than vice versa. Existing comparative historical evidence, for example, shows that core industrialized areas of Europe (France and England) were not the first to expand systems of mass education in the nineteenth century; rather, states in the semi-periphery of Europe (Prussia, Denmark, Austria, and Scotland) expanded mass education earliest (Ramirez and Boli 1987). In the United States, many rural farming states had enrollment rates as high as and sometimes higher than urban, industrialized states in the nineteenth century. In the post–World War II period, industrialization and level of economic development have weak effects on crossnational educational expansion. In short, the origins and expansion of mass schooling may have more to do with cultural institutional forces promoting individualism and new definitions of citizenship than with industrialization and the concentration of wealth (Boli et al. 1985). In a crossnational study employing simultaneous equation techniques, Wheeler (1980) did find that primary schooling has a strong effect on economic growth even when the reverse effect is held constant.

3. The main reasons for using energy consumption rather than GNP data for the period 1930–1950 are availability and comparability. Economic historians have yet to estimate national growth rates for a broad range of nonindustrialized nations in this period. Estimates of GNP for the 1913–1929 panel are taken from a paper by Bairoch (1981) and are supplemented with estimates from McGreevey (1968) and Mitchell (1983). GNP figures for the 1955–1970 and 1970–1985 panels are taken from the third and fourth editions of the *World Tables* published by the World Bank (1983, 1988; see also Morawetz 1976).

4. The inclusion of a strongly correlated lagged dependent variable assures a large R^2, which, while a positive result in cross-sectional analyses, is of less importance in panel models. Instead of evaluating the results of panel regression models based on the value of R^2 obtained, emphasis here is placed on the size, direction, and significance of the partial regression coefficients. Note also that by explaining a large portion of the variation, lagged dependent variables work against the explanatory power of the other dependent variables in the equation, providing a conservative test of schooling effects (Meyer and Hannan 1979).

5. Given the small number of cases in the 1913–1929 panel, estimating a constant-case sample beginning in this first panel is not justifiable.

6. Additional evidence for the declining impact of education on economic growth can be discerned from individual rate-of-return studies. If the figures published by Psacharopoulos (1989) are reorganized by historical period (1955–1970, 1970–1985), we find that the social rates of return at all levels of education have declined for low-income countries. For the early period they averaged 29.4 for primary, 18.3 for secondary, and 15.1 for tertiary; in the later period they averaged 25.6 for primary, 15.8 for secondary, and 12.8 for tertiary.

9

The Economics of School Expansion and Decline

Walter W. McMahon

Formal education is a widely desired and very successful enterprise—if success is defined as the continuing expansion of enrollments over the last two decades as child populations have grown. The increase in the proportion of children enrolled in every age bracket across many countries, be they rich or poor, has been equally spectacular. Over the last decade, however, enrollment rates have begun to decline in the poorest countries of sub-Saharan Africa and Latin America—countries making the largest budget cuts in social services under economic adjustment policies.

The economics of school expansion—or decline—is concerned not only with enrollments but also with both expenditures per capita in real terms and educational quality. When these elements are introduced, the economics of educational decline in the poorest countries, which I also explore in this chapter, should become the dominant issue. As will become apparent, the processes of school expansion and decline are not mirror images of one another.

The most dramatic fact is that educational investments per capita by governments have declined sharply in real terms in the thirty-nine poorest countries over the past two decades. In middle-income countries school investment has grown rapidly, more than doubling over the same period. Yet even here spending often fails to keep pace with child population growth. Empirical evidence suggests that as per pupil spending erodes, declining school quality depresses student achievement (Fuller 1987). As measured by internationally standardized Cambridge and baccalaureate exams, student performance in basic subjects (and literacy rates) are falling in African countries where real expenditure per pupil has been declining (Lockheed et al. 1991).

We should be able to explain these kinds of stylized facts regarding the economics of school expansion and decline within a more general theory of school expansion. This chapter focuses on the important economic forces contained in Bruce Fuller and Richard Rubinson's model of school expansion presented in Chapter 1.

First, I offer a brief overview of these economic aspects of the general model, followed by a more specific presentation on worldwide school expansion and decline. Second, I develop the conceptual framework in more specific terms. This includes the feedback mechanism: per capita income growth contributing to the growth of investment in schooling, followed by feedback as these individuals enter the labor force and contribute to further national (and per capita) income growth in later years (as introduced in McMahon 1984; 1987). My basic model incorporates the logic of individual family investment decisions, including how household budget constraints influence effective demand for schooling and why continuing school expansion depends heavily on the state's capacity to finance human resource investment. Third, I conclude by reviewing the implications of school expansion and contraction for efficiency and equity.

ECONOMIC FORCES DRIVING SCHOOL EXPANSION AND DECLINE

A brief overview of what forces determine family and government investments in education and child enrollments will be presented first. This basic framework will then be related to the dynamic process of growth or decline over time followed by an empirical modeling and interpretation of these economic processes.

Family Preferences, Costs, and Demand for Schooling

The term *investment in education* will be used rather than *expenditure*, since school investments yield returns later in life for the individual and family. Parents are aware of this, and although younger children are normally quite myopic, there is evidence that the "generalized preferences for schooling" (which energize Fuller and Rubinson's general model of school expansion) depend on family aspirations.

The basic framework holds that the family's expectations of current and future monetary and nonmonetary returns are not sufficient to result in effective demand or actual enrollment unless the family's economic resources are sufficient to sustain investment costs. Major investments made by the parents include farming or cash-earning labor that could be provided by the child but is foregone while the child is in school. This opportunity cost is a major factor in explaining high dropout rates among children in developing countries, and it operates quite apart from direct costs of schooling (tuition, textbook, uniform, and fees), which are seldom fully subsidized by the state.

The key economic fact here is that "generalized preferences" alone are not effective until there is a joint determination consistent with the family's economic constraints that results in real resources being invested in support of actual enrollment. Only then are generalized preferences converted into effective demand.

Therefore, the two most important determinants of the level of investment expenditure on education (and the rate of its expansion) are real per capita income of families (Y) and the number of children five to seventeen years of age as a percentage of the population (C) (McMahon 1970). Where per capita income and the number of children as a percentage of the population decline, we can expect investment in education and enrollments to decline. However, if population is growing rapidly and per capita income and public expenditure are falling, as in much of Africa, then enrollment pressures can be expected to grow while education expenditures fall.

Population growth intensifies social demand for schooling. Government leaders struggle to respond to this pressure, and sometimes they raise taxes to finance school expansion (which might otherwise occur privately but to a more limited extent). Finally, a feedback effect operates as education contributes to earnings growth later in the child's life and to national income growth. In turn, this income growth—if augmented by physical capital formation, rising economic efficiency, and technical change—supports further school expansion. Private borrowing by families to support their investment in human capital is not a realistic alternative, especially for families near subsistence levels of income, because of imperfect capital markets. The main sources of support to finance educational expansion (apart from external donors) are either current parental income or public tax revenues (McMahon 1984).

Basic Empirical Patterns of School Expansion

The number of children six to seventeen years of age more than doubled worldwide between 1950 and 1980, with the most rapid population growth occurring in the poorest developing countries (Table 9.1). What is more remarkable is that the percentage of children engaged in formal schooling increased at primary, secondary, and higher education levels in countries at all levels of economic development (Table 9.2). The large 25 and 29 percent gains in enrollment rates at the primary level in the lowest- and lower-middle income countries are particularly remarkable in light of static per capita income in many of these countries. This is consistent with the hypothesis that growth in the number of children as a percentage of population is a major factor creating enrollment pressure on governments and schools. A weighted average (not shown in Table 9.2) indicates that the total years of schooling demanded, and provided largely by governments, increased by 32 percent in the lowest-income countries, 46 percent in middle-income countries, 50 percent in upper middle-income countries, and 16 percent in high-income industrial countries.

Table 9.1

Income and Population Growth: Average Annual Growth Rates

		Real GNP Per Capita 1965-1986	Population Growth Rate 1980-1986
Lowest Income Countries (Not including China and Indonesia)	(37)	.5%	2.8%
Low Middle Income	(28)	2.5%	2.6%
Upper Middle Income	(23)	2.8%	1.9%
Industrial Economies	(18)	2.3%	.6%

Source: World Bank, *World Development Report* (1988, pp. 222, 274).

Table 9.2

The Expansion of Schooling and Change in Real Spending

Country Groups		Percentage Point Increase in Percent of Age Group Enrolled 1965-1985			Percent Change in Real Expenditure Per Capita on Education 1972-1981
		Primary	Secondary	Higher	
Lowest Income	(39)	25	12	4	- 67
Lower Middle Income	(33)	29	26	9	+ 22
Upper Middle Income	(23)	8	28	9	+140
Industrial Countries	(18)	0	30	18	+ 87

Source: Computed from World Bank, *World Development Report* (1988, p. 280).

The percentage of children enrolled is tied very closely to government per capita spending on education. For twenty-three African countries from 1975 to 1985, Gallagher and Ogbu (1989) find a positive and significant relationship ($r = .58$). There have been some sharp setbacks in enrollment ratios, however, in thirteen of the twenty-nine poorest countries for which data are available. These declines occurred regardless of a nation's structural adjustment status and appear to be more closely related to declines in per capita income (and to civil wars in the cases of Angola and Somalia, where declines were greatest).

Real investment in education per capita, depicted in the last column of Table 9.2, shows an even more drastic pattern of decline. There has been a sharp 67 percent decrease in government's real per capita support for education in the lowest-income countries, a 22 percent increase in the lower middle-income countries, and a 140 percent increase in the upper middle-income countries.

This variation in changing levels of per capita expenditure, taking enrollment growth into account, is reflected directly in per-pupil spending. The fall of teacher salaries in real terms during rapid expansion is an engine driving erosion in quality. As reported by Gallagher and Ogbu (1989), for example, average test scores on internationally standardized exams for both primary and secondary schools in Burkina Faso were worse in the 1980s than in the 1970s and are still declining. This was associated with a decline in per-pupil expenditure. In Senegal, test scores of primary school graduates declined by 9 percent and secondary school students' scores increased by over 8 percent, prior to the decline of primary school spending per pupil and when secondary school expenditures were still growing. In Botswana, the one place in Africa where expenditure per pupil has been growing dramatically, the pass rate on the Cambridge internationally standardized exams increased from 52 percent in the 1970s to 83 percent in the late 1980s.

In the absence of sufficient per-pupil spending, the best teachers cannot be attracted and retained, and adequate teaching materials and facilities cannot be secured. This particular indicator reveals that expenditures per pupil are falling in thirty-nine low-income countries, suggesting a deterioration in related indicators of educational quality (Lockheed et al. 1991). In low-income countries the contrast is dramatic between slower per capita growth and rapid population growth, as opposed to middle-income countries where economic growth is stronger and population growth is much slower. Clearly, rapid population growth and faltering economic expansion in the poorest countries put tremendous pressure on governments and schools.

A GENERAL ECONOMIC MODEL OF SCHOOL EXPANSION

The Flow of Causation: Joint or Recursive?

Has the increase in educational investment and improvement in school quality (to the extent that this is associated with increased expenditure per pupil) contributed to higher productivity of graduates and higher economic growth in middle- and high-income countries? Or, instead, have high rates of economic growth in these countries contributed to more rapid school expansion? Similarly, for the poorest countries, have falling per capita incomes and more severe population pressures been responsible for falling expenditure per pupil? Or is it the other way around: Have low rates of investment in basic education driven the very low rate (one-half of 1 percent) of per capita economic growth?

Logically, there would appear to be a two-way flow of causation so that both effects are true, given sufficient lags before effects are actually felt. But this kind of causation can never be inferred from the data. It can only be inferred from how the process is represented in theory and in empirical models. Within a life-cycle context, when parents invest in education for their children, this does not raise parental income. It raises children's earnings later, and the direction of causation is clear. But when parents' income is higher, they are likely to invest in more education for their own children. Both directions of causality occur in real life.

The General Model and Empirical Test

The general economic model seeks to capture the main economic effects on school expansion just discussed, as well as the feedback effects from this expansion on per capita income and output growth. This economic growth in turn contributes to further school expansion through a second round of feedback whereby growth in per capita income boosts further investment in education (after a time delay). This reciprocal process—set out more formally in three equations given in Appendix A at the end of this chapter, accompanied by a detailed definition of the variables—can be explained simply.

Rates of investment in basic and higher education by families that forego earnings of their children, and by governments that are supported by taxes paid by families, are influenced heavily by the household's per capita income. Level of investment also is influenced by the number of school-age children as a percentage of the total population, and by increased earnings expected as a result of education. Other influences on the rate of investment, and hence expansion of the quantity and/or quality of education, are less systematic. Such forces include religious and cultural attitudes, and the shocks of wars or major changes in oil prices. This investment in human capital, in turn, contributes to productivity growth and hence growth of per capita income. The higher earnings transfer back into greater support for school expansion. Rising education levels are not the only cause of growth by any means; higher rates of investment in physical capital, technology, and economic infrastructure (conducive to strong incentives and efficiency) are crucial. But increased education facilitates adaptation to new technology and productive utilization of capital goods. Without the advance of education, diminishing returns to physical capital soon set in, and growth does not spread. The vast amount of technology available today has little effect on production methods in many poor countries, such as those in sub-Saharan Africa, where many laborers remain illiterate and unable to understand how to utilize this technology.

I estimated this basic model for thirty sub-Saharan African countries for the period 1965–1985 (McMahon 1987). The data consist of five-year average rates of growth in real gross domestic product and population. Effective investment in schooling was measured by the sum of expenditure by governments, private expenditure by families, and the value of that investment spent by families in the form of foregone earnings. There are controls for investment in physical capital (I_k), and for oil price increases (in μ_1, μ_2, and μ_3) in the production function. For purposes of estimation, instead of C, a lagged endogenous variable was introduced on the right side of each equation. This captures delayed effects from increases in the number of children in prior years while simultaneously reducing possible problems with serial correlation in the residuals.

There are 120 observations (thirty countries, five observations for each country across the five five-year periods). Note that thirty observations are lost in Equation 3 as the result of the one-period (five-year) lag. The mathematical derivation of the production function (Equation 6) from a Cobb-Douglas form is shown in McMahon 1987, where other technical details also are explained. These include explanations of the use of the ratios to facilitate inter-country comparisons, and the use of other controls that did not prove to be significant.

Implications for Educational Expansion and Decline

Results for this model of school expansion for Africa are shown in Appendix B at the end of this chapter. The specification takes into account the two-way flow of causation that is implied in the real process. The thirty African nations included in the analysis are among the poorest in the world; they have high population growth and low per capita economic growth.

It is clear from the results that even in this low-income country group, the income elasticity of effective investment demand for schooling is somewhat greater than unity. As income increases, a constant I/Y ratio would imply that a 10 percent increase in income makes possible a 10 percent increase in school investment. Above and beyond that, increases in per capita income in Equations 4 and 5 contribute positively to an increase in this ratio of investment to income. This is in addition to the lagged effect from initial investment levels which reflect generalized preferences and tastes made effective through earlier investment decisions in each country.

Positive contributions of primary and secondary education to the growth of per capita income after a five-year lag also are observed. When this is converted into a one-year (rather than a five-year) rate of return, it constitutes a 21.2 percent social rate of return on investment in primary and secondary education in these African countries—comparable to the 21.7 percent social rate of return obtained on average by numerous studies using individual-level earnings functions in the same countries (computed from Psacharopoulos 1985). Higher education is negatively associated with short-term growth in these countries, perhaps because it drains resources from other uses with no short-run return. However, long-term lags of ten to fifteen years are consistent with the hypothesis of a net positive contribution of higher education to growth.

Since per capita income has been falling in many of these countries in recent years (World Bank 1988), it should be noted that the positive relation to per capita income revealed in Equations 4 and 5 would predict a decline in the ratio of investment in education to gross domestic product (GDP). This is consistent with what appears to have been happening in the thirty-nine lowest-income countries shown previously in Table 9.2.

I do find clear evidence of a feedback effect in these data. The evidence is consistent with the twin hypotheses that growth of income contributes directly to increased investment in education (even in poor countries), which in turn contributes to further economic growth and further school expansion. Conversely, falling real per capita income (which is likely to follow oil price shocks in the future) contributes to the decline of education and to falling productivity.

Individual Family Investment Decisions

Underlying these overall economic effects is the life-cycle model of household decisions at the mircoeconomic level, which focuses on the decision to consume in the present versus choosing to refrain from consumption and invest in education to increase both earning capacity and other satisfactions in the future. Although expected monetary and nonmonetary returns from education may be high, families cannot normally borrow to finance basic education for their children and therefore are limited by their own total income and by schooling provided at lower cost by the state. The net effect is to force the effective decision to invest in education to be limited by the family's current total income. Thus, if family income is low, there will be serious underinvestment in education, that is, the family's effective demand for education will be low.

The school-leaving age, when the choice is made by families to invest in more schooling or not, is one decision point that is important to study. In the United States this is faced by most families as a student is leaving high school. At this time a decision is made whether to go on; if so, should the student attend a two-year community college or a four-year bachelor's degree program? Earlier empirical results based on a sample of 5,200 individual students who reported the nonmonetary returns they expected from college as well as their expected earnings, and whose families reported their income, assets, sibling aspirations, and parental education levels, are detailed in McMahon 1976.

This model estimates simultaneously the investment-demand function, which includes generalized preferences for schooling, along with the supply-of-funds schedule for white males and white females separately. Since the sample is large, it is possible to control for many influences on these schooling decisions, including the schooling of the mother, S_M schooling of the father, S_F ability level of the student, A; and uncertainty, μ. All variables have the expected sign, except some of the nonmonetary returns (N_2, N_1, and N_6).

A summary of these results is quite pertinent to the present discussion. Forces that are most important in determining the amount to be invested (and hence the effective demand for schooling) are expected monetary returns (r*, $t = 14.92$), schooling of the mother (S_M, $t = 3.49$), and only one of the components of expected nonmonetary returns, "finding a spouse with college-developed values" (N_7, $t = 4.57$). The demand function does slope downward as expected, reflecting higher foregone earnings and lower implicit rates of return (albeit higher absolute returns), when the more advanced levels of education are contemplated.

Other factors one might expect to be important determinants of demand for further schooling simply were not significant. For example, ability as measured by test scores has a very low level of significance ($A, t = .48$) when controlling for parents' education level and income. Uncertainty about expected returns had a negative effect on the amount of planned investment, but it was not significant ($\mu, t = 1.36$). A whole range of possible expected nonmonetary satisfactions simply were not significant influences on these actual decisions, or they simply were reported as not being important. The pattern revealed for females was similar to this pattern for males, with the one exception that ability was a more significant factor for females in the decision to go farther in school ($A, t = 4.42$).

The most important factor by far in determining effective demand for more schooling is the level of financial resources available to the family and the student. All t-statistics relating to the supply of resources available to both males and females are highly significant. The income of the parents ($Y, t = 21.80$) is an important internal source of funds to the family, as are scholarships and subsidized tuition, room, and board ($S, t = 6.42$ for males and 20.35 for females). Subsidized and government-guaranteed student loans significantly reduce impediments to borrowing to finance human capital formation ($L, t = 23.18$). Remaining variables control for other effects on the decision such as the number of siblings, which reduces the financial resources available to the family for each child ($B, t = -4.67$). Other controls include hours withdrawn from investment in education due to work ($W, t = -45.41$) and birth order, which has a small coefficient for males but a larger positive coefficient for females.

Government Decisions to Invest in Education

Next I analyze the economics of government decisions to invest in, expand, or contract school supply. The unit of analysis will be the individual governmental unit, that is, the combination of legislative and executive agencies that make basic decisions to invest in education and determine the level of taxation to support expenditures. The conceptual framework and more rigorous empirical tests will be developed as they apply to determinants of public school supply in the United States, where data are more adequate. This will be followed by an analysis of an analogous process in developing countries.

Admittedly, educational expenditure and tax rate decisions in the United States and other Western countries are considerably more democratic than those in many developing countries. They are also more decentralized, in contrast to highly centralized national financing structures typically found in low-income countries. Individual citizen participation is more common—in voting for representatives on school boards where expenditure decisions are made. This suggests a relatively high degree of responsiveness to citizens' generalized preferences for education and to citizens' willingness to pay taxes to convert their preferences into effective demand (Bowen 1948; Buchanan 1966). Nevertheless, in developing countries governments also are responsive—in differing degrees, to be sure—to enrollment pressures at the local level. There also exists a responsiveness to economic capacities as taxing decisions are made.

Although the specific public expenditure model to follow in a developing country would need to place "national development goals" in a more prominent role as one of the determinants of effective demand for public education, other elements of the model would be quite similar. The basic model, first developed for application to the expansion of public expenditure on education in McMahon 1970, focuses primarily on the analysis of interstate differences in the United States, where ample data permit more complete models. I then adapted the model to analyze growth of public expenditure on education over time as well as the joint determination with the tax side of expenditure over time (McMahon 1975).

First, the data show a long-run income elasticity of real expenditure on primary and secondary education, I_H, that is greater than one (the line in Figure 9.1 that bends upward). But the short-run cyclical elasticity (and slope) is less than one (the solid lines with a flatter slope). The cross-section income elasticity is also less than one (Figure 9.1). This common pattern needs to be kept in mind when making short-run and cross-sectional comparisons or when interpreting the recent long-run intertemporal income elasticities of 1.4 and 1.5 as computed by Schultz (1988).

Underlying structural demand and supply functions are illustrated in Figure 9.2. Estimates of the reduced-form end results of solutions at points like E that are shown in Figure 9.2 are presented in Appendix C at the end of this chapter. This is essentially the same model as the one estimated recently by Schultz (1988), who used data for eighty-nine developing countries from 1950 to 1980. Thus it is possible to compare the results.

Demand for education is the quantity demanded by the median family, ignoring those who do not vote or do not hold political influence. More specifically, the amount invested in schooling depends on Y, the taxpayers' real disposable income; C, children five to seventeen years of age as a percentage of the population; N, children not attending public schools, as a percentage of C; D, urbanization; and μ, random disturbances (see McMahon 1970). The desire for economic development by national planners may also add to these educational demands, but for our purposes this is included in the disturbance term. Similarly, technical change and income growth may shift total derived demands for educated labor, thereby increasing the rate of return to education and hence the demand for schooling. Identifying these structural parameters is not attempted here, and shifts in the expected returns due to technical change or other factors are also left in the disturbance term. This demand function is illustrated as $\overline{DD}$ in Figure 9.2. It is expected to shift outward in response to increases in income (Y) and in the school-age population (C), and downward in response to a larger percentage of students in parochial or private schools (N).

The *production cost* of education underlies the supply side of educational services. These costs are illustrated by the average cost curve in Figure 9.2. The

Figure 9.1
Family Income and State School Expenditures

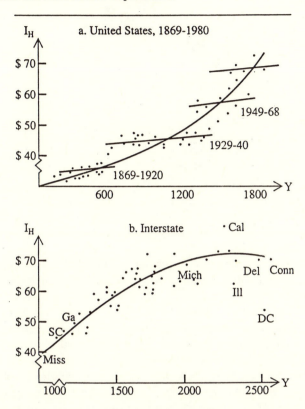

underlying production function for educational services together with the optimization process is shown in McMahon 1970 and in Schultz 1988. If the public school system minimizes costs, then the solid line that forms the lower boundary of the scatter of observations in Figure 9.2 is the average cost curve. However, if costs are "padded" due to internal inefficiencies, then the dashed line that forms the upper boundary (and points in between) is made up of points on the actual average cost curve, and the solution is at point E in Figure 9.2.

If internal efficiencies can be increased, the output of educational services can be increased at no extra cost. This new solution of demand with the supply side would use the solid line average cost curve, appearing to the right of I_H. The supply of education services by school districts depends upon P_E, the price per unit of educational services of given quality; Q, the number of pupils per school district as an index of net economies of scale; W, the real wage of teachers; Z, the number of pupils per teacher; D, the density of population; and μ_8, the disturbances.

It is true that the price of teacher salaries declines relative to average income

Figure 9.2
Effective Demand for and Supply of Schooling

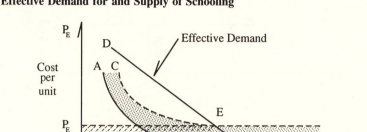

Quantity of Educational Services

and tends to lower the unit cost of providing schooling, shifting the cost curve in Figure 9.2 downward as growth occurs. This is a major engine of educational growth, as Schultz (1988) points out. However, significant economies of scale in education also occur as population density, D, increases, which is observed as a highly significant term in the models appearing in Appendix C.

Finally, although demand and supply-price give a solution for the desired level of expenditure, this is not effective unless there are "tax handles" available to provide necessary revenues. Therefore, tax decisions depend more specifically upon A, the assessed value of taxable property; S, local government support for schools; F, federal or central government support; r, the interest rate cost of funds borrowed from donors or the public; R, nontax revenue sources; and μ_9, disturbances. This represents the supply of funds or the government budget constraint. Parameters in the tax function can be interpreted as tax rates about which decisions are being made. In developing countries, most funds come from central governments, donor agencies, and various fees. In the United States, local property tax sources and provincial-level financing predominate.

A comparison can now be made of the empirical estimates obtained for this model using U.S. cross-sectional and time-series data separately along with estimates of a similar model using pooled cross-sectional and time-series data for a set of poor and middle-income countries in Africa (thirty nations), Asia (twenty-three) and Latin America (nineteen).

The evidence again is consistent with the hypothesis that growth in per capita income is a major determinant of school expansion (or decline). Shorter-run income elasticities are smaller than longer-run elasticities. But as per capita income rises in the United States, it is associated with an approximately equal increase in expenditures on primary and secondary education after a lag, with long-run income elasticities of approximate unity. When many lower-income countries are included in the analysis, Schultz finds an even higher responsiveness to long-run income growth with income elasticities of 1.35 and of 1.47 for primary and secondary expenditure per pupil, respectively. This is not inconsistent with a simultaneous feedback effect from school expansion on productivity and income growth, as suggested previously. The effects of more rapid population growth on school expansion are revealed mainly through increases in the number of school-age children as a percentage of the population, C (as shown in Appendix C). More children are associated with larger expenditures. And tax effort, expressed as a percentage of GNP, also is highly significant (as may be seen in Appendix C).But larger proportions of children are also associated with lower expenditure per child (and presumably lower quality) as indicated by the highly significant negative coefficients. Urbanization exerts a relatively weak influence. This is consistent with the hypothesis that it has both a positive effect on demand (as governments respond to politically vocal, higher-income urban dwellers) and a negative effect as the benefits of the economies of scale in urban areas and school consolidation are realized. The net effect of urbanization on ''effort'' is insignificant in the United States and is consistent with the relatively weak negative relation observed in Schultz's study of eighty-nine countries.

As per capita income rises, teacher salaries also rise, but at a slower pace over time. Schultz (1988) finds an income elasticity of the relative price of teachers of .87 at the primary level and .94 at the secondary level. This suggests that the relative salary of teachers (W/Y) actually declines by 6 to 13 percent as average income in a country doubles. This reduction in the relative real cost of teachers represents a decline in the real price of schooling (assuming that the quality of education is unaffected by the loss of able teachers to other callings). The pattern suggests that the lower relative price of this salary input is associated with a lower unit cost (involving a smaller reduction in quality) and, given a price elastic demand that is less than unity, with a lower expenditure per pupil than would otherwise be the case. It does not necessarily follow that going in the other direction, during contractions, proportionately large teacher salary cuts will occur, given wage stickiness.

IMPLICATIONS FOR INTERNAL EFFICIENCY AND EQUITY

Efficiency is not the same as low expenditure per pupil. As I have indicated, the recent evidence for Africa suggests that declining expenditure per pupil is associated with falling student achievement. Conversely, as income rises, total expenditure on education, expenditure per child, and quality all can be expected to increase. Although it is beyond the scope of this paper, it does appear that excessively rapid expenditure increases lead to diminishing returns and marginal quality gains become slight.

Under continuing population pressure in Africa, Latin America, and much of

Asia, along with low or no growth in real per capita income, enrollments will grow but expenditure per child will fall. Considering that budgets for teaching materials and texts tend to be cut first, then teacher salaries or posts, and finally administrators, this results in a less efficient input mix. With lower spending per pupil and less-than-proportionate cuts in salaries, quality falls. And larger percentage cuts often are made at the primary education level rather than in higher education, and in rural areas rather than higher-income urban areas. Equity as well as efficiency appear to be adversely affected.

APPENDIX A: RECIPROCAL MODEL OF EDUCATION INVESTMENT AND ECONOMIC GROWTH

Investment in Education as Desired by Families and Governments:

$$I_H/Y = I\left(\frac{\partial \ln (Y/N)}{\partial t_{-s}}, C, \mu_1\right) \tag{1}$$

$$I_{HE}/Y = I\left(\frac{\partial \ln (Y/N)}{\partial t_{-s}}, C, \mu_2\right) \tag{2}$$

Education's Contribution to Growth of Income per Capita:

$$\frac{\partial \ln(Y/N)}{\partial t} = Y(I_H/Y_{-s}, I_{HE}/Y_{-s}, I_K/Y_{-s}, \mu_3) \tag{3}$$

$\partial \ln(Y/N)$ = Percent rate of growth of real GDP (Y) per capita (N)

I_H = Investment in primary and secondary education by families and by government

I_{HE} = Investment in higher education by families and by government

C = Children of school age as a percentage of the population (for I_H); children who have completed prior schooling levels (for I_{HE})

I_K = Investment in physical capital goods

$\mu_1 \ldots \mu_3$ = Disturbances, including religious differences, wars, oil price shocks, and technology transfer. The model abstracts from allocations between public and private education.

APPENDIX B: EFFECTIVE INVESTMENT DEMANDS FOR SCHOOLING

(t-statistics in parentheses)

$$I_H/Y = \frac{.044}{(2.88)} \frac{\partial \ell n(Y/N)}{\partial t} + \frac{.104}{(1.58)}(I_H/Y)_{-5} + \frac{.027}{(7.40)} + \mu_4 \tag{4}$$

$$I_{HE}/Y = \frac{.011}{(1.50)} \frac{\partial \ell n(Y/N)}{\partial t} + \frac{.383}{(2.53)}(I_{HE}/Y)_{-5} + \frac{.008}{(4.15)} + \mu_4 \tag{5}$$

$$\frac{\partial \ell n(Y/N)}{\partial t} = \frac{1.62}{(2.19)}(I_H/Y)_{-5} - \frac{5.02}{(-1.53)}(I_{HE}/Y)_{-5} - \frac{.65}{(3.06)}(I_K/Y)_{-5}$$
$$+ \frac{.43}{(4.12)} \left(\frac{\partial \ell nY/N}{\partial t} \right)_{-5} + \mu_6, \ R^2 = .43 \tag{6}$$

APPENDIX C: COMPARISON OF DETERMINANTS OF SCHOOL EXPANSION AND DECLINE

Dependent Variable	Demand Influences			Production Costs				Tax Sources			R^2
	Y/POP	C	N	Z	Q	D	W/P	A	S	F	
U.S. Interstate											
p I /Y E H	.013	.15	-.02	-.09	.04	-.01		-.02	.01		.74
	(.024)	(.04)	(.01)	(.02)	(.01)	(.01)		(.02)	(.02)		
p I /Y E H	(see col. 1)	.155	-.029	-.087							.73
		(.016)	(.007)	(.004)							
U.S. Time Series											
p I /Y E H	(see col. 1)	.13	-.01	.08	.05		-.08	.04	.86	.41	.99
		(.05)	(.03)	(.08)	(.01)		(.01)	(.03)	(.2!)	(.40)	
p I /Y E H	(see col. 1)	.208	-.159	-.149						D-W	
		(.026)	(.028	(.049)						1.78	.984
89 Developing Countries, Primary School								W/Y			
p I /C E H	1.35	-1.12					-.25	.16			
89 Developing Countries, Secondary School											
p I /C E H	1.47	-1.68					-.26	.24			

p I / E H = Expenditure on education in constant U.S. dollars
C = Children in the relevant school-age bracket
Y = GNP in local constant U.S. dollars
N = Not attending public schools as a % of C
Z = Pupils per teacher
Q = Pupils per district

W/P = Teachers real wage
A = Assessed property
D = Density
S = State aid
F = Federal aid
Pop = Population

Sources: McMahon (1970), Schultz (1988).

Notes: Standard errors in parentheses. Coefficients in bold type are significant at the .05 level or above.

The Political Construction of School Supply

Strong States and Educational Expansion: France versus Italy

Jerald Hage and Maurice Garnier

The school expansion literature has sought to explain enrollment growth by focusing on broad societal changes that foster rising demand (Craig 1981; Boli et al. 1985). Because of this emphasis on demand, previous studies have omitted the agency of the state and the specific institutional character of the educational system, factors that determine supply (a notable exception is Archer 1979). We propose to look at the relationship between the strength of the state, the openness of its educational system, and enrollment expansion by focusing on the cases of France and Italy between 1881 and 1975.

France and Italy are important for several reasons. France has had a strong state, whereas Italy's has been comparatively weak (over this period), although their institutional arrangements are quite similar (Fried 1963; Germino and Passigli 1968; Suleiman 1976). In addition, France's educational system has traditionally been closed, while Italy's has been relatively open (Prost 1968; Barbagli 1982). The class structure of both countries is quite similar. Thus, we are contrasting educational dynamics under a strong versus a weak state.

Empirical studies of educational expansion have paid scant attention to the role of social class (Ralph and Rubinson 1980; Fuller 1983; Walters 1984). Studies that do include social class have tended to analyze it in isolation from other institutional arrangements (Tyack 1974; Carnoy and Levin 1985). A recent exception is Rubinson (1986), who argues that social class and the political process interact, using Europe and the United States as illustrations.

We argue that strong states can impose a class-based educational structure that is open to some and closed to others. As Boudon (1974) has argued, members of different social classes must take such a structure into account when deciding how long to stay in school. The implication is that the relative importance of demand models (institutionalized values as opposed to changes in labor force demand) will be affected by this type of institutional arrangement. Weak states, by contrast, are not in a position to dictate a closure of educational opportunities, since such a closure would mitigate against some class interests. Therefore, demand models are more likely to explain educational expansion under such a condition.

THEORETICAL FRAMEWORK

Rubinson (1986) argues that one of the most fundamental differences between Europe and the United States involves the class-based system of education in Europe. He does not explain how such a system developed, nor does he discuss differences in the class nature of European educational systems. We assume that a strong state plays a key role in creating and maintaining a class-based system of education by restricting access to the most prestigious tracks, especially to higher education. This assumption does not mean that education need be free of class biases when the state is weak. Rather, the key difference is that the strong state can *magnify* the importance of class forces.

In the following section we discuss the strength of the French and the Italian states and their capacity to craft influential educational policies. We then consider the impact of these educational policies on growth to understand how state supply of education affects demand.

The State

Strong states can impose a class-based educational structure that is open to some but closed to others. Bureaucrats can dictate curricular requirements, such as Latin or Greek, that make it difficult for many to obtain access to education (Ringer 1979). Weak states are less able to restrict or open educational opportunities, or to impose a particular educational agenda. Extremely weak states may not be able to enforce attendance in primary schools. The state and its ability to shape educational institutions represents a key intervening variable between the determinants of demand and educational expansion.

When a strong state follows such policies, it can thwart the wishes of both middle- and working-class parents. The middle class wants its children to be educated, since education represents a condition of membership in that class. The state may set strong limits on middle-class demand for education by imposing very high standards of academic performance and by restricting the number of places. Such a policy may also reduce working-class aspirations for mobility— particularly where education represents a scarce opportunity, as with highly skilled workers. Only a strong state can "establish formal rules stratifying school- ing into different status streams" (Rubinson 1986, p. 521). Such a practice usually limits school expansion and imposes a system that reproduces the class structure by limiting access to school and, ultimately, to prestigious jobs.

A strong state can resist pressures from the middle class to further expand schools and from working-class groups who may not wish to see their children educated. Such policies clearly stem from perceived state interests that transcend class concerns. But, as we have already noted, such a practice may reinforce already existing class arrangements because middle-class children will come to school better prepared and with strong incentives to remain in school.

What Enables a State to Be Educationally Strong?

First, the legislature as a center of power must be relatively weak, because a multiplicity of parties frequently makes it impossible for one party to dominate. Coalition governments enhance this tendency. State bureaucrats may dominate because they can set the agenda for policymaking and will also supervise the implementation of policy. Indeed, sometimes senior bureaucrats must approve the terms of policy implementation before it can be executed.

State bureaucrats are not automatically powerful. They gain autonomy and, thus, power if they are perceived as effective, competent, and disinterested. Such a system can be self-perpetuating: Autonomy and high rewards will attract the best graduates from the most prestigious schools who, in turn, will be trusted with important decisions. Their high level of legitimacy allows these bureaucrats to follow policies (such as restricting admissions, for example) that will be accepted (willingly or not) by the legislature. These bureaucrats can become significantly isolated from political pressures, although part of their continued legitimacy will depend on their ability to adapt to new circumstances, such as the need for technical education or the movement toward greater equality of opportunities (Talbott 1969).

The Relative Strength of the French and Italian States

It may seem obvious that the French and Prussian states were strong, but the concept is difficult to measure (Wilensky 1976; Quadagno 1987; Hage et al. 1989). We will establish the strength of the French state and the relative weakness of the Italian state in the area of education by examining the following indicators: the relative power and legitimacy of state bureaucrats, creation of a highly differentiated educational system, closing of access to some parts of the educational system, emphasis on the quality of education, enforcement of attendance laws, and the state's ability to handle educational crises (the continuous overproduction of educated personnel in Italy, for example). Indeed, it is in periods of crisis that the state demonstrates its ability to resolve divergent class interests.

A key difference between the French and Italian political systems lies in the relative power of the civil servants. In France, higher civil servants enjoy significant autonomy; their Italian counterparts must answer to parliamentary leaders, each one of whom tends to control a different sector of the bureaucracy (Germino and Passigli 1968). In Italy, a system of patronage has led to widespread distrust of state bureaucrats, who are poorly paid. Recent attempts to establish rigorous civil service requirements brought down two governments within one year.

A strong state can maintain a highly differentiated school system that reinforces the class structure. As Suleiman (1976) demonstrates, French society is dominated by a political elite recruited through the educational system, specifically through the *grandes écoles* (Polytechnique, Ecole Nationale d'Administration, Centrale, Mines). Admission to these schools is highly selective. Their graduates are perceived as highly competent and enjoy great legitimacy. In Italy, no such ruling elite exists nor does the school system insist on a similarly rigorous selection. The basis of political power in Italy rests more with barons, whose power is geographical and personal.

The differentiation of French education is not limited to the distinction between the *grandes écoles* and the university, but it carries into secondary education as well. Prior to World War II, six kinds of secondary schools existed: *lycée, collège, école primaire supérieure, cours complémentaires, écoles professionnelles*, and *école pratique du commerce et de l'industrie*. The Italian system is much simpler, having two major tracks: the *lyceo* and the technical secondary schools. Unlike their French counterparts, these schools enable their graduates to enter the university. This openness of university admission distinguishes the Italian system from other European countries. The French system restricts the number of places in most of its advanced tracks. For example, the number of physicians being trained is limited and so is the number of engineers. A secondary school will not accept more students than its allotted number of places allows. By contrast, Italian schools are more flexible in their admission policies.

Such limitation of educational places requires a legitimating ideology (Clignet 1974). In France, quality arguments fulfill that function. It is because Polytechnique recruits "the best" that it must restrict admission. Such ideology is also used in the case of a number of old *lycées*, which act as feeders for these *grandes écoles*. But quality is more than an ideology; it is a real concern. Educational legislation is replete with alterations of teacher-training programs, requirements for particular curricula, changes in the availability of resources to students (Prost 1968). This concern is translated into the allocation of resources that maintain low student/teacher ratios: three students per teacher in the *grandes écoles*, about fifteen in the *lycées*, and about thirty in primary schools. In Italian universities there are fifty students per teacher (depending on the area), and in primary schools there are between forty and fifty students per teacher. Both countries rely on examinations to measure the progress of students, but the Italian examinations are provincial, not national, in scope.

The power of the state also manifests itself in its capacity to enforce attendance laws. The French state mandated attendance in 1881 and saw to it that its decrees were enforced. The motivation was to construct both a nonclerical state and a strong army. Italy, however, repealed its compulsory education law of 1859 when local property owners complained about the burgeoning costs of primary education. Italian children were not required to go to school for more than three years, and then only if there was a school no more than two kilometers from the home. The state did not require Italian communes to build schools, nor did it provide significant financial assistance until 1906. Illiteracy was not eradicated until after World War II, largely because the landed gentry in the South resisted the building of schools and enforcement of school attendance laws.

The distinctive indicator of the weakness of Italian educational bureaucrats is their inability to resolve crises. For over a century, the Italian National Assembly has debated the problem of overproduction of educated personnel as well as the problem of illiteracy. Despite agreement by all social classes and political parties that these were (and continue to be) major social problems, no effective action was taken except for the Gentile reforms of 1924. However, these reforms were repealed eight years later as a result of middle-class pressure. The Italian National Assembly remained stalemated over education issues because opposing class interests could not be resolved. Secondary schools and universities continued their policy of admitting ever-increasing numbers of students.[1]

State Strength, Educational Policies, and Enrollments

The strength of the state enables it to follow certain educational policies that then affect enrollments and the dynamics of growth. A strong state can control its administrative apparatus and thus has many more policy options at its disposal than does a weak state. Because it must respond to the demands of all classes, a weak state must increase spending on education; a strong state, however, can resist such pressures. Indeed, the single best predictor of growth in educational expenditures in Italy has been enrollment, while in France expenditure levels are not affected by enrollment (Hage et al. 1988). In addition, since the beginning of the twentieth century, Italy has spent a greater percentage of its GNP on education than France. These findings indicate the inability of the Italian state to resist class pressures and the ability of the French state to do so.

Institutional Arrangements and Educational Demand

Given the presence of a strong state that mandates that education be class-based, members of various social classes will face different contingencies. In turn, contingencies and decisions made by individuals will alter the nature of demand for schooling.

For members of the working class, there are few opportunities. The working class realistically does not see education as an avenue for mobility if occupational opportunities are limited. Members of the middle class, however, enjoy educational opportunities and hence have access to the richest occupational rewards. Thus, they will respond to changes in the labor force, at least insofar as these

changes affect the creation and distribution of middle-class jobs. The old aris-
tocracy may not accept the educational charter and may wish to maintain educational offerings outside the state system, thereby resulting in a gradual loss of
power. When a power elite dominates a strong state, the most talented young
people will be attracted to that elite rather than the capitalist class, thereby
reinforcing the legitimacy and power of that class (Suleiman 1976).

When the state is weak, members of the different social classes face different
contingencies. The middle class can demand that educational opportunities be
created (the American model), and, in turn, their demands will be affected by
changes in the economy. The weak state cannot force reluctant members to
attend school, especially during early industrialization, when the modernization
process has not yet made education seem to be a necessary step on the ladder
of social mobility.

In open systems, educational demand also will be driven by status considerations. In closed systems, however, state policies requiring education will constitute one dominant source of demand; the other is the slow diffusion of values
concerning education, a diffusion resulting from the modernization process.
Status also implies a life-style heavily influenced by education (including marriage patterns). In other words, education becomes salient and valuable. To the
degree to which the benefits of education are only subjective (due to perception
rather than reality), the term *myth of education* may be appropriate (Collins
1979).

We have thus identified the following models: When the state is weak and
the educational system open, both middle and working classes will respond to
the changes in the labor force and to the spread of status competition linked to
school credentials (itself resulting from modernization). The state will be pres-
sured to meet that demand and enrollments will grow. This growth may be quite
uneven, however, for different classes may expect different types of education
or none at all. Thus, in Italy, the middle class will demand secondary and
university educational opportunities, while the working class, particularly in the
South, will not seek educational opportunities. An open system may thus create
opportunities for some but simultaneously exacerbate gaps between segments of
the population.

In France, however, because the state is strong and able to impose its own
educational agenda, two systems of secondary education are maintained side by
side. The working-class system does not provide opportunities for mobility.
Students who participate in this system will not respond to changes in the labor
force because the best rewards are not available to them and because attendance
is compulsory. In the elite part of the system, however, opportunities abound
for its participants and they will likely respond to changes in labor demand.

DESIGN AND METHODS

We consider the years 1881 to 1975 for secondary education in France and
Italy, and the years 1881 to 1932 for primary education in Italy. The choice of

1881 for both France and Italy is dictated by a series of events in France. Only in 1881 were at least some opportunities for secondary education open to the working class. The year 1881 represents the time when the *cours complémentaires* and *écoles primaires supérieures*, secondary schools catering to the working class, were established, while 1882 represents the time when middle-class female schools were created in France (for historical discussions, see Maillet 1974; Anderson 1975). The two systems were merged at the secondary level in 1975. In contrast, the Italian system had secondary education for women and technical education prior to 1881, but the unification process during the 1860s makes 1881 a reasonable choice for Italy as well. A number of variables could not be measured during World War II. As a consequence, the years 1939 to 1945 have been eliminated from the analysis.[2] Time series often contain auto-correlated errors. Equations were estimated using the Cochrane-Orcutt procedure to correct for first-order auto-correlated error. The Durbin-Watson statistic indicates the presence of first-order auto-correlation in the final equations.

An important problem when using time series involves specifying the length of lags. Our best judgment in this case is that educational expansion requires a period of three years before it responds to policies or changes in demand. One reason is that most curricula are organized on three-year cycles, and educational decisions usually involve not how many years a child will stay in school but in which curriculum that child will participate.

Measures

To standardize primary and secondary enrollments in the two systems, we subtracted primary enrollment in the middle-class *lycées* and *collèges* (the dual track system meant that middle-class schools had their own primary schools and working-class schools their own secondary schools). We defined the first five years of schooling as primary and the next seven as secondary. For a long time, most of the growth in the working-class secondary schools involved growth in the sixth, seventh, and eighth grades. Likewise, there was considerable dropout in the middle-class schools after age sixteen. All vocational schools were included in the category of working-class secondary. In addition, enrollment figures have to be standardized as a percentage of the relevant cohort, otherwise the numbers would merely reflect fertility changes (Craig 1981). We used ages six to fourteen as the denominator.

Our models specify the effects of economic, political, and institutional variables on educational expansion. The measurement of job opportunities is relatively straightforward. Unemployment and the proportion of the labor force in industry and service are used. Modernization was measured by urbanization, communication, and transportation indices. The sources for these data are discussed in Hage et al. (1989).

Family values about education were estimated by parental enrollment twenty-five years earlier. We reasoned that parents will want their children to receive at least as much education as they themselves received. In other words, school attendance on the part of the parents teaches them the value of education. The data were constructed back to 1800 for both systems and for both sexes using the various reports of the Ministry of Education.

The policy variables were created in the following way. Some policy changes are reasonably straightforward. For example, in 1942, the Vichy government reclassified the *écoles primaires supérieures* as *lycées*, that is, they transformed working-class secondary schools into middle-class schools, at least formally. This kind of change can easily be handled by moving the enrollments into the appropriate category. The creation of entirely new tracks represents a more complex problem (for example, the modern track in secondary schools, which made the transition from mass to elite secondary schools possible). Our procedure estimated the number of persons who would be affected by the change. For example, we estimated that when female elite schools were created in 1882, the maximum potential for enrollment would equal the number for males in the same kind of track, namely, the modern curriculum. That potential, in fact, was not realized for fifty years. While such numbers reflect a discrepancy between supply and demand, we realize that the supply could not be filled overnight; we therefore spread the number of persons affected by the policy change over a period of eight years. In short, we gave the state time to build schools and train teachers.

It is particularly difficult to estimate policies that hold egalitarian intentions. We attempted to model the two most important changes to occur during the entire century: the creation of CEG (*college d'enseignement general*, basically a comprehensive junior high school for all French children) in the 1960s, aimed at integrating the two-track system, and the abolition of fees in the middle-class schools starting in 1931. We created dummy variables for the years 1963 to 1975 and for 1931 through 1975 to represent the first policy and the second. The measurement of the government's concern for quality represents yet another problem. We computed per capita student expenditure in each track.

Few expansionary policies in Italian education were observed, since many programs were created early. The major change was the lengthening of the compulsory school age, which was only three years in the 1880s. In 1904 the age for school leaving was raised to twelve, and then to fourteen in 1923. This upper limit, however, was not enforced until the 1950s and 1960s (Barbagli 1982).

FINDINGS

Before examining the results of our models, it is instructive to consider the evolution of enrollments in both France and Italy. The most striking difference lies in relatively low enrollments in Italy until the fascist government began to enforce attendance, resulting in an enrollment increase to 50 percent of the child cohort, age six to fourteen. Italian primary school enrollments grew slowly despite the presence of laws mandating compulsory education. In the French

Figure 10.1
Primary School Enrollment Rates for France and Italy

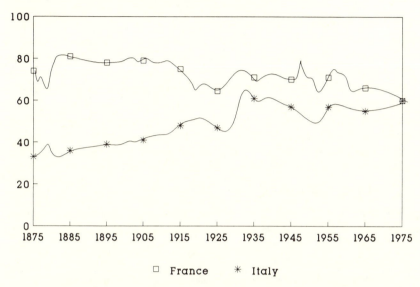

□ France   * Italy

Note: As a percentage of cohort age six through fourteen. The French primary schools involved
seven to eight years until the reforms of the comprehensives in the 1960s, while the Italian primary
schools involved five years. Thus if there were universal enrollment and all children enrolled were
within the specified cohort, enrollment would be 75 percent in France and 50 percent in Italy.

case, the decline in primary enrollment was due to the creation of *cours complémentaires, écoles primaires supérieures*, and technical schools that gradually
syphoned off sixth graders. Thus, by the time Italian primary schools were finally
including all young people, French education had created a mass system of
secondary education for the lower (sixth through eighth) grades (Figure 10.1).

Figure 10.2 plots enrollment changes for secondary education. Total enrollments in French secondary schools were higher than those in Italy. The two
states achieved these levels in quite different ways. France required attendance
in the mass system by raising the leaving age to fourteen in 1936 and to sixteen
in 1959, while the Italian system has grown almost exclusively because of demand
or self-selection. Italian secondary enrollments grew quickly after World War
II, as did the French; both responded to expansion of economic opportunities
and the processes of modernization. The real difference lies in the controlled
expansion, indeed restriction, of the French elite system. If one assumes that
the same pressures affect the French elite as the Italian or the French mass
system, then the restriction in growth is all the more striking. We might even
define unmet demand as the difference between the growth rate in the open
Italian system and the growth rate in the French elite system.

Next we examine the findings for Italian primary schooling. We suggested

Figure 10.2
Secondary School Enrollment Rates for France and Italy

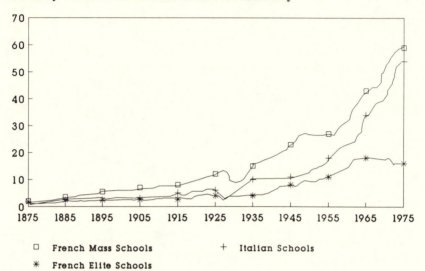

□ French Mass Schools   + Italian Schools
* French Elite Schools

Note: As a percentage of cohort age six through fourteen.

that a weak state is slow to enforce attendance in primary school, but state policies can still make a difference in the growth in enrollment of the system, as can be seen in Table 10.1. The best predictor of primary school expansion is indeed the changed Italian law regarding attendance. Not quite as important are student-teacher ratios. In smaller classes the retention rate, especially of working-class children, is likely to be higher.

Once one controls for state policies, the prime determinant of expansion is urbanization, which facilitates the spread of the "myth of education" (Ramirez and Boli 1987). We referred earlier to the development of the myth of education when industrialization creates a shift in the occupational structure. Many high-status jobs—including those in the expanding public sector—are in cities; hence the association between education and status is easily perceived in cities. Also, schools tend to be located in urban areas, thereby facilitating access. Growth in real wages affects enrollment, but job opportunities in general do not explain growth in primary enrollment. Leftist votes drive enrollment presumably because of the willingness of leftist parties to allocate funds to education. The fascist regime in Italy tried to restrict admission into universities, a policy that may have motivated parents not to send their children to primary school because opportunities were being closed off.

In Table 10.2 we examine the determinants of growth in Italian secondary and French elite and mass secondary education. Consistent with the control over the elite system, less variance is explained in the model for elite education than in the one for mass education. The impact of state policies on both mass and

Table 10.1
Factors Influencing Italian Primary School Growth, 1881–1932

	Primary School Enrollment Rate	
	betas	T-ratios
Institutional Values		
Parental Enrollment	.07	1.14
Communication	-.16	-1.67
Transportation	.18	2.38
Urbanization	.33	3.33
Material Incentives		
Wages	.17	2.85
Industrial Jobs	.05	.65
Service Jobs	a.	
Unemployment	-.02	-.55
State Policies		
Expansion	.40	4.61
Student-teacher ratio	.18	2.67
Political		
Left Vote	.25	4.32
Center Vote	.01	.24
Right Vote	.01	.29
Fascist Regime	-.16	-3.05
Adjusted **R²**	.95	
D-W	1.56**	

a. Multi-collinear with service sector employment.
**Indeterminate zone of auto-correlated error.

elite French systems is strong. In particular, the beta for expansion is .41 in the elite system and .26 in the mass system, reflecting the slowness of the French state to make educational opportunities available. In contrast, the open Italian system made the modern curriculum and technical education available decades before they were created in France. The only variable that has an impact in the Italian case is expenditures, which reflect class pressures to which the state responds. In contrast, this variable has little impact in the two French systems.

Table 10.2

Factors Influencing Secondary Education Growth in France and Italy, 1881–1975

| | FRANCE | | | | ITALY | |
	Mass		Elite		Secondary	
Demand Models	betas	T-ratios	betas	T-ratios	betas	T-ratios
Institutional Values						
Parental Enrollment	-.07	-2.98	.25	2.56	.09	3.32
Communication	.13	1.69	-.16	-.91	-.02	-.45
Transportation	.45	4.76	-.10	-.61	.34	10.89
Urbanization	.20	2.88	-.05	-.40	.31	6.97
Material Incentives						
Wages	-.11	-1.94	.45	4.44	.24	9.75
Industrial Jobs	-.10	-2.06	a		.10	2.99
Service Jobs	-.11	-.28	.08	1.06	.04	2.01
Unemployment	-.07	-2.17	.02	.18	.01	.45
Supply Models						
State Policies						
Expansion	.26	5.53	.41	4.81	.04	1.22
Expenditures^c	.13	1.48	-.00	-.01	.07	2.85
Comprehensives	.09	3.89	d		e	
Political						
Left Vote	.10	2.97	.09	1.23	.01	.72
Center Vote	.02	.58	-.02	-.22	-.00	-.42
Right Vote	a		a		-.01	-.57
Fascist Regime	b				-.04	-2.37
Historical Outliers						
1937					.01	5.26
1938					.10	0.25
1966	-.09	-5.04				
1967	-.14	-7.44				
1971	.05	2.89				
Adjusted R^2	.98		.71		.99	
D-W	1.58**		1.94***		1.59**	

a. Multi-collinear. Right and center votes positively related at .80 or above in France. Expansion in industry and service at the same level in French elite secondary schools.

b. Fascist regime does not apply to France.

c. For Italy, expenditures represent total educational expenditures divided by secondary enrollment. In the future we hope to estimate expenditures on secondary education more precisely. For France, expenditures are actual expenditures in each track in the pre–World War II period. After World War II, they are estimated by student-teacher ratios.

d. The comprehensive policy does not apply to the elite system in France. For both France and Italy it started in almost the same year.

e. Tuition was free for the mass secondary system in France from 1881, except for some elite technical schools, and largely free for the technical tracks in Italy throughout the whole period. Fees for the secondary tracks were much lower in Italy than the corresponding fees for *lycées* and *collèges* in France, which became free in 1930. Fees were totally eliminated in the 1960s. Furthermore, Italian secondary schools had many fewer boarders than was the case for the elite secondary schools in France. Of course, free tuition does not eliminate the economic hurdle of the rest of room and board for the boarders.

f. Outliers discerned with OLS runs. For Italy, they reflect the rapid expansion after the repeal of the Gentile reform and the aftermath—the Ethiopian War. For France, they reflect the explosion in enrollments in C.E.G.s in some years and the unevenness of this growth.

**Indeterminate zone of auto-correlated error.

***Free of auto-correlated error.

We have argued that growth in a restrictive educational system will be determined by different factors from those in an open system. There is one aspect in which the Italian secondary and the French elite systems are similar: Both provide access to jobs. The French mass system also leads to jobs, but these are not high-status jobs and thus do not provide as strong an incentive. It is therefore not surprising that the Italian secondary and the French elite enrollments are driven by material incentives, while the French mass system is not. We also note that French elite enrollments respond heavily to material incentives, because graduates of that system have access to the very best higher education (*grandes écoles*) and to the best jobs.

The elite French secondary system and the Italian system are also alike in being driven by status considerations. Although the beta is much stronger in the French elite system, it is still significant in the Italian system. In contrast, the mass French system is driven by the diffusion of the myth of education through the process of modernization.

IMPLICATIONS: WHAT STATE POLICIES YIELD ENROLLMENT EFFECTS?

We began this chapter with the argument that the dynamics of educational growth differ, depending upon whether the state is strong and able to restrict access to higher education. In such a case, growth in secondary education is driven primarily by supply and secondarily by material incentives and the myth of education. For primary education, the strong state insists upon universal attendance. In contrast, weak states are dominated by demand. Of the two explanations, the myth of education is more important than material incentives at both the primary and secondary levels. The myth of education is especially striking in Italy because the country was established in the 1860s by elites who believed that education provided the road to modernization.

The relative importance of these two explanations varies when there are multiple systems, some closed and some open, and when the state is strong. The establishment and maintenance of two school systems, one providing access to university (but limiting the number of students), leads to the growth of education in response to material incentives, but not to the myth of education (as measured by our various indices of modernization). In contrast, the mass system, where access to high-status jobs is closed, is driven by state requirements and by the myth of education. Material incentives have little impact on the working class because its members know that there are few opportunities available to them. The strong state responds by steadily increasing the number of years of compulsory education, thus increasing human capital.

It is interesting that the Italian system is able to achieve almost the same enrollment levels, in spite of a lower level of economic development, by letting demand drive the system. It does not have to raise the school-leaving age; indeed, it may not even be able to enforce attendance laws. In the Italian case, all social classes attend the same secondary system and each class may respond to different forces. One interpretation may be that the working class and peasants in Italy are responding to the myth of education and status competition, as is the working class in France, while Italian middle classes respond to material incentives, as does the middle class in France. More research on this issue is needed.

What is true at the secondary level in Italy is not true at the primary level. Left to their own devices, many families would not choose to send their children to school. Thus, the paradox is that state policies, both compulsory education laws and financial support, explain the growth in primary enrollments. Weak states, such as Italy, rely more upon positive than negative incentives and may only reluctantly move toward enforced sanctions. Primary enrollments grew as the myth of education spread to the South via the development of a modern transportation system and rising urbanization. Material incentives, in this case wages, also facilitated this process. Thus, in some respects, primary and secondary education in Italy are of a piece. The same forces drive the expansion of both systems. Weak states allow demand to dictate the dynamics of growth and they respond by spending money. Modernization processes (including the spread of the myth of education) and the presence of material incentives explain growth in demand.

One of the most important contradictions involves the failure of unemployment to predict school expansion in Italy. In an extensive cross-sectional analysis of data for 1961, Barbagli (1982) demonstrates the tendency for enrollment rates in the upper secondary system to be higher in the South (where unemployment is high) than in the North, especially for children from working-class families. He argues that higher unemployment in the South encourages retention in school; he calls this the "parking" effect. What accounts for this difference between Barbagli's findings and ours?

The temporal growth of the economy overrides regional differences in levels of economic development. In fact, the unemployment fluctuations across time are much smaller than variations in secondary school enrollment. However, we did not have youth unemployment data and these figures might be instructive, showing a greater impact of unemployment on enrollment. Finally, the parking effect is visible if one compares the impact of unemployment on the closed secondary system (not leading to the university) with the effect of unemployment on enrollment in the open system. In the French open system and in Italy (an open system), unemployment marginally increases enrollments. In the closed system, however, unemployment reduces enrollments because there are even fewer reasons to stay in school. The difference between the two betas represents the magnitude of the parking effect.

Another contradiction involves the relative lack of impact of those educational policies creating comprehensive schools on enrollments in Italy. These policies were successful in France (Prost 1968). Barbagli (1982) sees this structural reform as having an impact on the proportion of students moving on to the upper secondary level in Italy. Our analysis indicates that more of the expansion results from increased expenditures and from an expanding economy rather than from the policy itself. In contrast, in the mass secondary French system, the reform raised students' expectations. Prost's (1968) analysis of equality in secondary education indicates that, indeed, all of these changes in the 1950s and the 1960s had an impact on the proportion of children from the working class going into the more prestigious tracks. The comprehensive policies unleashed pent-up demand in the relatively closed French system, but they did not have such effects in the relatively open Italian system.

School Institutions That Signal Mobility

Implicit in our analysis is that an open system is likely to signal more upward social mobility than a closed system. What consequences does the presence of a (closed) elite and (open) mass secondary system have on working-class university enrollments? Or, how much do institutional barriers imposed by a strong state contribute to the class barriers that result in self-selection?

By comparing the two systems we gain some insight into this process. Fees (though small) were charged in Italy until the reforms of the 1960s (Barbagli 1982), whereas secondary education in the French elite system was free after 1930 and in the mass system after the 1880s. Despite this economic hurdle, the representation of the working class in Italian universities grew from 11 percent in 1953 to 21 percent in 1967. In France, 2.5 percent of the university students were from the working class in 1953, that is, less than one-fourth the proportion in Italy, and this figure had grown to only 8.3 percent by 1965. These figures do not truly express the extent of the impact of institutional barriers on upward mobility. France has an elite higher education system, the *grandes écoles*, which largely determines access to the political and economic elite positions; Italy does not. In the 1960s, the average working-class representation varied between 2 and 5 percent, except for the *école des arts et métiers* (which is not really a *grande école*), where it rose to 17 percent. Of course, the latter recruits students from technical schools (Ringer 1979). The difference between universities in France and Italy suggests that half the working class representation in universities, or about 10 percent of the enrollment, is a consequence of an open system or the absence of institutional barriers.[3]

We also noted that strong bureaucratic states are shielded from political pressures. There is much quantitative data to support this assertion. The role of politics in postsecondary education was important in Italy (Barbagli 1982) but not in France. Although one could argue that the slow movement toward equality in the 1960s started with Zey and the Front Populaire in 1936, politics appears to have had more of an impact (at least indirectly) on expansion than we had anticipated, particularly in France. Vote shifts to the left affect enrollments in both mass and elite systems of France. We suggest that when the working class is mobilized and wins at the ballot box, this expands aspirations because the system appears to be opening.

The negative impact of fascism is also worth noting. The Gentile reforms of 1924 had a chilling effect on secondary enrollments because these were the only reforms that closed the Italian system. While they only lasted for eight years, the betas are negative and significant. What is particularly interesting is the ripple effect on primary education as well. Even though the government was trying to increase attendance in primary schools, its policies at the secondary level had a negative impact.

CONCLUSION

These findings clearly indicate that educational systems can fruitfully be studied as systems and not as collections of separate and independent parts. We have shown that the expansion of educational systems is affected by the strength of the state, by the charter of the educational system, and by politics. The comparison of France and Italy sheds light on the U.S. case. The openness of the system and the weakness of the state in educational issues suggest that expansion is driven by demand in the United States, and this contributes to opportunities for mobility. However, the U.S. state may be stronger than the Italian state in educational matters, and therefore material incentives may be more critical than the myth of education or status competition in the United States.

Future studies will need to take into consideration characteristics of state involvement and strength in education and how this may condition the influence of economic and other institutional forces on school expansion.

NOTES

1. Some readers might wonder why we do not rely on more rigorous quantitative indicators of state strength. For example, why not rely on the percentage of GNP spent on governmental activities or the proportion of civil servants in the labor force? The issue involves not the extractive capacity of the state but rather the percentage of total wealth under the direct control of the state. In France and in Italy, the single largest budgetary allocations involve welfare expenditures. In France, the state determines how funds will be spent because the minister who controls these agencies is part of the government. In Italy, however, welfare administration is a separate enterprise in which the state has nominal participation. The heads of public enterprises (Renault in France, ENI [Ente Nazionale Idrocarburi] in Italy) are appointed by the government in France, but not in Italy. Furthermore, Wilensky's (1976) analysis of the capacity of the state to resist welfare backlash found that centralized administrations such as the French were able to do so, but the percentage of GNP spent on welfare was not a good predictor of resistance to backlash. While on the surface France and Italy seem to have similar administrative structures with high centralization, in fact Italy's provinces remain powerful sources of influence in the education sector.

2. We inspected the residuals after ordinary least-squares (OLS) runs to determine if there were any other outliers (± 2 standard deviations). We discovered that there were, and we added dummy variables to prevent these years from disturbing the analysis.

3. If one asks how this occurs, much of the answer focuses on the special role of technical education as an avenue of upward mobility for the working class. A comparison of the enrollments of students in classical, modern, and technical/vocational tracks reveals striking similarities between the two countries in the 1940s through the 1960s. For example, the proportion of working-class enrollment for France in the period 1961–62 was 16 percent in classical and modern *lycées*, 33 percent in technical *lycées*, and 35 percent in general secondary. In 1967, the graduates of comparable systems in Italy were 11 percent in classical, 33 percent in technical, and 28 percent in teacher training.

11

Who Should Be Schooled?
The Politics of Class, Race,
and Ethnicity

Pamela Barnhouse Walters

This chapter examines the politics of access to public education in the United States, focusing on the Northeast and the South in the early twentieth century. I have three purposes. First, class analyses of the politics of education have been called into question recently, both by those who reject the class imposition claims of revisionist historians' analyses of the Northeast (e.g., Ravitch 1974) and by institutional theorists who argue that neither class structure nor class conflict affected state support for an expansive system of public education (e.g., Ramirez and Boli 1987). I argue here that class inequalities and class interests did affect children's access to public education in the United States.

Second, class analyses of public education have been commonly applied to the Northeast, but theories of race and racial inequalities have generally been used to explain the politics of education in the South. I argue that a class model of the politics of education applies in the South as well as the Northeast. The dominant classes in the Northeast and South did not share the same educational agenda, nor did subordinate groups in the two regions. Yet in both regions, groups' interests and abilities to act on their interests were influenced by class position and inequalities.

Third, the experience of the South has been treated as exceptional vis-à-vis the U.S. model developed with respect to the North (see Walters et al. 1990). I attempt to show that the same factors were related to educational politics in both the North and South.

A *politics of inclusion* prevailed in the North: Neither working-class groups nor elites made attempts to deny working-class children access to public education. Educational conflict existed between elites and working-class groups, but it was over the content of public education, centering on issues such as Taylorism, vocationalism, the language of instruction, and the implicitly religious content of the curriculum. In the South, elites were opposed to the education of blacks and poor whites beyond rudimentary levels; and subordinate groups, particularly blacks, had much less power to press their own educational agenda than did subordinate groups in the North. Consequently, a *politics of exclusion* prevailed in the South. The regional differences in class interests and action vis-à-vis public education are rooted in regional differences in production relations, means of labor discipline, reliance on child labor, definitions of citizenship, and the availability of alternatives to the public educational system. These factors determined whether elite groups found it in their interest to incorporate subordinate groups into the public educational system, affected the degree to which subordinate groups pressed for greater access to education, and influenced the outcome of struggles over educational access. I illuminate regional similarities and contrasts throughout this chapter.

THE FORCE OF CLASS INTERESTS

Class affects education in two principal ways. Class conflict affects the provision of educational opportunities, or the supply of education (see Garnier et al. 1989; Walters et al. 1990). Class politics of educational supply is the focus of this chapter. Assuming that school "spaces" are available, however, the constraints of class membership (e.g., differences in the ability to afford the costs of education, or to afford a child's foregone labor) and possibly cultural differences among classes (see, e.g., Perlmann 1988) produce class differences in children's preferences and abilities to attend school, or social demand. Therefore, class differences in school enrollments or attainments are the result of one set of class constraints operating within another set: class inequalities in the availability of educational spaces, and class differences in the rate of utilization of class-specific educational opportunities, due to class inequalities in family resources. Under certain conditions the first set of constraints may be minimal, but the relative absence of class constraints on educational supply is as deserving of explanation as their presence.

Since the South has been largely excluded from theorizing about North American education, and since it is the only region in which a politics of exclusion prevailed in the struggle over access to education, scholars have generally assumed that growth in enrollments or attainments was due to an increase in demand. In other words, educational supply is presumed to have been adequate to meet the demand for education expressed by the U.S. population (Rubinson 1986). While this assumption may be valid for other regions of the United States, researchers have paid little attention to the theoretical question of why sufficient educational opportunities existed outside of the South.

It is important to determine why the supply of education was adequate to meet demand in the Northeast and why educational opportunities were insufficient to

meet demand in the South.[1] By examining a greater range of institutional arrangements than existed in either the North or South alone, we can learn more
about the relationships between political and economic structures on the one
hand, and education on the other (for elaboration, see Walters et al. 1990). In
particular, we can determine whether some conditions that were invariant in one
region (e.g., the availability of the franchise in the North) were conditions under
which other institutional arrangements had particular effects on education. I argue
that (1) the essential regional difference was a shared politics of educational
inclusion in the Northeast versus a contested politics of access in the South that
was dominated by plantation owners' politics of exclusion, and (2) the same
theoretical model can explain these seemingly divergent sets of educational
policies.

WHY AN ANALYSIS OF CLASS POLITICS?

It might be asked why I would pursue a class-based explanation of divergent
educational practices in the turn-of-the-century North and South. After all, the
class-imposition models of educational change that were popular in the 1960s
and 1970s, arguing that capitalists used public education to socialize and control
the urban working class and Americanize potentially disruptive immigrants (e.g.,
Katz 1968), are now out of favor among many sociologists and historians. These
models certainly paint an overly simplistic picture of elite domination. However,
all forms of class analysis of education reform need not be discarded along with
the strongest claims of class-imposition theorists. A number of more textured
accounts of class conflict over educational structure have been published recently
that stress the contested nature of school reform movements, emphasizing that
the working class enjoyed at least some partial successes in their struggles with
capitalists and professional educators over the form and content of public education (e.g., Apple 1982; Katznelson and Weir 1985).[2] Nonetheless, these analyses still maintain that capitalists won more than their share of the battles over
public education.[3]

Moreover, some of the reasons for rejecting class models are invalid. Many
empirical studies that claim to reject class-imposition models of school reform,
for example, evaluated class-related arguments with respect to outcomes that
were not the focus of the original theories. Class-imposition accounts speak to
elites' interests vis-à-vis educational policy, claiming that elites embraced the
working class in the public schools, albeit clearly in a position subordinate to
the children of elites and with an educational curriculum intended to prepare
them for working-class jobs. The theories do not speak to the issue of whether
the working class was so gracious as to avail itself of the opportunity to attend
public school. Yet the many studies showing that public school enrollments were
lower in areas in which industrial work and/or immigrants were concentrated
have often been taken as proof that the class-imposition accounts of school reform
are wrong, missing the fact that determinants of enrollments may be quite dif-

ferent from determinants of the educational opportunity structure. This is fundamentally a confusion over supply versus demand. Analyses of enrollments, which are determined to a large extent by the demand for education, cannot be the basis for accepting or rejecting theoretical claims about who controlled educational policy (supply). Moreover, studies of class and education all but ignore the South, leaving us with little knowledge about whether class dynamics affected schooling there.

That brings us to the question of whether a class model of education is applicable to the experience of the South. Theories of U.S. education that deal with class are almost always based on the historical record of the Northeast (or sometimes the Midwest), resulting in what Richardson (1984) calls the "northeasternization" of theories of U.S. education.[4] Theories of education in the South generally pose race rather than class as the central cleavage in southern educational politics (see, e.g., Bond 1934; Harlan 1958; Bullock 1967; Margo 1987). As my colleagues and I argue elsewhere, however, racial criteria were used to create classes in the South, although the abolition of slavery made it impossible to draw the equation between race and class as perfectly in the postbellum as in the antebellum South (Walters et al. 1990). Planters defended black subordination in large part because it ensured them an adequate supply of low-wage labor, decidedly a class-based consideration. Poor whites were also racist, perhaps because in a system in which they had so little hope of escaping poverty they "could take pride only in color" (Flynt 1979). Another reason for developing a class model of educational politics is that education is a central activity of local governments, and a large body of research in both sociology and political science shows that locally dominant classes and ethnic groups often are able to wield a disproportionate influence over local policies. Local government institutions (the local state) have been the organizations primarily responsible for the creation and maintenance of public school systems and for the development of public school policy since the establishment of common schools in the United States.[5]

If local states shape educational policies, it is obvious that an adequate model of the determinants of educational supply cannot be developed without taking the role of the local state into account. Ironically, even those studies that highlight the class politics of education typically fail to identify the local state as the mechanism by which contending classes either succeeded or failed in translating their interests into educational policy. James and Walters (1990) argue that analyses of the determinants of school policy should take into account "the same kinds of mobilized political forces and institutional constraints that affect other local-state outputs" (p. 82), primarily those related to class structure and conflict.

CLASS INTERESTS IN EDUCATION

The North

It is significant that class-imposition or class-conflict theorists do not suggest that any classes or ethnic groups involved in northeastern conflicts over public education advocated a politics of exclusion. The debate was always over what type of public education should be offered to working-class and immigrant children: classic or vocational, Catholic or implicitly Protestant, instruction in English or in children's native tongue, and so forth. But no social group doubted over time the wisdom of providing the working class with greater access to education. To elites, the problem was how to attract the children they aimed to socialize into the public schools.

Despite much disagreement among scholars about whether industrialists, the dominant elite in the North, were able to implement their educational agenda in a straightforward manner, there is little disagreement about the specifics of their publicly expressed educational agenda. Immigrants were the primary targets of elites' formal socialization efforts. The Americanization of those elements viewed as dirty, disruptive, and even dangerous was high on the elites' agenda, and they viewed the school as the best institution to accomplish this purpose (the immigrant family, itself the presumed source of the problem, could not be trusted to accomplish the task). In terms of industrialists' interests in workers qua workers, as Hurn summarized it, industrialists

were especially concerned to see compulsory schooling because they believed that only schools could guarantee them the kind of stable, industrious, and compliant work force on which their prosperity depended. . . . An educated worker, they thought, would be a worker who was less likely to be unreliable, rebellious, or disrespectful of authority; less inclined to drunkenness and disorderly behavior, and more inclined to be a stable and industrious worker. (1985, pp. 89–90)

Industrialists certainly experienced a large degree of success in molding the schools according to their vision. Outside of the South, and especially in the Northeast, "business values" dominated the schools by the turn of the century (Callahan 1962), just as big business had become dominant throughout non-southern society. The penetration of northern schools by business values is apparent in some of the major reforms that were widely adopted in the early twentieth century, at least in the cities: scientific management (Taylorism) and industrial education, for example. Similarly, the major buzzword of the (non-southern) school reform movement in the early twentieth century was *efficiency*, reflecting the desire to model the organization of the school after the organization of the successful factory.

In the minds of many industrialists and school reformers, the optimal school was an efficient sorting machine that would take students of a particular social class and prepare them for their assumed adult social roles. Progressives also were concerned with "social efficiency," which "meant social harmony and the leadership of the 'competent' " (Haber 1964, p. x). Social harmony was a big concern in a society that was presumably at risk of becoming unraveled due to rapid urbanization and industrialization and a massive influx of immigrants (Tyack 1974).

Working-class interests in the content of education differed, but they were in agreement with industrialists and school reformers that more education was desirable (at least as expressed by organized labor). In its first statement about public education, the American Federation of Labor (AFL) argued in 1911 for the passage of compulsory education laws so that

all children between the ages of six and sixteen years should be provided with at least a common school education and given at least the ordinary opportunities for preparation in childhood to meet the duties of life. . . . The time is long since past when the ignorant and uneducated stand any chance against the educated, active and well developed man. (p. 360)

Labor was not as enamored of efficiency and sorting as industrialists were, however. A few years later, for example, the AFL lobbied for a reorganization of the school upon a democratic basis. It argued that the ideal education

begins with those things which appeal to the child and arouses his curiosity in . . . daily life. . . . These things the schools of the future are to explain to the child in order that he may have full and complete understanding of his daily life and thereby be master of himself and his environment. . . . The effect of this sort of education will be to lay the basis for economic democracy, a democracy in which each individual will have equal opportunity. (1915, p. 159)

Labor, in sum, supported expanded education and industrial education, but it wanted a measure of control over it; it expected that improved education would give workers more control over themselves and their work environments.

The South

There were major conflicts in the South about access to education for poor whites and for blacks. The economy of the South was dominated by plantation agriculture, and politics was dominated by the Democratic party, the party of the plantation-owning class (Key 1949; Kousser 1974). Planters were able to successfully resist the populist challenge to their economic and political hegemony in the 1880s, and they consolidated their power over both poor whites and blacks in the late nineteenth and early twentieth centuries. Planters viewed "too much" education for either of these subordinate groups as a potential challenge to their continued hegemony. Nonetheless, it was in their opposition to education for blacks that planters were most vehement, and they were joined by poor whites in their opposition to black political and economic power, as manifested in educational opportunities. Indeed, Key (1949) claimed that the only matter on which the (white) South was solid was the issue of race:

[T]here is one, and only one, real basis for southern unity: the Negro. . . . The maintenance of southern Democratic solidarity has depended fundamentally on a willingness to subordinate to the race question all great social and economic issues that tend to divide people into opposing parties. (pp. 315–316)

The reasons why planters opposed education for blacks were related to the importance of blacks as low-wage agricultural workers and the use of coercion rather than free markets as a means of labor discipline. First, whites had no intention of allowing blacks to have access to the types of jobs that required formal education. Thus, blacks had no need for the skills they might acquire through education to perform their allotted economic roles (Bond 1934; Harlan 1958).

Second, and more important, since the assumption that blacks were best suited for low-wage, unskilled labor went unquestioned by most whites, it was worse than a waste of resources to educate blacks. It was downright dangerous. Too much education would make them rebellious and dissatisfied with their lot, because it would unreasonably raise their expectations (Bond 1934; Harlan 1958; Anderson 1988). This position can be illustrated by the polite statement of an Alabama school administrator to the National Education Association in 1890:

But the most formidable opposition we have to negro education, is the positive declaration made by a *large and respectable class of citizens* that education is a decided detriment to the negro's best interests. It is claimed by these opponents that just as soon as the negro obtains a little learning, he is disposed to abandon manual labor, and seeks to engage in politics, preaching, or teaching . . . and uses his acquired talents in stirring up and perpetuating hatred and strife between the races. (quoted in Tyack 1967, p. 289, emphasis added)

These first two reasons also account for poor whites' opposition to black education. Basically, giving blacks too many skills challenged poor whites' already tenuous economic position. The certainty that blacks occupied a lower economic and social position than themselves also may have made poor whites less interested in education for themselves as a means of gaining economic advantage. There is little evidence that poor whites strongly advocated improved education for their own children; if anything, they were unconvinced that it provided many benefits (Hall et al. 1987; Tullos 1989). Writing about the Piedmont (a textile-producing area) of the 1920s, Tullos reports that whites commonly thought that "schooling beyond the sixth grade might cause children to 'rise above their raising,' becoming, in effect, strangers to their friends and families" (1989, p. 185).

Planters profited by defrauding illiterate tenants and sharecroppers, who could not read their contracts; in their frequent role as merchants, white elites also profited by overcharging and otherwise cheating illiterate tenants and share-croppers who bought supplies on credit (Johnson 1934). Thus, another reason why planters opposed education is that if agricultural workers became literate, they would lose these forms of exploitation.

Finally, planter political control depended on the political disenfranchisement of blacks and many poor whites. In fact, the "one-party South" was created by revoking citizenship rights of these groups who had challenged planter political power (Kousser 1974). Because of U.S. constitutional guarantees, southern whites could not use explicitly racial criteria to deny the vote to blacks. But they could, and did, use other criteria as a basis of disenfranchisement. Between 1890 and 1910, all southern states enacted legislation that limited voting rights, restricting voting to those who were literate, who could demonstrate "understanding" of a clause in the state constitution, or who were able to pay a poll tax to vote.

Southern blacks exhibited a strong desire for education from Reconstruction through the early twentieth century (Anderson 1988; Tyack 1967). One of the main motivations among blacks for education was to "uplift the race." On the part of some blacks, this was a desire to prove to whites that they were worthy of rights and responsibilities equivalent to whites', and a conviction that once they proved this worthiness they would achieve social and economic progress.[6]

Perhaps the most eloquent demonstration of blacks' commitment to education is their surprising financial support of schooling given their extreme poverty. Significant black efforts were undertaken to establish and maintain educational institutions outside of the public sector, starting with grass-roots school movements during Reconstruction, continuing with attempts to establish private black secondary and postsecondary schools when it became clear that the public system would provide few opportunities, and including substantial private contributions to "public" schools to counteract woeful underfunding of black education by white authorities.[7]

Industrialists are the final southern group whose interests must be taken into account. Like their northern counterparts, southern industrialists (in a coalition with northern elites, philanthropists, and some southern educators) supported expanded access to education for the region's subordinate classes (both blacks and poor whites). Industrialists assumed that education (at least at the elementary level) would provide useful skills to industrial workers. Moreover, industrialists were less threatened by an educated work force than planters since they relied less on coercive means of labor control (including fraud and deceit), and they primarily employed whites. White labor unrest could be controlled by the ever-present threat of replacing whites with black workers. Yet industrialists were by no means advocates of racial equality in education. Industrial education was promoted as a means to socialize blacks for subordinate economic roles (DuBois [1903] 1968; Harlan 1958). This advocacy sounded much like that of their northern counterparts. In fact, northern industrialists and their agents entered the educational conflict in the South during the Progressive era, but their efforts accommodated the prevailing tastes and interests of the regionally dominant interest group, the planters.

Planters dominated the struggles over education in the South. Ample evidence indicates that they dominated the South economically and politically from the 1890s until at least the 1930s. It was their political agenda of black disenfranchisement and black educational subordination that was instituted. Anderson, for example, claims: "[I]n the early twentieth century whites all over the South seized the school funds belonging to the disfranchised black citizens, gerry-mandered school districts so as to exclude blacks from certain local tax benefits, and expounded a racist ideology to provide a moral justification of unequal treatment" (1988, p. 154). Writing in 1911 about the consequences of disen-franchisement, W. E. B. DuBois declared:

Not only has the general enrollment and attendance of Negro children in the rural schools of the lower South and to a large extent the city schools been at a standstill in the last ten years, and in many cases actually decreased, but many of the school authorities have shown by their acts and in a few cases expressed declaration that it was their policy to eliminate the Negro school as far as possible. (Anderson 1988, p. 154)

The sharp drop in funding to black schools relative to white schools following black disenfranchisement in the South (Maxcy 1981; James and Walters 1990) is further evidence of planters' success in implementing their educational agenda, since disenfranchisement can be seen as the decisive point at which planters regained their political hegemony over poor whites and blacks.

TOWARD AN EXPLANATION OF DIVERGENT CLASS POLITICS OF EDUCATION

This section provides a direct comparison of the politics of education in the North and South, the goal of which is to determine whether a common framework can be used to understand the class politics of education in both regions. The focus, as before, is on the factors that produced differences in class interests and in class resources affecting local school policy.[8]

I have described the differences in class configurations between the North and South, and the varying interests in education voiced by the contending classes in each region. The most important factors that influenced elites' interests in education were the means of production and prevailing methods of controlling labor. In the North, with its more capital-intensive, industrial form of production, there was a place for a moderately educated work force; but in the South, with its labor-intensive, low-skill agricultural production, a need for even a moderately educated labor force was seldom expressed. The primary means of disciplining workers in the North was a free labor market, with the threat of unemployment and dependence on wages rather than subsistence production. But plantation owners in the South relied heavily on coercion to motivate workers and to maintain an adequate supply of low-wage labor (Walters et al. 1990). Debt peonage and severe restrictions on the activities of northern labor recruiters, for example, were important means of labor discipline in the South (Ransom and Sutch 1977; Mandle 1978). Schooling in moderate amounts did not threaten labor discipline in the North, but planters' means of coercion, particularly of black workers, would have been compromised by widespread literacy.

The relationship between coercion as a means of labor discipline and limitations on education is further illustrated by the change that occurred in plantation owners' stance toward education when their control over agricultural labor started to break down in the face of black migration from rural to urban areas (first in the South, then later in the North) beginning in the mid–1910s.

[W]hite landowners, fearful of losing a critical mass of cash tenants, sharecroppers, farm laborers, and domestic servants, returned larger shares of public tax funds to support the construction of rural schoolhouses for blacks, which whites felt would serve as an incentive to blacks to stay. This fear was well founded as almost half of Georgia's black males from fifteen to thirty-four years of age left the state during the 1920s (Anderson 1988, p. 159).

The ethnic composition of the subordinate class also influenced the educational agenda of elites. Northern elites faced a subordinate group that was racially similar but ethnically different, which was probably a factor in their willingness to attempt to "shape them up" by bringing them into the public educational system. Southern elites faced a subordinate group that was composed of both blacks and poor whites, but they faced little class antagonism between themselves and poor whites because of their unifying belief in white supremacy. Education would only be wasted or, worse, would give blacks ridiculous ideas about social advancement that could only be frustrated, possibly leading to insurrection.

Probably the most important political factor that led northern elites to favor a politics of educational inclusion and southern elites to favor a politics of educational exclusion, however, was the enormous difference between the two regions in the availability of citizenship rights.[9] (Male) immigrants in the North could become citizens after a period of time, but in the South virtually all blacks and many poor whites were deprived of the vote by the early twentieth century. One of the motivations for incorporating immigrants into public schools in the North was to ensure that these would-be voters were properly prepared for the responsibilities of citizenship. In the South, in contrast, because virtually all blacks and many poor white tenant farmers and sharecroppers could not vote, local elites did not have to worry about whether the subordinate class was sufficiently well educated to make "responsible" electoral choices. Elites in the North were preoccupied with the potential cultural and political threat posed by the "hordes" of immigrants who "invaded" the cities in the late nineteenth and early twentieth centuries (e.g., Higham 1955); given that these outsiders could vote, there was little choice but to assimilate them into elite social and political values. Education was seen as the primary vehicle to accomplish this purpose.

The degree to which citizenship rights were available to the subordinate group affected elites' interests in education (Rubinson 1986). But it also affected the ability of the subordinate class to act on its interests, and thus elites' ability to implement their educational agenda without significant opposition from below.

Education is part and parcel of local politics, and if subordinate groups could not vote, they had no institutional voice in the formulation of educational policy. Prior to disenfranchisement, black political power did affect the availability and quality of education for southern blacks. In the 1880s and 1890s, for example, blacks successfully pressed for the replacement of white teachers in black schools with black teachers (Rabinowitz 1974).

Two other factors, not heretofore discussed because they are generally not seen as determinants of class interests, help explain the divergent class politics of educational access. The first was the degree of reliance on child labor. Industry in the South was much more dependent on child labor than was industry in the North. The textile industry was the major industrial employer of children in the United States.[10] In 1908, for example, 20 percent of southern textile workers but only 5 percent of northern textile workers were under sixteen years of age (U.S. Department of Labor 1916). Outside the South, the Progressive-era drive to eliminate child labor and get children into school was fairly successful (perhaps because industry was no longer dependent on child labor and because immigrants now constituted a huge pool of low-wage labor in most nonsouthern industrial areas). A "cardinal article of the Progressive creed . . . [was that] schools were to help solve the problems of child labor and child welfare" (Cohen 1968, p. 97). Northern elites did not face a loss of a large number of actual or would-be workers if they backed the expansion of public schooling, unlike southern industrialists. And southern planters were even more dependent on child labor than were southern industrialists.[11]

The final factor that influenced the class politics of educational access is the degree to which an alternative to the public educational system existed. Catholics constituted a large portion of the working class in the North at the turn of the century, and they were successful in building a large school system that challenged public education. Catholic opposition to the public schools was based in large part on their "pan-Protestantism" (Reese 1986). It is quite likely that competition from the Catholic system in the North resulted in greater access to the public system because elites were worried that Catholic schools would not properly socialize their students into the values of the dominant Protestant culture (see Chapter 12).

No such large-scale alternative to public education existed in the South. Outside of Texas and Louisiana, there were few Catholics in the South, and few private educational alternatives existed other than elite academies patronized by children of the wealthy. Various religious denominations supported some private schools for blacks in the South, but these efforts were concentrated primarily at secondary and postsecondary levels, where public school opportunities were most inadequate (Jones 1917).[12] Relatively few southern students attended private schools. In Georgia, private schools accounted for only 1.4 percent of all schools for whites and only 0.8 percent of all schools for blacks in 1910 (calculated from Georgia Department of Education 1911). These proportions are small compared to figures for the North. For example, in the same year, 16.1 percent of all Massachusetts students were enrolled in academies or private schools (calculated from Massachusetts Board of Education 1911).

SUMMARY

The literature on the development of education in the United States has not seriously questioned why educational opportunities in the North were adequate to meet demand in the late nineteenth and early twentieth centuries, a period of crucial institution building in U.S. education. The literature on the South, in contrast, clearly recognizes that educational opportunities were limited during the same period, especially for blacks, but has not advanced much beyond racial prejudice as an explanation for why these limitations existed. Analyses that connect racial inequalities in economic, political, and educational institutions have been lacking. Moreover, the case of the South has not been used to understand theoretical conditions under which limitations on educational opportunity existed, or how direct limitation of school supply expansion may have depressed popular demand.

The main point is that analyses of U.S. educational development must pay attention to educational supply. Decisions about providing public schools, teachers, books, and so forth, and about what type of public educational program to provide, are political decisions made by local elites acting through local state institutions. I place class politics at the center of the politics over access to public education.

I agree with many analysts of nonsouthern educational expansion that outside of the South supply was generally adequate to meet demand.[13] But I question what the conditions were that facilitated a politics of inclusion outside the South. Even if there was little variation outside the South in the adequacy of supply, it is still important to determine why this relatively constant condition prevailed. Standard correlational-based analyses cannot explain an outcome with a constant, but comparisons between regions that differed in the adequacy of supply can help to explain the condition that was constant within regions.

The need to explain why the supply of education was limited in the South is more often acknowledged. My main point vis-à-vis the South is that the politics of exclusion was fundamentally a class politics, although racial criteria and racial prejudices were used to further class interests and race also may have held effects independent of class.

Finally, I argue that the same theoretical model can explain both the politics of inclusion in the North and the politics of exclusion in the South: The North and South were not two completely separate social systems, governed by different "laws." One must understand the interests of the locally dominant and locally subordinate classes in education, and the resources that the competing classes had at their disposal for influencing the local political process, coalesced in and maintained by the local state. The first step is to identify the most important classes related to the politics of education: industrialists and an urban working class in the North; planters and a rural agricultural work force in the South. In the North, industrialists and the urban working class shared an interest in educational access, albeit for different reasons. In the South, however, the politics of access was contested: Planters wanted to limit educational opportunities for their subordinate class, especially blacks, whereas southern blacks were generally committed to educational improvements and poor whites often were indifferent. Planter interests prevailed.

Much of my argument centers on the question of why local elites' interests in education differed between the North and South, and why subordinate groups' resources for implementing their own educational agenda varied. I argue that differences in elite interests in public educational access are explained by differences in prevailing means of labor discipline, in the availability of the franchise, in the prevalence of child labor, in the composition of the subordinate class (were they racially or ethnically different from elites?), and in the existence of an educational system that posed an alternative to public schools and that threatened to "improperly" socialize subordinate-class children. Differences in subordinate groups' resources for affecting education policies are explained by differences in the availability of voting rights, in the availability of an ally to support an alternative to the public system of education, and in the composition of the subordinate group itself. For instance, race muted poor whites' opposition to planter interests in the South, but in the North ethnic politics largely reinforced or were an additional base of working-class opposition.

The arguments I present suggest the necessity of (1) specifying the conditions under which educational supply has, or has not, been adequate to meet demand, and (2) affording a central place for class politics in future investigations. Analyses of educational outcomes such as enrollments or attainments that plausibly result from both supply and demand should take each into account and make a clear distinction between the determinants of each.

NOTES

An earlier version of this chapter was presented at the 1990 annual meeting of the American Sociological Association, Washington, D.C., August 1990. This research was supported by a grant from the National Science Foundation to the author and David R. James. My collaborative research with Mr. James on education in the South provided the motivation for this essay; my thinking about these issues has been greatly influenced by extended discussions with him. I am grateful for his input. I also thank Maurice Garnier, Regina Werum, Michael Wallace, David Post, and the editors for helpful comments on an earlier draft, and Regina Werum for her research assistance.

1. It is also likely that demand for education was lower in the South than elsewhere in the United States, due to a variety of factors including greater poverty, greater reliance on child labor (in both agriculture and industry), and greater illiteracy. Nonetheless, both quantitative (Margo 1990) and qualitative (Knight 1922; Harlan 1958; Anderson 1988)

historical evidence suggests that the inadequacy of educational supply in the South depressed school enrollments and attainment.

2. Not only did the working class win victories in their struggles over the form and content of education (supply), but they also possessed an important resource of resistance—they sometimes chose not to go to public school. In other words, elites could not directly control subordinate groups' demand for education. Many working-class children "voted with their feet" (Walters and O'Connell 1988) and either worked instead of attending school or patronized Catholic schools (Ravitch 1974).

3. In his study of the Progressive era, William Reese (1986) shows that conflict over the goals and curriculum of public education was intense and that elites were unable to shape schools completely to their liking. He nonetheless concludes that "schools were especially responsive to economic elites, the professional classes, and school officials, whose shared values strengthened the public system and whose political power gave their ideas added weight" (p. 19).

4. Conflicts among ethnic groups, between immigrants and native-born Americans, and between Catholics and Protestants were also important in struggles over northeastern education. Ethnicity and religious differences often produced similar cleavages, however, and more recent ethnic groups, immigrants, and Catholics were disproportionately represented in the working class. Although many studies of education and mobility in the Northeast have struggled to determine whether class or ethnicity, for example, were more important factors in educational and occupational success (for a recent example, see Perlmann 1988), it is very difficult to disentangle the effects of class and ethnicity.

5. Outside of the South, the common school movement of the first third of the nineteenth century succeeded in placing most primary education under public control (Fishlow 1966). In the South, however, a system of free public primary education was not established until after the Civil War (Bond 1934). Public education remained almost entirely in the hands of local governments until the 1960s, when local governments were forced to yield some control over educational policymaking to the federal government.

6. Booker T. Washington, for instance, espoused this view. But it is important to note that he never advocated social equality between blacks and whites. In his famous "Atlanta compromise" speech of 1895, Washington declared to an audience of white southerners: "In all things that are purely social we can be as separate as the five fingers, yet one as the hand in all things essential to mutual progress" (Tyack 1967, p. 271).

7. The latter effort is most telling. The Rosenwald Fund, a private northern philanthropic organization, subsidized the construction of 4,977 rural black schools throughout the South in the period 1914–1932 (Anderson 1988). Anderson reports sources of funding for ninety-two rural black schools that were built in southern states between August 1914 and February 1916 with support from the Rosenwald Fund. In this initial period, public tax monies accounted for only 16 percent of total expenditures, contributions from the Rosenwald Fund accounted for 33 percent, private contributions from blacks accounted for 46 percent, and contributions from whites constituted 6 percent.

8. The classic explanation of the South's educational underdevelopment hinges on nonpolitical problems such as an inadequate tax base, a sparsely settled population, and a high ratio of children to adults. This explanation has been offered by, among others, the most important institutional historian of southern education of the early twentieth century, Edgar Knight (1922). However, these characteristics do not necessarily limit the availability of education. Schools were provided to children in the rural Midwest under conditions of spare population settlement.

9. The effect of citizenship rights is unexamined in most studies of northern education, but its availability may be a crucial scope condition under which variability in other factors produced variation in the politics of education in the North.

10. In 1905, for example, more than one-fourth of all child wage-earners in manu- facturing were employed in textiles (U.S. Department of Labor 1916).

11. Harlan (1958, p. 125), for example, reports that some white landlords testified during debates about compulsory education in the South that they would not hire blacks as tenants if the tenants' children went to school. They were expected to work instead.

12. For example, according to federal sources not a single public high school existed for blacks in North Carolina in 1910. But even though private educational opportunities for blacks were greater at the secondary than at the elementary level, only 549 black students were enrolled in private high schools in the state (U.S. Bureau of Education 1911).

13. Actually, we do not know whether supply was adequate to meet demand for specific subpopulations, such as female students, Mexican Americans in the Southwest and West, Asians in the West, and so forth, because the question has not yet been addressed.

12

The Politics of American Catholic School Expansion, 1870–1930

David P. Baker

Throughout the "long nineteenth century" modern nation-states built formal public school systems, but significant nonpublic systems also emerged (Archer 1979).[1] Perhaps the most intriguing case—given its prodigious growth and educational politics—occurred in the United States between the time of the Civil War and World War II. This chapter presents synopses of several episodes in the history of the American Catholic system and relates these to central themes in the study of school expansion, showing how the consideration of sector development can refine theories about school supply and demand.

To begin with, consider briefly the comparative evidence in Table 12.1 of the nonpublic school sectors in five countries. Worldwide, an average of 13.5 percent of primary enrollments are in the nonpublic sector (Cooper 1982), but even among these five systems there is great variation. Ireland has the largest nonpublic education system, which is a state-supported but Church-controlled system. France and Canada have nonpublic enrollments close to the world average. The United States trails these systems, and last is England/Wales with only a small proportion of primary nonpublic school enrollment. Behind each case is a history of sector development revealing the forces of educational supply and demand within each country.

In Ireland, for example, a dominant nonpublic system was transformed into a state-religious system. The Irish Catholic Church aligned with state building and national schools more than the Church in other European nations. Thus, an early and fledgling national educational system was usurped by a sectarian system primarily controlled by the Catholic Church, schooling a large portion of the

Table 12.1
Percentages of Pupils Attending Nonpublic Schools

	Percent of Primary Enrollment in Non-Public Schools	Percent of Secondary Enrollment in Non-Public Schools
Canada	12	19
England/Wales	4	8
France	13	21
Ireland	98	91
U.S.	10	10

Source: Cooper (1982).

population with support from most social and political interests in Ireland (Larkin 1976).

In quite opposite fashion, educational sector development in France was shaped by various anticlerical movements during the eighteenth and nineteenth centuries. The resulting flexibility of French Catholic schooling influenced both educational supply and demand. As the main supplier of nonpublic schooling in France, Catholic schools served a strong minority of interests and adapted themselves to conflicts over social class interests by providing special educational opportunities that the larger and less adaptive state system could not organize. A supply example was the mid-nineteenth century development of Catholic primary schools for the petite bourgeoisie, who were dissatisfied with both the lower-class dominated, state primary schools and the lengthy education required by elites. In terms of educational demand, tuition to nineteenth-century Catholic schools was a status distinction used by the middle class, and it therefore increased demand for nonpublic schooling (Gildea 1983).

England has had a small amount of nonpublic schooling ever since an early and consensual arrangement of church and state control over schooling reduced the chances for continued competition between sectors. In the main, English school development was a slow erosion of Anglican prestate educational activities after the merging of the English state with the Anglican Church in the sixteenth century. The Catholics did control a school system and entered into school politics, but their actions were often oriented toward the Irish question during the nineteenth century. By the middle of the twentieth century the British Catholic system was financially sponsored, organized, and partially controlled by the state (Lee 1967; Vaughan and Archer 1971).

AMERICAN EDUCATIONAL SECTOR DEVELOPMENT

Educational sectors emerged differently in the United States. The history of American Catholic schooling introduces several themes to school expansion research that are generally overlooked in analyses limited to public schooling.

The first theme is the role of competition both across and within educational sectors. Schooling in the United States is a long story of competition between groups over control of supply. Over time, as this competition increased, larger collectives dominated the contest. The lack of restrictive regulation by the states, and competition produced by this arrangement, led to school expansion and a rich mixture of public and nonpublic schooling.[2] The antebellum educational history is rife with competition. For example, the Society for the Propagation of the Gospel in Foreign Parts, organizing schools for the Church of England, often competed with the Puritans over schools; Protestant Home Mission societies competed with one another; and the Western Literary Institute used vitriolic anti-Catholicism to promote schooling.

By the postbellum period the stage was set for large-scale competition for schooling. An 1894 Annual Report to the Commissioners of Education reveals at least six major nonpublic systems of schooling and several minor systems. Some of these were quite complex; for example, both the Lutheran and Catholic systems had their own teacher training, educational associations, and publishing houses for textbooks (Jorgenson 1987). The imagery of competition between groups (mostly public versus Catholic schools) is the standard historical interpretation (e.g., Tyack 1967).

A second and less considered source of competition over schooling emerged at this time. Conflict within corporate bodies that control school supply has often been overlooked, although it may be an even greater potent force behind the expansion of organizations like the American Catholic Church. Within a large and complex organization, internal conflict over the control of resources expands institutional building, in some cases even more rapidly than competition between organizations. For instance, once a collective's clientele (e.g., congregation) has the right to request resources (real, but also symbolic, such as a charter) for school supply, education is likely to increase. Competing factions within a school system often generate both higher demand and higher supply of schooling. The following description of the expansion of the Catholic system will focus on the effects of intra-corporate conflict on school supply as an alternative explanation to the more common image of conflict between Catholic and Protestant interests as the primary mechanism behind school expansion.

A second theme is institutional isomorphism, or more simply, the convergence of competing systems of schools on a similar model of schooling (DiMaggio and Powell 1983). Competing organizations, such as systems of schools, often produce a standard type of schooling. As we shall see, American Catholics developed a mass school system very similar in organizational design to its public counterparts even though the Catholics took strenuous steps to maintain institutional borders between educational sectors.

A final theme about the growth of nonpublic schooling is the relationship between corporate resources and school supply. The religious corporate bodies involved in the expansion of American nonpublic schooling provided basic ideological frameworks as well as networks for resource distribution and personnel supplies. As will be discussed in more detail subsequently, American Catholics combined the Church's governance structure and formidable resources to increase the supply of nonpublic schooling during the last half of the nineteenth and first half of the twentieth centuries.

The remainder of this chapter examines four aspects of the history of the American Catholic school system in light of these themes. First, I review the system's growth and organizational development. Second, I present several examples of the Church politics behind early expansion and conflict over the use of a broad base of resources that fueled expansion well into the twentieth century. Third, I discuss why and how Catholics transformed a loosely connected set of schools created largely for elite religious personnel into mass schooling for a wide range of children with different educational goals. Finally, I delineate the influence of national Catholic organizations and resources on the supply of Catholic schools.

ANATOMY OF A NONPUBLIC SCHOOL SYSTEM

Demography of American Catholic Education

To protect itself from encroaching liberal European states and other perceived modern evils, the Church issued a series of pronouncements during the First Vatican Council (1869–1870) that directly increased the supply of Catholic schooling in the United States. To monitor the institutional growth of the American Church and strengthen its control over the American congregation, the Vatican (through the offices of the Congregation De Propaganda Fide) commanded the American Catholic hierarchy to form Catholic schools and coerced Catholic parents, with the refusal of absolution, into sending their children to these institutions (Plenary Council of Baltimore 1866). The American Catholic hierarchy softened the language of the Vatican's decree but kept its original intent during the Third Plenary Council of Baltimore (1884) by legislating that every parish was to have a school within two years of the meeting of the council (Fogarty 1985). This ruling provided official backing for a fifty-year-old movement striving to supply schools for an increasing Catholic demand.

Although American Catholics at the end of the revolution were only the tenth largest religious group, by 1850 they had become the largest single denomination

Table 12.2
Relative Share of Nonpublic Religious School Systems, 1890 (total nonpublic enrollment equalled 1,028,843)

	Percent of Total
Roman Catholic	77
Evangelical Lutheran	20
German Evangelical Synod	2
Episcopal	*
Holland Christian Reform	*
Other Churches	*

*Less than 1 percent.
Source: Report of the Commissioner of Education, 1894.

in the country. Institutional development accompanied this growth. Table 12.2 lists the relative share of nonpublic schooling that each of the major religious systems reported in 1890.[3] The Catholic system was over three times the size of the second largest nonpublic system, which was run by the Evangelical Lutheran Church.

Enrollment in most Protestant religious school systems declined with the consolidation of the American public school movement. But the Catholic system increased in size and complexity during the years following the Civil War. As Table 12.3 shows, the Catholic percentage of all primary schooling doubled during the sixty-year span beginning in 1870, so that by 1930 over 9 percent of primary enrollment was Catholic.[4] As early as 1884, when the Third Plenary Council worried about increasing supply, the system was extensive, with 40 percent of American parishes operating a primary school (Hennesey 1981).

Catholic secondary education also grew. Catholic high school enrollment increased more than fivefold from 1890 to 1930, expanding a system of 52,000 students into one of over a quarter of a million students by 1930. Table 12.4 shows a decreasing share of Catholic high school enrollment, but this is due to the dramatic rise in public high schools during this period and does not reflect an absolute decline in Catholic secondary schooling.

While the Catholic system was developing primary schooling during the first few decades of the twentieth century, the public system was expanding secondary schooling. In the 1940s and 1950s, the Catholics followed the public system by expanding secondary education. This lagged, but parallel, expansion is replayed often in the history of Catholic schooling in the United States.[5] and can be seen in the decade growth rates of each system in Tables 12.3 and 12.4. The Catholic primary system grew at a greater rate than the public system, but the reverse is true for secondary schooling. The average Catholic percentage growth in primary

Table 12.3
Percentage Catholic of Total Elementary School Enrollments, and Decade
Growth, 1870–1930

Year	States Reporting	Percent Catholic Enrollment	Decade Growth Rate - Catholic	Decade Growth Rate - Public
1870	21	3.9	--	--
1880	37	4.2	69.8	53.9
1890	40	4.9	56.4	34.9
1900	44	5.3	35.9	23.6
1910	46	6.4	39.7	14.6
1920	48	7.9	40.0	11.8
1930	47	9.4	32.8	9.7

Sources: *Official Catholic Directory*, 1870–1930; *Report of the Commissioner of Education*, 1870–1920; and *Biennial Survey of Education*, 1930.

enrollment was about double the public primary growth rate, but the average public percentage growth in high school enrollment was over twice the Catholic secondary growth rate.

Why did the American Catholic educational system expand? While there was anti-Catholic sentiment within the American nativism movement, the United States did not sustain anticlerical reforms aimed at limiting organizational power such as those that occurred in France. Unlike their French counterparts, American Catholics were not propelled by anticlerical movements to develop schooling for the recruitment of clerics. At the same time, American Catholicism was not the cornerstone of the American state, as Irish Catholicism was of the Irish state. American Catholics could not align themselves with the state and develop federally supported, church-controlled schools, as the Catholics did in Ireland.

Why American Catholics did not produce a small set of schools for its elite and then give way to the growing public system to school the mass of Catholic children is a function of several factors. These include the particular way the American Church was organized, the results of central organizational struggles within the Church, the pressures of a predominantly Catholic immigration, and the Church's ability to generate institutional power in the decentralized political environment of the United States. These are considered in the subsequent discussion.

Table 12.4
Percentage Catholic of Total Secondary School Enrollments, and Decade Growth, 1890–1930

Year	States Reporting	Percent Catholic Enrollment	Decade Growth Rate - Catholic	Decade Growth Rate - Public
1890	32	22.3	--	--
1900	45	14.1	61.0	180.9
1910	45	11.9	44.4	75.4
1920	46	7.2	32.7	129.7
1930	47	6.1	76.5	112.4

Sources: *Official Catholic Directory*, 1870–1930; *Reports of the Commissioner of Education*, 1870–1920; and *Biennial Survey of Education*, 1930.

The Apparatus of Catholic School Supply

From its inception, American Catholic schooling was organized within the existing structure of the Church; thus, school supply became inseparably tied to the diocese. Under the control of a bishop and his staff, the diocese (made up of a group of parishes) is the basic administrative unit of the Church. Decisions about the local supply of education are made at this level.[6]

The number of dioceses in the United States increased through two mechanisms, each of which had an unintended effect of increasing school supply. At any time, all settled portions of the United States were under the control of a network of dioceses. One way to create new dioceses was to split an existing diocese in two. A split was a function of the density of the Catholic population and resulted in two smaller dioceses that were easier to administer and control. As with other religious and governmental units, to maintain an existing level of administrative control, the Catholic Church expanded the number of dioceses as density increased (Suggs 1977). The process of dividing dioceses helped to intensify the local control of bishops and, in turn, helped to implement a bishop-level policy of school expansion.

In addition, the formal organization of the Church grew with the general expansion of the American state. Regardless of Catholic population density, the policy of the Church was to place an area under the administrative responsibility of an existing diocese. Wedding Catholic administration to westward settlement by a contiguous spread of the Church organization encouraged institution building, particularly the building of schools. The Church established a school even with a small initial population of students and, in doing so, attempted to "create demand" through supply of schooling opportunity. This is evident particularly in those areas in which non-Catholics, such as Indians and blacks, were enrolled in the system. The Catholics could expand their system and in a sense wait for the growth in Catholic populations, which occurred with the westward movement of Catholic immigrants.

The entire apparatus of Catholic school supply was relatively easy to develop because Catholic schooling generally ran at minimal expense. The semi-autonomous religious orders brought women and, to a lesser degree, men from Europe to serve as essentially unpaid (except for minimal living costs) teachers and child care workers. In 1901, average tuition for Catholic primary schooling was $37 per year (National Catholic Educational Association 1901).[7] Parish funds, usually obtained by direct pastoral lobbying, were also used to fund schools. For example, in 1914 half the high schools for boys were supported by funds other than tuition fees.[8]

The funding of the Catholic hierarchy and more specifically the Catholic school was a bottom-up operation and was centralized only at the diocesan level. Except within some orders, there was no central source of school funding beyond what the diocese could raise through the efforts at the parish level. Bishops expected parishes to raise the funds for instructional materials. Because instruction costs were minimal and capital costs of school buildings were spread over a number of years and across all parishioners, these expectations could be met without a central source of funding. Therefore, although Catholic schooling was nonpublic schooling, it was not a solely tuition-driven system. Opportunity costs were low; thus, the demand for this type of schooling was not seriously limited by resource constraints. This, in part, explains the large growth of the system among people with lower incomes.

Church Factors and the Politics of School Supply

Because the postbellum American Church was large and relatively rich, it experienced numerous internal struggles over the control of resources, ideology, and internal power. It is interesting that many of these battles concentrated on Catholic education, and the outcome of these conflicts had profound effects on the dynamics of nonpublic school supply.

Two of these struggles show how conflicts within systems of education propel schooling. The first was a struggle over how much cooperation between Catholic schooling and public schooling the American hierarchy would allow, the result of which was a victory for the forces wanting a completely separate Catholic system. The second conflict was the struggle for a mass rather than an elite system of Catholic high schools. In this case, the conflict arose out of an attempt to mirror public development, rather than to ward off a direct challenge by the public system. The Protestant-Catholic conflict over schooling, a major theme during the period, played only a minor role in these internal Church battles. The underlying internal battle for Church control expanded Catholic schooling.

War of the Prelates

During the last decade of the nineteenth century, two factions of the American hierarchy and the Vatican entered into a struggle over Catholic schooling and its relationship to the public system. The result was a consolidation of the Catholic system as a freestanding entity prepared to receive the large wave of immigrants in the early portion of the twentieth century (Fogarty 1985). On the surface, the battle was over whether various cooperative efforts between parish and public schooling, such as the Faribault-Stillwater Plan, were acceptable to the Church's hierarchy.[9] Underneath this seemingly straightforward question of school administration was a battle between the liberal and conservative U.S. bishops over the nature of the American Catholic Church as it faced the new century.

At the heart of the issue was the Vatican's fear of losing ground to liberal nation-states. A partial response to this was to "Romanize" (i.e., bring under clear hierarchical authority) the loose American collegial hierarchy and gain more access to future Church resources (Fogarty 1985). In this struggle the Vatican aligned with the conservative bishops, who were interested in having a separate Catholic school system.[10] On the other side, the liberal bishops were more willing to cooperate with the local public school system and in so doing increased the local bishop's control over the diocese. Additionally, the liberals believed that an "American" Church instead of a "Roman" Church could best survive and prosper in the anti-Catholic climate of postbellum America. The conservatives fought for a separate and ultra-Catholic school system, in partial response to anti-Catholic movements, but also to support the German Americans' concern for cultural preservation, to appease conservative pro-Catholic sentiments among conservative Irish Americans, and to organize general opposition to the broadening American state. It was this final concern that pushed the Vatican to support the conservative stance and reestablish its earlier position for separate Catholic schools in each parish. The conservative position prevailed; the liberals were unable to convince Rome that the American Church would not be compromised, as it had been during its painful accommodation to the liberal European state. The way was opened for a consolidated and purely Catholic school system. This situation increased the school supply of Catholic education over the ensuing several decades.

If the liberals, who aligned themselves much less with systemic school expansion, had won, it is very likely that a consolidated system of Catholic schooling would not have emerged at this point. In this case, nonpublic school supply rested on the outcome of an internal struggle over corporate power. Here the specific struggle was over the larger question of the symbolic nature of the corporation itself; expanded nonpublic school supply was an indirect outcome of this argument. This initial school controversy between liberal, pro-American leaders and conservative, pro-Rome leaders would be replayed often in the history of the Church. Each time the conservatives won (and with the Vatican's help they won often), some aspect of Catholic institutional construction expanded, and in many instances this was some aspect of Catholic schooling. In each case, however, it was not the external Protestant-Catholic rhetoric of the times that was the main force behind the internal conflict. The anti-Catholic movement was certainly a foil for the Church's mobilization, but as illustrated in the struggle just described, both sides used this foil when convenient. Nonpublic school supply grew from internal conflict within the controlling body of the system; anti-Catholic tensions may have done less to stimulate growth than is usually assumed.

Central Catholic High School Movement

The movement to establish mass, comprehensive schools within the Catholic system was a prolonged struggle, but it embodied far less dramatic conflict between Church leaders than was evident during the school wars of the prelates. This chapter in Catholic education history is instructive for school expansion research for two reasons. First, it shows how uniform school management spread through a network of schools without direct state intervention. This movement was the Catholics' first and most extensive use of "modern" rational planning and overt scientific central management of their system during the first half of the twentieth century. It was piloted by a newly established corps of professional Catholic educators, analogous to the professionals who were instrumental in controlling public schooling (Tyack and Hansot 1982). Second, the Catholic reformers relied on a model of secondary schooling developed first in the public system. This case illustrates how a convergence of organizational form between nonpublic and public systems took place.

The movement centered around a fifty-year effort, beginning in 1905, to establish large diocesan-managed high schools, or the so-called Central Catholic High School (CCHS), as an extension of parochial primary schooling. The Catholic professionals, starting with the newly formed National Catholic Educational Association (NCEA) and running through numerous commissions, developed a plan for mass Catholic secondary education that was to consolidate the school system. Consider the resolution of the 1905 meeting of the NCEA:

that it is the sense of the College Department of this Association that the high school is and should be considered an integral part of the Catholic school system. . . . [I]t is desirable that some arrangements should be devised which will enable the authorities in the existing Catholic high schools *to cooperate with the diocesan authorities and to arrange with them some way of articulating the parish school with the high school,* so that all our Catholic educational institutions may be knitted together in closer union and unnecessary waste of money, men and effort may be eliminated. (NCEA 1905, p. 59, emphasis added)

A series of surveys, using "state of the art" sampling methods and analysis procedures, were written at various points during the movement to justify the CCHS on the grounds of efficiency, scientific management of school supply, and, most important for our notion of convergence, the use of the large consolidated public high schools as a model of development.[11] For example, one such report from 1951 suggests the following: "There is some similarity between the public and Catholic school system in organization and administration. The parish resembles the local school district in being the base for elementary schools; the diocese is like the union or county district for secondary schools. Both systems depend upon private and State resources for higher education" (Spiers 1951, p. 16).

The development of the CCHS was an attempt to change two preexisting structures in Catholic secondary education. First, the movement attempted to consolidate the small parish high schools into the larger, cost-efficient CCHS. Second, the CCHS allowed the diocesan hierarchy to control school supply and wrest control from the established elite high schools managed by the religious orders.[12]

There was some resistance to this movement, but the opposition is less documented than other educational controversies within the Church. The CCHS reformers fought a two-sided battle. On one side, they attempted to alter a direct outcome of earlier expansion, namely, the tendency of high schools to be a small, local extension of the parish school. And on the other side, they directly confronted the control of elite high schools by clerics. The strength of the resistance is evident in the fact that by 1947 CCHS made up only 8 percent of all Catholic high schools, with the largest share (55%) still separate parish schools and the remainder (37%) cleric-run schools (Spiers 1951). There was, however, a gradual and steady increase in CCHSs that had an influence on the supply of Catholic secondary education.

The movement for the CCHS illustrates how, through a corps of professionals, a nonpublic school system attempted to consolidate its school supply into a centralized organization. Obvious political implications of this plan (i.e., recovering control of schools from the parish and the clerical orders) were shrouded by the neutral, scientific veneer of studies about CCHSs' cost-effectiveness and the notion of educational efficiency. This reform was not the result of fierce warfare between bishops as had occurred fifty years earlier; rather, it was a cool professionalization of the system's bureaucracy. The Protestant-Catholic conflict played no part in this struggle. Instead, the Catholic reformers embraced the public high school as a model for their own schools.

If this reform had not taken place—and without the new institutional power provided by the Catholic University of America and the NCEA it easily might not have occurred—Catholic secondary schooling could have been greatly restricted. The expanded and modernizing public secondary system would have become very attractive to Catholic students in the face of the alternative: small, traditionally structured, parish high schools. This reform also led, somewhat unintentionally, to more organizational flexibility within the system that helped it survive declines in the size of cohorts of Catholic students later in the century.

Nonpublic Schooling for the Masses

On the eve of the Jacksonian period, the Catholic school system was a motley collection of impoverished schools on the frontier; the first stirring of a small, stable set of elite academies; and separate parochial schools often beleaguered by various local political and religious conditions (Beutow 1970). Nevertheless, there existed the rudiments of a system of schools that expanded with each consecutive wave of Catholic immigration over the next one hundred years (Lieberson 1980).

What is most obvious about immigration to the United States, namely its size, may not be the most important factor for understanding Catholic school supply. Beyond its magnitude, several qualities of nineteenth-century immigration directly influenced the supply of Catholic schooling. First, multiple ethnic immigration to the United States condensed the patchwork ethnic structure of nineteenth-century Europe into an American Catholic population nominally uniform but with an underlying diversity that presented the Church with an unwieldy, dispute-ridden, stratified congregation. Second, immigration to the United States resulted from a global transformation of agrarian labor into industrial labor, and Catholic immigrants were at the center of this change, often shifting from peasant to industrial worker in as little time as it took to travel to the new land. Third, this movement and transformation of labor brought with it substantial social disorganization, both in terms of family structure of the immigrants themselves and in the effect that this disorganized mass had on American institutions. For different reasons, each of these aspects of immigration increased the Catholic school supply.

Much of the administrative history of the Church examines attempts to manage its polyglot, multiethnic congregation. Vibrant ethnic stratification, including distinctions between old and new arrivals, and a range of socioeconomic standing spawned several unique American Catholic organizational structures. Chief among these was the national parish. An administrative structure originally developed by German refugees of the Kulturkampf to maintain language and cultural traditions in the new land, the national parish evolved into a widespread structure that the Church could use to give recognition and, most important, appease the demands of ethnic groups.[13] Local ethnic groups formed (often with diocesan funds) a parish dedicated to their particular language and culture (Dolan 1987). Staffed by national priests and other personnel from the ethnic group, these parishes intensified the homogeneity of ethnic neighborhoods and—most important—increased ethnic institution building, of which schools were a fundamental part. National parishes contained both symbolic and physical resources and legitimated a particular ethnic group's claim on a diocese to provide resources for their use.

Table 12.5
Institution Building by Ethnic Catholics as Reflected by National Parishes

Percent of National (ethnic) Parishes of all Parishes within Dioceses
(Number of Dioceses in Parenthesis)

Regions	1850	1900	1930
Northeast	6.0	15.0	19.0
	(7)	(21)	(24)
Midwest	15.0	14.0	11.0
	(8)	(31)	(40)
Southeast	8.0	4.0	4.0
	(16)	(16)	(16)
Pacific	--	4.0	2.0
	(0)	(6)	(9)

Note: *Compiled from data reported in Dolan (1987, vol. 1, pp. 381–401).

As shown in Table 12.5, national parishes proliferated in dioceses serving immigrants (in the Midwest and Northeast). These regional figures mask even more dramatic growth of national parishes at the local levels. Thirty percent of all new parishes established between 1880 and 1930 in the Northeast were national. In both New York City and Philadelphia, 50 percent of all new parishes opened in the first several decades of the twentieth century were national, with one-third in New York formed by Italians and one-third in Philadelphia formed by Poles.

Catholic immigrants to the United States, particularly during the second wave, came more as imported labor than as political or religious émigrés.[14] These people entered an agricultural society undergoing industrial transformation and settled in the cities of the Northeast and Midwest. The striking social disorganization resulting from the forces that attracted late nineteenth-century immigrants to the United States also played a direct role in the development of Catholic schooling. Industrial development, expansion of urban residence, decaying independence of an "archipelago of rural centers," and a rapidly growing federal state, all part of the modern transformation of the United States, shocked many American citizens into a persistent antimodern panic (Skowronek 1982). One of the only remaining salient consistencies between their origins in Europe and the urban industrial cities of the United States was the Catholic Church. The Church was a paternal institution in their lives, and Church-sponsored schooling was a cornerstone of the immigrants' dependency.

The Catholic Church, however, felt the effects of social disorganization well beyond the sting of vitriolic anti-Catholic attacks from nativist groups. In many ways the Church, through its attempts to incorporate into its ranks successive waves of immigrants, experienced more immediately the disorganization of the times than did many other American institutions. Even though the Church had relatively few resources, the pressure from the upheaval of immigration motivated the Catholic hierarchy to build institutions to administer to its growing constituency, and this focused primarily on Catholic schooling (Lazerson 1977). The parish school was a central tool for the Church to control ethnic Catholics and expand its own institutional base within the country.

Many documented cases exist of the Catholic Church building organizations among immigrant communities as a result of aggressive anti-Catholic campaigns.[15] But being an institution heavily dependent upon successful socialization, the Church had its own interests, separate from anti-Catholic competition, in constructing institutions. As always, to survive as a religious body the Church had to socialize Catholics, but during the great waves of immigration the Church was equally interested in socializing American Catholics. For the same reason that a nation-state turns to formal education to reduce ethnic barriers and social disorganization, the Catholic Church turned to schooling as it faced the staggering weight of Catholic immigrants. Americanized Catholics were important to the Church for both external reasons (easing Protestant attacks) and internal reasons (maintenance of a stable congregation).

The Church concentrated on molding immigrants into American Catholics. In 1938, the American bishops gathered in Washington, D.C., to form the Commission on American Citizenship. The commission focused on producing American Catholics through education, with such guidelines as the following: "The aim of the Catholic elementary school is to provide the child with those experiences which are calculated to develop in him such knowledge, appreciation, and habits, as will yield a character equal to the contingencies of fundamental Christian living in *American democratic society*" (*The Catholic Education Review*, cited in Beutow 1970, p. 231, emphasis added). The commission's report contained rhetoric stressing educational goals that would mold culturally manageable and politically astute citizens of the United States who were fundamentally committed to Catholicism.

Both external and internal pressure to form an American Catholic citizenry out of immigrants encouraged the Catholic educational system to emulate the public system to a greater extent. Holding the twin goals of Americanization and religious socialization, Catholics plunged into the business of mass education and therefore, in an important organizational sense, into the building of a mass system of schooling. Local competition with public schools and other institutions, particularly for state funding, contributed to specific instances of school supply, but it was not a simple formula of Catholic reaction to anti-Catholic pressure. The Catholic educational system was developed as a socializing agent for ethnic peasants to ensure the Church's own survival in the institutional world of modern America.

Governance of the System

Central to the history of governance of the Catholic system is the creation, at the turn of the century, of the NCEA and its consolidation of an emerging corps of Catholic professional educators. The NCEA was a coalition of three early Catholic educational associations, each representing a powerful segment of the system—the Educational Conference of Seminary Faculties (1897), the Association of Catholic Colleges (1898), and the Parish School Conference (1902) (McCarren 1966). Although the association was originally organized on a voluntary basis, it soon became the central organization of the system, entering into battles over Catholic high school development, state funding of nonpublic schools, and accreditation of nonpublic schools. In each case, NCEA fought for the expansion of the system as a whole. Three points about the birth of the NCEA, briefly described in the following discussion, illustrate how governance influences the supply of nonpublic schooling in the United States.

NCEA's formation and development in 1904 was similar to that of the National Educational Association (1870) and the National Teachers' Association (1857). Because both the public and Catholic systems operated in the same political environment, the voluntary association, which was initially weakly tied to control of schooling, was the first step toward centralization. The public associations led to the loose federalization of American public education, and the NCEA led to the loose centralization of Catholic education. Attempts to increase centralization in both systems provide a recurrent theme in each system's governance rhetoric. As late as 1960, the following description of the lack of centralization of the Catholic system was offered by an official of the NCEA:

The parochial school as an independent, parish-controlled and parish-financed operation is an anachronism. For the greater good all parochial schools should become diocesan schools. This will mean, of course, that pastors will have to yield control over their schools. We speak loosely of the Catholic school "system," but only a few dioceses approach education systematically. (McMlusky from NCEA in 1960, cited in McCarren 1966, p. 202)

This kind of discussion of the local organization of the system moved the issue of school supply beyond the general rhetoric of the Church and solidified the control of the Catholic schools in the hands of Catholic professional educators. Whether or not the presence of the NCEA increased Catholic schooling or merely reflected the system's growth owing to other causes is difficult to determine. It is clear, however, that as the NCEA became an organization that represented the system as a whole, its presence became an issue of conflict within the Church.

The NCEA, like its public counterparts, did have some centralized power that influenced school supply, and consequently the development and formation of the organization was contested within the Catholic system. The internal Church politics within the NCEA was a mixture of the earlier split between liberals and conservatives over how separate and distinct Catholic education should be from public education, and the increasing influence of an emerging corps of Catholic education professionals. By and large, issues of professionalization were more important in NCEA's development than raw political disputes. Thus, as Catholics developed their higher education system and professional corps, they linked together bureaucratic control of the entire system.

In addition to attending to the task of internal restructuring, the NCEA acted as the primary political arm of the system, thus representing the entire Catholic system within the larger public arena. One of the earliest examples of this function was NCEA's involvement in limiting the effects of local educational legislation that curtailed Catholic schooling. The following is a statement of the NCEA's secretary general in 1906 about the value of the association in opposing external threats to the system:

The value of the Association is now recognized by Catholic educators generally and the Association is organized on a satisfactory and secure basis. . . . There is need of a sense of solidarity of Catholic educational interests. Every year State legislatures go more widely and more deeply into educational projects, and there is a tendency on the part of the state to absorb and dominate the educational interests of the people. The legislation which is enacted each year in the several States tends in this direction, and the educational interests of Catholics are often unfavorably affected by these measures. These conditions have made it necessary for Catholic educators to be alert in taking cognizance of their rights and in protecting their interests. (*NCEA Proceedings* 1906, cited in McCarren 1966, p. 230)

The NCEA was the central organization by which Catholic educators defined, protected, and extended these Catholic interests in supplying nonpublic schools. This institutional power was particularly important in maintaining the earlier expansion of the system. Without it the Catholic system of schools would have weakened. The formation of this power was not greatly opposed, however; this illustrates how a decentralized political environment can foster educational sector development. By directly copying the institutional arrangements of the public system, the Catholics gained (on a smaller scale) similar benefits from school expansion.

CATHOLIC SCHOOLING AND FUTURE SCHOOL EXPANSION RESEARCH

This chapter began with an argument for the study of educational sector development in general and of American Catholic schooling in particular as a way to expand theory about educational supply and demand. The themes that run through the history of American Catholic schooling are beneficial to refining our theories of school supply and demand. Two are particularly helpful.

First is that the Catholic system is an excellent example of systemic development. Most research on school supply has focused on enrollment, the most basic indicator of school expansion. We know less about the systemic development of education. We need to understand how a system of schools begins and becomes increasingly more complex, how issues of system governance influence supply, and how concerns of large collectives mingle with school expansion policies. Understanding how systems of education expand greatly increases our knowledge of school expansion in general. Systemic development often stands between large-scale societal forces and schooling. Systems of schools can transform grand forces into numerous local educational opportunities.

A second and related theme is the role of conflict in increasing school supply. The diffusion of conflict throughout the Church and its ensuing influence on the production of a large national system of schools is an important historical feature that theories of school expansion must explain. Clearly, in the most general of terms, Catholic school supply supports the image of a loosely linked American capital interest unable to control the proliferation of schooling (Rubinson 1986). But this general argument does not explain the influence of internal organizational conflict and its impact on schooling.

Conflict over education, particularly within corporate bodies with a direct interest in formal socialization, is a recurrent issue in the history of nonpublic schooling in America. Control over this domain becomes a source of organizational power to be wielded both internally and externally. The institution-building quality of social conflict is not a monolithic sociological force. As the account of the anti-Catholic pressure versus internal Church politics demonstrates, conflict and its influence on school expansion comes from different sources with varying degrees of strength of impact upon educational demand and supply.

NOTES

1. The more general term *nonpublic* is used throughout this chapter to represent both private, tuition-supported schooling such as American Catholic schooling and subsidized, semi-private schooling such as Catholic schools in many western European countries.

2. This is, of course, the main argument (minus certain refinements) offered to explain the proliferation of public schooling in the postbellum United States as compared to European states (e.g., Meyer et al. 1979; Rubinson 1986). But the same argument can be made about schooling in the United States before the common school movement ran its full course. Colonial America and the Jacksonian era produced a large growth in schooling (private and religious) as compared to other states in similar development (Smith 1967; Fishlow 1966).

3. The total nonpublic share of all U.S. schooling in 1890 was 8 percent (Blodgett 1894).

4. The first four decades of the twentieth century witnessed a continued growth in Catholic schooling followed by stable enrollments and then a decline during the middle of the century, so that in 1930 there were more Catholic schools than there were in 1980.

5. There are also incidences in which the public system followed the Catholic system in educational expansion, although these tend to be isolated and local events. For example,

see Tyack's (1974) description of the common school movement and Catholic schooling in Oregon.

6. Although a diocese's parishes are the basic congregational units of the Roman Catholic church, the diocese, particularly under the strong collegial bishop organization of the nineteenth-century American hierarchy, controls parishes' institutional development, personnel, communication, policy, and resource flows.

7. The NCEA also reports that among "public schools" charging tuition that year, the average cost was $52.

8. The percentage of nontuition support for Catholic high schools for girls was much lower and therefore they relied more on direct tuition; this apparently reflects a lower priority within the system for secondary education of girls (NCEA 1915).

9. The Faribault-Stillwater Plan in Minnesota, undertaken by Bishop Ireland in 1891, arranged for the local school board to rent the parish school and pay the nuns their teacher salaries. In return, the parish agreed to have the nuns certified by the public system and to provide religious training only after school hours. This would recoup money for the local parish, always a concern for the pastor, and maintain a core of nuns for teaching at a higher level than was usually found in most parishes, both at the price of yielding a certain amount of control of Catholic schooling to the local public authorities.

10. The conservative bishops were generally the German bishops, the conservative Irish bishops, and the bishops of original English Catholic stock. The liberal bishops were the more liberal Irish and bishops from the eastern European regions (Cross 1958). This characterization of the bishops into two parties, one hostile to the American state and the other more progressive, probably oversimplifies the complex divisions of bishops on the Americanization issue. But it will suffice for our immediate purpose of describing the intra-corporate effects on school expansion. See Moore (1986) for a more detailed account of the division among the bishops.

11. The reports were similar in tone and recommendations to that found in the later Conant Report about public secondary schooling resulting from the Sputnik crisis. Many of these reports were done as part of graduate training undertaken by diocesan personnel at The Catholic University of America, the core institution for training of professional Catholic educators. For examples see Janet (1949) and Spiers (1951).

12. Orders of brothers have separate hierarchies from the diocesan structure, and the resulting semi-autonomy of order personnel working in diocesan organizations is often a management problem for bishops and parish priests. For example, the Jesuits were an autonomous force during the 1890 school battle, siding with the conservative bishops.

13. Competition and conflict between ethnic groups among the Catholic congregation are often overshadowed by accounts of Protestant-Catholic tensions. The latter were certainly formidable, but they were generally national and diffuse. By contrast, Catholic interethnic conflict was local and at times intense, and the national parish furnished a way to manage this within dioceses. Consider the fierce confrontation between American German and American Irish Catholics over the issue of non-English-speaking priests and ethnic control. The battle was so salient and representative of widespread concern that the Church named the issue "Cahenslyism" after the German who led the fight.

14. That these immigrants were part of a world labor market is illustrated by the fact that many were male temporary laborers who planned to return to their native country.

15. For example, consider the often cited reaction of Catholics to the child-saving programs of New York City's Protestant elite.

13

Historical Expansion of Special Education

John G. Richardson

The topic of special education has been peripheral to the study of mass schooling. This marginality parallels the social status of exceptional children. Yet special education may usefully be viewed as a means to comprehend the beginnings of mass education and its various historical trajectories. Indeed, the symbolic power of certain groups played an essential role in placing the legitimacy of popular education beyond dispute. This chapter argues that in the United States, deviant and special groups played a strategic and decisive role in the formalization of common schooling. And over the past century a widening array of interest groups has pushed the state to incorporate exceptional children into public education.

Despite some resistance, special education has attained near-universal acceptance. Two facts confirm this: first, the dramatic increase in the number of school-age children receiving special education. In 1938 there were 299,257 children receiving special education, representing just 1 percent of the total school-age population. Since 1950 the growth has been exponential, rising to 3,256,633 in 1976, and to 4,094,108 in 1985, accounting for nearly 10 percent of the school population. Second, mandating an appropriate education in a "least restrictive environment" for handicapped children has pulled previously labeled "deviant" children into the mass (common) school. This was accomplished by passage of the All Handicapped Children Act of 1975 (PL 94–142). These changes should not be taken to imply that special education is a recent achievement. In fact, states extended formal provisions for "exceptional children" at different times from 1911 to 1974, and rates of placement expansion have been uneven since 1938.

I first review various interpretations of the origins and growth of special education. To guide the review, three related areas are identified: common school formalization, institutional reform, and urban growth/cultural diversity. The first confines discussion to the formation of common school systems; the second moves attention outside common schooling to the reform of delinquency and to physical and mental exceptionality; the third focuses on demographic and institutional contexts of states that bear on the formalization and expansion of special education inside public schools. I then analyze the timing of formalization and of the rate of expansion between 1957 and 1978 across the American states.

This chapter addresses a main theme of this volume, assessing those causal claims that are valid under specified conditions. For this, special education is strategically situated. It is an institution within an institution; its own origins and growth reveal to us the conditions that have militated for a wider membership in common schooling. And the study of special education is a particularly good test of an interpretative guideline of this volume, the need to distinguish underlying conditions from fluctuating actions of institutions. As the means to identify the specific conditions that permitted the formalization of common schools, and as a barometer of its expansion, there is no better candidate than special education.

COMMON SCHOOLING AND THE ORIGINS OF SPECIAL EDUCATION

The distinction between the formalization of provisions and the expansion of placements in special education parallels the history of common schooling, albeit reversed. For common schooling, voluntary enrollments were high well prior to formal enactment of compulsory school attendance (Fishlow 1966; Meyer et al. 1979; Richardson 1987). Moreover, the timing of compulsory attendance legislation is not related to these enrollments, despite a presumption that such laws simply formalized already high enrollments. Rather, levels of enrollment and measures of formalization were only weakly related, and in young states and territories compulsory attendance was enacted in the absence of a substantial school-age population.

For special education, what matters most is the passage of compulsory attendance legislation. These laws enlarge the span of governmental responsibility, committing local and state authorities to some measure of enforcing earlier constructions of a "free and uniform system" of schooling. It is important to recognize that for nearly all states and territories, compulsory school attendance was preceded by elaborate statutes setting forth the outline, organization, and content of a uniform system of common schooling. Virtually every element of a state school system was in place, save for compulsory attendance. As long as school attendance remained voluntary, there was no pressure on local or state authorities to compel attendance or to extend instruction to those not yet reached. Those who came to school did so because they were able and willing, and any selection practices exercised by schools were informal at best.

All this changes when education becomes general and compulsory. Once schooling ceases to be voluntary, providing adequate instruction becomes problematic. Those who are compelled to attend strain the ability of schools to extend instruction. Thus, the origins of special education parallel the systematization of mass schooling, constituting an organizational reaction to pupils traditionally kept out (Sarason and Doris 1979; Lazerson 1977). A greater diversity of children can now enter. If they then fall behind, their inability to pass through the graded curriculum defines them as "backward" or "laggard." To meet the challenge of legally enforced attendance, local schools devised the internal mechanism of an ungraded or special class, reflecting a nascent system that was more local and informal than state-authorized. These early classes allowed schools to conform to compulsory attendance laws and yet preserve the daily workings of regular education.

Of course, states did keep categories of pupils out as part of enacting compulsory attendance. Built into these laws were exemptions that "excused" children from attending the common school. Virtually all compulsory attendance laws exempted a child "if it shall appear that [his] bodily or mental condition has been such as to prevent [his] attendance at school" (Massachusetts 1852, p. 849). In addition to the exemption of physically and mentally handicapped children, many states excused pupils who lived beyond two miles of the nearest traveled road, who were poor, who were employed, or who had "already acquired the branches of knowledge" given in the common school. Thus, social and demographic conditions joined physical and mental deficiencies as initial grounds for not being required to attend common schools.

Beyond exercising the right to exempt students unable to profit from a common schooling, several states continued the practice of segregating students on the basis of race. Up until at least the time all states had enacted compulsory school attendance (1918), twenty-one states held statutes that required the segregation of students of different racial origin (different from white). Six of these states were outside the South. Yet against these statutes requiring the educational separation of racial groups, fourteen states prohibited the exclusion of students on the basis of race, nationality, or religion.

In light of these opposing forces of exemption and inclusion, the formalization of compulsory attendance would be expected to exert an influence on the later expansion of special education through the medium of secondary education. It is here that increased numbers of "laggards" amplify the problem of school efficiency from a local idiosyncrasy to an issue of relevance to the state.

DEVIANCE AND INSTITUTIONAL REFORM

The view that special education was impelled by compulsory attendance is historically and intuitively plausible. The alignment of historical events reveals that with all but two southern states enacting compulsory attendance by 1900, city schools reported an increasing use of special classes for truant, physically and mentally defective youth (Van Sickle et al. 1911). Nonetheless, the alignment is itself part of a broader sequence of events that outlines a process beginning well before compulsory attendance. The formation of truant or parental schools at the turn of the century gives the strongest suggestion of a larger story. Setting up the truant school was a strategy forced on schools caught in the crossfire from strictly enforcing compulsory attendance. The traditional option of suspension increasingly "brought the school into disrepute" by adding to the burden of families, and it exaggerated youth delinquency by turning unruly students upon the street (*Report of the Commissioner of Education* 1901, p. 190). But truant and parental schools suggest more than troublesome pupils gaining entrance; they reflect on the failure of other institutions to constrain or confine them away from common schools. Within this broader view, compulsory school attendance becomes an intervening variable; it is related to special education by prior movements to reform the deficiencies of body and mind and the deviance of juvenile delinquents.

What is most significant is the sequence of institutional reform. The response to madness and to the physically handicapped comes first, in the form of "discovering" the asylum (Rothman 1971). Coming second was the state primary, industrial, or reform school for "disorderly youth." For these institutions to take root, juvenile truancy had to be distinguished from juvenile crime. The sequential pattern for these institutional reforms is well defined: All but three states established hospitals for the deaf, dumb, and blind prior to establishing the reform school. When the establishment of reform schools is compared to the timing of compulsory attendance laws, the sequential order is again striking: All but eleven states set up the reform school prior to legislating compulsory attendance, and nine of these were far western territories that did not yet face the problem of the urban delinquent.

URBAN GROWTH, CULTURAL DIVERSITY, AND SCHOOL MEMBERSHIP

The special class was an urban construction. As semi-autonomous systems, city schools exerted a defining influence on state policy. Within this context, children of foreign-born heritage were most often laggard in their ability to pass through the graded curriculum, and in Leonard Ayres's (1909) celebrated expression, they were counted as "retarded." In the face of cultural diversity, such recommendations linked the special class to problems of social control. As a practical and pedagogical strategy of public education, a precedent was set: Special classes were not necessarily linked to real physical or mental handicaps, but they grew out of the political issue of school efficiency and cultural trappings of Americanization.

The influence of urban growth and cultural diversity on the construction of special classes continues in this century as a determinant of expanding placements. This legacy finds its contemporary version in the "misclassification" of black and Mexican-American schoolchildren in classes for the educable mentally retarded (EMR) uncovered in the mid–1960s. These findings raised questions about the surge in special education, a growth that could not be attributed to meeting the demands of real prevalence rates of handicapped children. Rather, with the greater diversity and complexity of a school population, the professional autonomy of special education is undermined by exposing its organizational dependency on regular education. As regular teachers seek to keep pace with changes in composition and to maintain continuity in light of differences in learning modes, special education placement is particularly vulnerable to abuse.

In the contemporary period, special education is a regulator of changes in the political hierarchy that defines group membership in full-time, regular instruction. Historically, special education has reflected the intersection of sustained partic- ipation in secondary education with professionalization of the field. When at mid-century secondary education was transformed from a mass terminal to a mass preparatory system, the consumption of schooling became closely tied to the cultural hierarchy in the wider society via special education. Urban growth and the shifting composition of school populations are not the only measures of context that bear on special education. As segments of institutional life, insti- tutions for juvenile delinquents and exceptional children shift in both size and composition and become interwoven with the demography of common schools. Yet this interdependence is not limited to population redistribution. Rather, the populations of reform and residential schools, subject to movements of policy reform as well as demographic change, may exert an influence on the policies and practices of common schools.

EMPIRICAL ANALYSIS

Independent Variables

The independent variables are subsumed under three conceptual orderings: Common School Formalization, Institutional Reform, and Urban Growth and Cultural Diversity. The first variable set identifies characteristics that are internal features of state school systems: their date formalizing compulsory attendance, level of pupil expenditure, time of formation of a state board of education, statute language permitting or prohibiting a policy of pupil segregation (dummy variable, coded 1 if present up to 1900), and level of secondary enrollment. The second variable set organizes measures of a state's participation in nineteenth-century reform movements: date of formation of the (first) state reformatory, state asylum for the insane, and state hospital for the deaf, dumb, and blind. Additionally, this set includes the (timing) truant school, and the formalization of compulsory education for the deaf, dumb, and blind (dummy variable). Finally, the third variable set organizes the measures that reflect the societal composition of ur- banization, and foreign-born and black populations.

For the analysis of formalization, only urbanization, foreign-born and black composition are utilized. For the analysis of special education placements, residential populations are joined to these, for these institutional measures are available in consistent form beginning in 1950 (see Appendix A at the end of this chapter). Taken together, these variable sets reflect in some way the progression of the previous review, seeing measures of common school formalization as the more commonly encountered explanation for special education, and measures of institutional reform and composition as alternative explanations.

The Analysis of Formalization

The historical development of formalization can be analyzed using two indicators. The first is the legislation of truant schools that mark the incorporation of delinquent school-age children into the jurisdiction of common schooling. The measure is defined here by the timing of state-level legislation enabling or mandating the formation of a truant school by local districts. The truant or parental school was begun largely by medium to large cities whose initiative was then formalized at the state level. A review of statutes finds only twenty-five states formally enacting legislation for truant schools. Although the actuality of truant or parental schools (and classes) would be evident at local levels, we take this state-level formalization as the key event denoting a long course of institutional incorporation.

The second measure of formalization is the legislation of provisions for the education of physically and mentally handicapped children. As with the truant school, it is indeed the case that special education was a common practice in local school districts before the legislation of special education as a province of state authority. Two criteria distinguish formalization of state authority from local practice. First, this legislation linked (1) enabling authority extended to local school directors and boards to maintain classes for exceptional children to (2) a state formula for the funding of these classes. Second, these elements were grounded in the promulgation by the state board of education of a set of rules and guidelines for the regulation of local practice (see Appendix B at the end of this chapter). Thus, while most local districts have engaged in special education for some years and decades, the timing of a state's formal authority over local practice ranges from 1911 to 1974. This time range is shown in. Table 13.1.

The formalization of special education may be conceptualized as events that signify extension of state responsibility to the education of groups historically excluded or exempted from common schooling. The timing of state-level legislation for truant schools and provisions for physically and mentally handicapped students constitutes a qualitative change that is not observed directly. The technique well suited to such an interest is event history analysis, which has the ability to accommodate dynamic changes in variables over time and to isolate those factors that have a significant effect on the "time path" of change.

Because the truant school was formally legislated at the state level by only twenty-five states, half the potential cases are lost for the purposes of statistical

Table 13.1
Dates of State Legislation for Special Education—Provisions for Physically Handicapped

YEARS	N	%
1910-19	6	12
1920-29	7	14
1930-39	6	13
1940-49	12	25
1950-59	14	29
1960-75	3	7
TOTALS	(48)	(100)

Note: Alaska and Hawaii are not included; see Appendix A.

analysis. In contrast, enactment of special education legislation was experienced by all states. While legislation of classes for the physically and mentally handicapped was not in all cases introduced at the same time, the differences are negligible (the correlation for the respective years is .89). The analysis uses the date of introduction of provisions for physically handicapped students. The starting time for the observations is 1870, chosen because it represents a median year for the movement to formalize state school systems. The length of time in years from 1870 to the date of truant school and special education legislation is the duration time.

The Analysis of Expansion

Two measures are used in the analysis of placement expansion: Total Placements, and Educable Mentally Retarded (EMR) Placements. Of all the categories that constitute total special education placements, *educable mentally retarded* is the most sensitive marker of expansion. Those external social conditions and economic changes that bear on school systems are best measured by this category. Comparable data that distinguish educable from severe or trainable retarded are available for 1946, 1957, and 1978 (see Appendix C at the end of this chapter). All states experienced increases in Total Placements from 1957 to 1978. However, four states, California, Massachusetts, New York, and Pennsylvania, experienced a (proportionate) decline in EMR Placements over this time period and are removed from the analysis. As will be discussed later, these states foreshadow a pattern of change across handicapping categories that is an integral part of the overall expansion of special education.

The analysis includes both cross-sectional and panel designs. The first analyzes 1946 special education placements as a Beginning System; the panel analysis explores the period of major growth from 1957 to 1978, identified as Expansion and Turbulence. For the cross-sectional analysis, three separate regressions are performed that correspond to the conceptual ordering of independent variables. Given the number of variables constituting each theoretical set, for simplicity only variables that are individually significant are combined as a reduced set. In the final analysis, the southern states (dummy variable: South) are included as a control for their regional difference along dimensions expressed in each variable set.

For the panel analysis of expansion from 1957 to 1978, each variable is tested with the prior level of Total or EMR Placements in 1957 as the lagged dependent variable. The focus here is on the predictive strength of prior conditions on the rate of growth across the twenty-year period to 1978. For this analysis, state population and residential variables are measured at 1960. These results will be shown in Table 13.4.

RESULTS AND INTERPRETATIONS

The Formalization of Special Education

The bivariate effects on transition rates for truant schools and special education yield interpretations that conform strikingly with historical evidence and recent research. As shown in Table 13.2, state legislation of truant schools is linked to the prior establishment of reform schools, but not to the prior formation of asylums and state hospitals for the deaf, dumb, and blind. Timing of reform school formation and level of urbanization are consistent with the historical evidence that links urban delinquency and educational truancy. Moreover, the level of pupil expenditures is the only measure of common school formalization that influences the formation of truant schools. For truant schools, the sharp contrast between southern and midwestern states is consistent with empirical research on the adoption of reform schools. The southern states established the reform school comparatively late, a fact reflected in a delayed formation of the truant school. The significant effect shown for the black percentage of the school population is due as well to its strong association with southern states.

For the formal legislation of special education provisions, the pattern of effects is equally consistent with nineteenth-century antecedents. Here all three deviance reform movements have significant effects on the transition rate, as does the legislation of the truant school. Except for level of pupil expenditures, virtually no other measure for common school formalization has an effect on the legislation of special education. States that expressed a formal prohibition against any exclusion of students on the basis of race, nationality, or religion were no more likely to establish provisions for exceptional children than were states that endorsed or mandated racial segregation.

A significant effect is found for the foreign-born composition of states. A higher composition of foreign-born hastened state legislation of special education provisions. For this positive influence, the historical record is sharper. The impact

Table 13.2
Bivariate Effects on Truant Schools and Special Education Provisions

Independent Variables	Truant Schools	Special Education
Common School Formalization		
Compulsory attendance	.013	.004
Exclusion prohibition	.450	.195
Expenditures per pupil	.004*	-.001
Secondary enrollment ratio	.060	-1.490
Segregation clause	-.689	-.352
State Board of Education	-.004	-.005
Statehood	.004	.009*
Truant School		1.058*
Institutional Reform		
Compulsory attendance for Deaf		.300
Deaf, Dumb, Blind state hospital	-.013	-.025*
Insane asylums	-.003	-.015*
Reformatory	-.036*	-.026*
Institutional and Cultural Diversity		
Percent urban (state population)	.029*	.016*
Percent foreign-born (state population)	.020	.047*
Percent black (school-age population)	-.036*	-.007
Regions		
North	.272	.425
South	-1.004*	-.068
West	1.187*	.806*
Far West	-.273	-.820*

* $p < .05$

of foreign-born immigration on the introduction of special education attests to the negative incorporation of groups historically excluded or exempted. This path of negative incorporation represents a strategy of school tracking designed to guide a long-term process begun earlier in the reform school movement. This role of the foreign-born parallels similar evidence of a negative effect of immigration on common school enrollments from 1895 to 1925, when the composition of immigrants was predominantly from southern and eastern European countries (Ralph and Rubinson 1980).

As the bivariate relations suggest, specific historical paths emerge, from the reform school to the truant school, and from the institutional reform of the deaf and insane to the education of the physically and mentally handicapped. No measure of educational formalization, except for pupil expenditures, significantly affects the incorporation of excluded or exempted groups. Neither the internal expansion of secondary enrollments nor statute language permitting or prohibiting discrimination toward categories of students bears on the timing of formalization.

The Expansion of Special Education

Table 13.3 shows that for the analysis of special education as a Beginning System, the results for Total and EMR Placements are consistent. For both, higher school expenditures per pupil (measured in 1942) are significantly related to the level of placements in 1946. This is a strong influence, and it complements the same finding for the timing of formalization. Clearly, the initiation of a system of special education was in large measure determined by a state's financial capacity. This capability was itself tied to enactment of compulsory attendance, for these two measures are strongly negatively correlated ($r = -.73$). For this Beginning System, however, the financial expenditures per pupil are more directly related to initial levels of special education.

The significant effect indicated for an early achievement of statehood suggests a similar historical antecedent. After controlling for southern states, this measure remains strong. Nonetheless, year of statehood is a measure that disguises lines of regional difference. All but one northern state, and eight of the sixteen southern states, achieved statehood prior to 1800. To explore the resilience of this measure, the North was included without any substantive variables. The result was a sharp reduction in the magnitude of statehood, eliminating its statistical significance.

As with the formalization of special education, early participation in the establishment of reform schools is significantly related to the level of both Total and EMR Placements in 1946. In turn, earlier formalization of special education is linked to higher levels of both Total and EMR Placements. These findings reaffirm that the expansion of special education as a twentieth-century phenomenon has causal roots in nineteenth-century reform movements. The timing of a state's involvement in these movements set in motion a series of consequences expressed in levels of special education placements achieved by mid-century.

Finally, the variables of institutional and societal context again reveal historical continuities, but they demonstrate contemporary pressures on the growth in placements. Specifically, the size of the residential population of mentally handicapped children is positively related to both Total and EMR Placements.

When we explore the growth of Total Placements from 1957 to 1978 in Table 13.4, only the residential population of physically handicapped children is influential. Lower residential populations of physically handicapped children (measured in 1960) are associated with higher rates of expansion in Total Placements

Table 13.3

Results of Cross-Sectional Analysis: The Beginning System, 1946 [unstandardized/ (standardized) coefficients]

Independent Variables	Dependent Variables:	
	Total Placements	EMR
Common School Formalization		
Expenditures per pupil	.014 (.49)	.011 (.41)
Statehood	-.005 (-.24)	-.006 (-.27)
South	-.168* (-.01)	-.171* (-.09)
Enrollment base	1.14 (.65)	1.36 (.61)
Adjusted R²	.74	.72
Institutional Reform		
Reformatory	-.015 (-.37)	-.014 (-.41)
Special Education formalization	-.021 (-.34)	-.015 (-.26)
South	.018* (.01)	-.046* (-.02)
Enrollment base	.891 (.41)	1.02 (.46)
Adjusted R²	.77	.76
Urban Growth and Cultural Diversity		
Mentally handicapped children	.351 (.27)	.342 (.26)
Percent Urban	2.11 (.35)	1.99 (.36)
South	.096* (.04)	.141* (.08)

Table 13.3 (continued)

Independent Variables	Dependent Variables:	
	Total Placements	EMR
Enrollment base	1.56	1.49
	(.35)	(.68)
Adjusted R²	.79	.81

* p > .05

of special education. This association demonstrates the tie between common schooling and the alternative, residential sector for handicapped children.

The period 1960–1978 witnessed dramatic changes in the demographic size and composition of urban school systems. This was also the period of great expansion in special education, evident most of all in the growth in EMR Placements. As we see in the panel results, three nineteenth-century antecedents bear on the rate of growth: level of pupil expenditures, timing of compulsory attendance, and establishment date of the state reformatory. In addition, three factors of the contemporary period bear on the rate of expansion: the residential population of mentally handicapped children, the percentage of the state population that is urban, and the percentage of the school-age population that is black.

Comparing all variables, only level of pupil expenditures, date of compulsory attendance, and the black percentage of the school-age population reduce the significance of the South. The information embodied in these antecedents reflects a regional difference, for all but two southern states enacted compulsory attendance after 1900, and southern states were behind others in pupil expenditures. Other variables show a similar statistical tendency, but conditions of the contemporary period cut across the contrast that has distinguished the southern states. The compositional effect of minority populations on EMR Placements reaffirms cross-sectional analyses (see Gelb and Mizokawa 1986) but confirms here that the expansion of special education throughout the 1960s and 1970s was propelled in some measure by the conflicts and strain that schools faced as their environments became increasingly diverse.

The analysis of EMR Placements gives a viewpoint to the sequential expansion and contraction across special education categories. The experience of decline in EMR Placements by California, Massachusetts, New York, and Pennsylvania reflects the movement of state school systems out of a condition defined as mild retardation and into one defined as neurological disorder (learning disability). This sequential movement is exemplified by states that were early leaders in the

Table 13.4
Panel Analysis: Expansion and Turbulence, 1957 to 1978 [unstandardized/ (standardized) coefficients]

Total Placements

Independent Variables		Enrollment Base	Prior Level	South	R^2
		.542	.292	.196	.87
		(.49)	(.44)	(.20)	
Physically handicapped	-.229** (-.10)	.546 (.49)	.282 (.43)	.222 (.21)	.88

EMR

Independent Variables		Enrollment Base	Prior Level	South	R^2
		.692	.290	.301	.86
		(.52)	(.34)	(.28)	
Per pupil Expenditures	-.002** (-.29)	.585 (.44)	.382 (.45)	.102* (.09)	.90
Compulsory school Attendance	.006* (.19)	.701 (.53)	.268 (.31)	.138* (.13)	.87
Reformatory	.003* (.13)	.690 (.52)	.334 (.39)	.243** (.23)	.87
Mentally handicapped	-.165** (-.21)	.647 (.50)	.274 (.32)	.198** (.20)	.88
Percent urban (state pop)	-.008** (-.23)	.688 (.52)	.405 (.47)	.203** (.19)	.90
Percent black (school-age pop)	.009** (.22)	.589 (.49)	.242 (.34)	.180* (.14)	.88

* $p > .05$ ** $p > .01$

formalization of special education and that represent the arena for the major legal and intellectual issues that impel change in special education. These are "core" states whose debates and court challenges diffuse outward to others, influencing the direction of national policy.

The exemplary role of these core states contributes to the interpretation of the shift in the sign for the independent variables. As a measure of a state's economic level, urban concentration confers on each state a position in a national ranking of economic and political power (Richardson 1984). States that share common levels of population size and diversity, as well as similar levels of economic strength, share a defining role in setting national educational policy. In regard to special education, California, Massachusetts, New York, and Pennsylvania are "ahead" of national policy. States with demographic and economic affinities, like Texas, Florida, Arizona, and New Jersey, are not far behind. Such states were comparatively late in their enactment of compulsory attendance and their participation in the movement to establish reform schools, but they are "thrust forward" by virtue of their linkages to economically and politically core states.

These empirical analyses describe a system that began its growth with roots in the formalization of common schooling and was influenced by the state's participation in nineteenth-century movements of institutional reform. These patterns underscore the interpretative guideline noted earlier, the need to distinguish between deeper and more slowly changing conditions from their fluctuating institutional responses. Earlier participation in nineteenth-century reform movements hastens state involvement in the extension of provisions for exceptional students, setting parameters that defined the formal incorporation of historically exempted groups. Principal among these conditions was the financial capacity of states to sustain the incorporation of exceptional children. Yet the impact of these historical antecedents wanes. This initial event structure gives way to contemporary institutional relations and fluctuations in residential populations, both of which alter the political hierarchy of American education. By its dramatic expansion, special education becomes a power broker of these broader institutional relations and economic changes.

SUMMARY AND CONCLUSIONS

The significance of special education has always extended beyond its statistical boundary. The presence of deaf and blind or mentally handicapped children has not been sufficient to generate a system of special education. The formalization of this alternative system, and its expansion, are both tied to events and conditions that have little to do with the physiological facets of exceptional children. They are tied to the long course of change aimed at lowering legal and organizational barriers to participation in public education.

The expansion of special education is not simply the growth of a sector within general education. Rather, special education provides the best reading of systemic and ideological change in general education. The maturation of special education caps the long trajectory of the rise and institutionalization of mass education. It was the symbolic power of the blind, deaf, and mentally exceptional that provided the crucial ideological thrust for the venture of mass education. The possibility of mass education was first constructed as an idea of intellectual worth, and one with viable pedagogical results. Beginning in the Enlightenment, the education of the deaf and blind, and the moral instruction of the mentally defective, predates the political struggles over mass education. Debates over the educability of special groups conferred legitimacy on mass education, and the physiological method affirmed the promise of its results. The grand ideas of progress and the perfectibility of the human mind found their empirical, or experimental, ground in the limiting conditions of mental and physical handicap.

This critical role of special groups remains nonetheless obscure; they are the silent actors in the long narrative of mass education. For the American states, the expansion of special education breaks this silence. As this chapter has tried to show, the analysis of the roots of special education rests on historical antecedents that reverse the traditional way in which education has been conceived and explained.

APPENDIX A

Measures of institutional reform are four: the date that states (1) established a state insane asylum, (2) established a state hospital for the deaf and blind, (3) established a state reform school, and (4) enacted legislation mandating compulsory education for the deaf/blind. Although the actual opening date of a state insane asylum may be taken, the date measured here is the time of state commitment to this institution. Specifically, this commitment is encompassed in the legislative act that confirmed financial allocation for construction at a designated place. Dates for the state (lunatic) asylum are taken from Hurd ([1916–1917] 1973); dates for the state hospital for the deaf are taken from Best (1914); dates for the first state reform school were secured from a personal communication from John Sutton (see also Reports of the Commissioner of Education, 1882, pp. 756–63; 1911, pp. 1286–91; and Sutton 1988).

APPENDIX B

The dates when states legislated special education provisions within public education are neither fully nor reliably available in secondary sources. These dates were secured from a review of *Revised Statutes* for all states to identify the precise year provisions were formally outlined as part of the state public school system.

APPENDIX C

Data on placements in special education by state are available from the *Biennial Surveys of Education* for 1946–1948 (pp. 1–19), and 1957–1958 (pp. 1–25). These sources give total figures for classes in "local public school," distinguishing these numbers from exceptional children in residential institutions or homes. These sources give numbers by handicapping condition and, especially pertinent to this study, distinguish numbers of students classified as "educable mentally retarded."

The actual figures for both Total and EMR Placements are highly skewed. For Total Placements, the range for 1946 is 24 students in Montana to 86,245 in New York. The figures for the same states in 1978 are 9,007 and 111,706, respectively. Because of this difference in range, a log transformation is performed that is appropriate for OLS regression.

Conditions Underlying Legitimate and Strong Institutions

14

The Social Construction of Motives for Educational Expansion

John W. Meyer

The extraordinary expansion of education in the modern world clearly calls for explanation. Mass schooling is found in every contemporary country, enrolling the great majority of children. Over 90 percent of the world's children are enrolled at some point in their lives (Unesco 1983). Basic schools are, by and large, compulsory. And they are, historically speaking, recent and have grown and spread very rapidly.

Furthermore, schooling systems reek with purposiveness. Their participants and advocates see every aspect of schooling as filled with intentions—sometimes admirable, less often perverse; sometimes fulfilled, often unfulfilled (as with the dream of educationally produced equality). Occasionally, schooling arrangements are advocated because they are good in their own right, as when core religious rituals or materials are included in the curriculum. But most often every schooling feature is defended instrumentally, as vital to important individual and social purposes: Mathematics will improve individual and national productivity; discipline is necessary to cognitive and moral learning; coeducation will benefit future mothers (and now female workers) by providing proper socialization for modern family relations; universal standards produce group equality and sustain merited mobility.

In fact, it is hard to find opponents of schooling and its expansion. So many instrumental reasons have been assembled that it now seems obvious that individuals should want to attend schools, communities to demand them, and nations to provide them, all within some resource limits.

The chapters in this book take the motivated or purposive character of modern schooling for granted, and they wisely do not consider alternatives. It is not supposed that the rise of schooling is a simple accidental product of arbitrary gods or values. It is not reasonable to see schooling as resulting from the drift of human evolution, with those groups and societies that happened to have it winning out in a mute process of evolutionary selection. Wherever it is found, in the views taken here, schooling is the direct product of rather self-conscious human intentions (though the ideological origins of these intentions may not be conscious). These intentions were by and large directly fulfilled, though some deflections occur, and many unintended consequences accompany the fulfillment: Some of these unintended effects, such as intergroup competition, may themselves further the expansion of schooling.

The chapters here, as well as the broader research literature of which they are a part, are strongest in analyzing the expansion of schooling as the product of self-interested actors of various sorts: individuals, but especially organized interests in society, and state actors representing or imposing themselves on society. A major theme is that when education becomes an important social good, and a main dimension of intra-societal and international stratification systems, many different actors (from individuals to states) are motivated to create and acquire it for themselves. The line of thought well represents the *actor-centered* vision of most modern social theory and research.

I review the line of work involved, but I also emphasize an *other-centered* view. Clearly, under modern conditions, people play the legitimated modern role of self-interested actors pursuing education for themselves, their families, and their social groups. The modern system makes it much in their interest to do so. But this modern system creates great collective perspectives, too, in which people enter as others, or as agents of the collective good: a collective good that most prominently comes to include education for everyone in society.

All sorts of people in the modern world, acting as these others, have made education a general collective good and have built it into the stratified rewards and resources distributed to actors. They thus help to create the conditions under which these actors pursue schooling. Individual people throughout the world— even those without children—advocate education for other people's children, and indeed for everyone. Many or most social interests similarly subscribe to education, not only for themselves but for others: Prominent here are the assembled professional elites and state advisors who play these important roles, such as the economists and sociologists of education. Similarly, national states participate directly (via colonial enterprises, and now via foreign aid) and through world bodies in pursuing educational expansion in other countries: In the world system, they also come to be important others.

Indeed, most actors who pursue education for themselves do so with the understanding that it is a legitimate collective good, a credible way of surpassing one's fellows. One can find in the schools individual children who see the situation with a narrower rationality and try to hinder and stigmatize the accomplishments of their competitors out of self-interest, but this obtrusive form of competition is not as common as theories stressing only individual interest would predict.

Thus, I emphasize the way modern people, as "others" rather than "selves," have constructed schooling as a collective good, thus constructing and legitimating the motivations for its pursuit in each other, in interest groups, in national societies and states, and now in the world system. Overall, the most surprising feature of educational expansion around the world has been less that people and groups act to pursue education for themselves than that people as others have pursued education for everyone—and have made it the basis of both individual status and the collective good.

MOTIVES OF THE INDIVIDUALS WHO PURSUE SCHOOLING

The motives of young people who go to school, or of the parents who encourage them, are seen as unproblematic in the chapters of this book. In most of the discussions, these motives are taken for granted and do not appear explicitly at all: Walter McMahon is an exception. (When I refer to a chapter in this volume, for brevity I indicate only the author's name.) Variations in preferences are seen, mainly, as derived from social incentives rather than internal dispositions.

The reasons for this are clear. First, in contemporary societies educational attainment is directly valued and is the main factor leading to advantage along all other key dimensions of individual stratification. Essentially every incentive that modern systems have to offer is put at the service of educational participation. In going to school and staying longer, people tend to gain greatly in occupational status, income, political rights to fuller participation and to seek office, preferred marital partners, enhanced access to organizational participation, cultural capacity to act in preferred ways, informal social advantages, and the esteem of almost all who matter. For each of these goods, education is not simply one helpful resource; it usually is the primary factor.

Why modern stratification systems—supposedly creatures of class and power in very dynamic economic and political systems—turn into educational hierarchies becomes a main research question. Why individual people participate in education is not a burning issue: Every institutionalized social motive impels them to do so. The research question thus shifts from one of individual preferences to one of the social construction of opportunities and incentives.

Second, of course, modern systems not only offer incentives but compel people to go to school through legitimated institutional rules. This compulsion is both direct and indirect through (1) restrictions on other activities such as child labor and (2) pressure on parents to permit and require their children to go to school.

Individual motives, thus, are taken for granted. But their prevalence has important consequences for educational expansion:

1. The expansion of motives for schooling built into modernizing stratification

systems positively affects the expansion of schooling. People push more for access and—using social, economic, and political resources—produce more schooling, though other forces may successfully resist. As schooling gets linked to more and more desiderata, such pressures increase.

The massive modern shift of stratification to an educational base requires much explanatory work, which will be considered subsequently. We simply note here that given this shift, individuals (and their family supporters) who earlier resisted school expansion are increasingly likely over time to support and demand it. The impact of this on families is likely to be especially notable. In earlier periods, with families acting as corporate social groups and with family collective status being an extremely important element of stratification, families were likely to resist (1) foregoing child labor, (2) the school-based attack on the diffuse identity and authority of the family, and (3) the costs of schooling. The idea was to keep the child an agent of the family. Now, with families reconstructed as agents of their individual members (including their children), they are supporters of expanded education. In most places, now, parents push reluctant children to participate effectively in schooling, demand schooling from the state, and sometimes create schooling themselves, as David Mitch notes.

2. Popular pressure for stratificational advantage through educational expansion has more impact the greater the social power and collective legitimacy of such pressure. That is, such modern arrangements as democratic decentralization, under conditions of effective education-stratification linkages, enhance educational expansion. Under other conditions (e.g., when education was not closely tied to stratificational advantage), they might have aided resistance to the imposition of schooling. Since one of the many sources of the expanded modern power and legitimacy of popular pressure is the expansion of schooling itself, this mechanism suggests that educational expansion may partly feed on itself.

3. Under conditions of great stratificational advantage for the educated, individual pressures for education are likely to create educational inflation, as people struggle to be at the front of a continuously elaborating job queue (Rubinson and Fuller, this volume; see also Boudon 1974; Collins 1979).

Future Research on Individual Motives and Incentives

Contributors to this book hold a hard-headed conception of the individual. Such individuals have their eye out for the brass ring. And since education has increasingly become the main route to stratificational advantage, they increasingly pursue education.

Fair enough, but perhaps not far enough. Surveys of modern individuals show they not only recognize many advantages of education but also believe that these advantages ought to hold: That is, education should lead to status advantages. Along with this, they generally support education as having more diffuse and personal advantages as well. Such popular doctrines make it more legitimate for individuals to pursue education, which might otherwise carry more negative social meanings (e.g., as a form of status striving). Indeed, in many traditional communities, a certain natural suspicion attaches to educational ambition: It is easy to suspect people of trying to use educational attainment to surpass others, since they are obviously doing just that. This view has declined with modernization. Individual aspiration and success in educational matters now are treated with more admiration than envy, reflecting the underlying legitimation of education.

4. As education becomes more collectively valued, and as its legitimacy in the stratification process rises, individual incentives to participate (1) increase and (2) are more likely to lead to action. Both the motives involved and the activity acquire positive collective social value and reinforce the expression of individual interest.

The sense that education is a normatively or collectively valued good is a pervasive feature of more modern systems. It begins to address an issue about individual motivation that is hardly addressed in the literature or in the chapters here: Why do modern people advocate the education of other people's children? They clearly do so—over and over, they support the general expansion of education for everyone. Elites with the status, power, and income to privately educate their own children are often substantial supporters of compulsory mass education for everyone. And people with no children to benefit support education almost as much as those whose children will gain.

Hard-headedness will not easily do here. Educating the children of everyone else provides stratificational costs to oneself and one's own children. One can make up intricate arguments that people believe that only in this way will they protect their own rights, but this does not handle the case of the childless very well.

It is probably most sensible to imagine that modern people—as much research suggests—have the good of something like "society" in mind as they take public action and pay taxes, and that they share the general conception (widely held, for instance, by economists) that education is good for society.

5. As education comes to be legitimated as contributing to the public good, and as individual persons come to be incorporated as citizen-members of the public, individual pressures to expand education will increase. As the modern system develops, all the processes discussed previously—individual interest, individual commitment, and individual agency for the public good—increasingly lead to individual activity on behalf of the expansion of the schools. Their force increases as individuals gain power and standing in the modern polity.

6. Thus, overall, the forces producing educational expansion shift over time and increasingly reflect the socially constructed motivations of individuals.

The question of individual motivation is now unproblematic: So many social changes build in this motivation and make it highly legitimate that individual motives have become routine and obvious. But this raises questions about the collectivities that structure these now-unproblematic motivations. Why do modern collectivities build education into their stratification systems? And why do they define education as contributing to the societal good?

MOTIVES OF COLLECTIVE ACTORS FOR THE EXPANSION OF SCHOOLING

The chapters in this book only infrequently address the two great questions presented here: Why education is a collective good, and why it is the appropriate vehicle for stratifying people. They concentrate on a more immediate mechanism: organizational competition and resulting competitive isomorphism. It is generally assumed that education is an important collective good; it then follows that organizational competition enhances its pursuit.

Thus, David Baker discusses (1) the efforts of the American Catholic Church to build an educational system to compete with the secular one, and (2) the further expansionary internal competition within the Church for effective control. In a remarkably parallel discussion, William Morgan and Michael Armer consider the adaptation of Islamic interests in Nigeria to the success of education by creating rather modern schools and penetrating the existing system—in both cases enhancing overall support for education and its expansion. Bruce Fuller and Richard Rubinson consider a wide range of competitions in different domains (roughly, class, status, and power, following Weber) as leading to educational expansion in Europe. Jerald Hage and Maurice Garnier include competition with other powers as one of the forces producing the use of expanded schooling. Such a mechanism is clearly involved in Francisco Ramirez and Marc Ventresca's discussion of the expansion of compulsory education around the world. And similar organizational struggles are involved in Pamela Walters's arguments about educational expansion as affected by class and status competition. If we treat the modern interstate competition for economic growth as playing a similar role, the chapters by Walter McMahon, Aaron Benavot, and John Boli also can be included here.

All of these arguments are built on the assumption that the two great principles discussed previously are firmly in place: Education is a most valuable collective good, and education is central to stratification. Note that the specific arguments work because these doctrines are cultural principles, not because they are necessarily true in practice. The competitions proposed are not long, slow evolutionary ones in which education works out to be successful: They are self-conscious and planned competitive strategies, working out from cultural assumptions. Baker's American Catholics know what they are doing, and they act in terms of modern cultural theory to enhance control over their population and to aid this population for stratificational advantage. So do Morgan and Armer's Islamic groups. So do the states discussed by Boli, McMahon, and Hage and Garnier. Thus, the core arguments of the chapters in this book are about organizational competition, and they view the motives involved as exactly parallel to those of the modern individuals discussed previously.

7. As education comes to be seen as a societal good and as the core of social stratification, organizations and groups (driven both by their individual members and by organizational agents) will compete for education, resulting in its expansion. It must be recognized, though the authors here (aside from David Mitch) tend to be mute on the subject, that organizations and groups within society often act as agents of society itself.

8. As education comes to be seen as a societal good and as central to social stratification, more organizations and groups, perceiving its legitimacy, will pursue educational expansion.

9. Under the same conditions, the modern shift of power and status to participatory groups and organizations within society will facilitate their effectiveness in producing educational expansion.

10. As education comes to be seen as a general societal good and as central to world stratification, national societies and states will compete for education, resulting in its expansion. Again, though the authors here do not discuss the subject, national societies and states are likely to act as agents of what they perceive to be worldwide good. It is important to bear in mind that nation-states, both directly (through aid programs later and colonization earlier) and indirectly (through world movements and such organizations as Unesco, the World Bank, and the United Nations system), attempt to enhance education elsewhere (McNeely 1989).

11. Under these conditions, national societies and states are likely to pursue (as agents of the general human collectivity) education worldwide as a general good.

12. Under these conditions, state formation—the rise of the legitimacy and power of national societies and states—is likely to enhance effectiveness in the state production of worldwide educational expansion.

None of these arguments, however, really explains why education is seen as a general collective good and as a legitimate basis for individual (and organizational, and intersocietal) stratification. We have simply seen that these conditions build motives and incentives for education in individuals, organizations, and national collectivities. All these entities come to see education as advantageous for themselves as an interest and right, and for everyone as a matter of the social good; and they come to be empowered in the modern system to take action along appropriate lines.

EDUCATION AS A COLLECTIVE GOOD

We have seen why education, if defined as a collective good, is pursued by individuals, interests, and national states. Why is it viewed as a collective good in the first place?

We have dismissed one answer out of hand: that people have learned, over a long, slow evolutionary process, that education in fact provides great collective benefits. The authors reviewing the matter (McMahon, Rubinson and Fuller,

Hage and Garnier, and Benavot) believe that modern societies economically benefit from more education: They treat the scientific investigation of this matter as recent and ongoing, and as requiring much additional research. The discoveries in question long postdate the actual historical expansion of education and its institutionalization as a virtue. The same situation would hold if we consider the putative benefits of education for political development or social integration— one cannot refer to anything as clearly established, or to earlier periods as having possessed evidence that would lead reasonable people to such conclusions as a matter of fact. We are, clearly, discussing doctrines here.

Then what is the doctrine? The chapters on the economic effects of education (Part II) are clearest in articulating it. First, society contains an economic system—a complex set of interdependent activities making up an overall action project that can be assessed as more or less successful on a single dimension (abstractly valued product and its growth): Here growth is an important and valid purpose of the collectivity. Second, the overall economic project is produced by the purposive and rational activities of individual people, each of whom makes a contribution: The contributions aggregate. Third, better people (more effectively devoted to the important purposes and more competent at rational activity) produce more. Finally, education can create more committed and competent people.

The economy is not really evaluated in terms of its overall product or growth in this product (though before the democratic revolutions it was common to try to think this way). The product is calculated, in all modern schemes, per capita. Otherwise, we might have the vision, which is common in agrarian systems, of expanding the product simply by expanding the numbers of peasant producers. The modern replacement sees the virtuous economic society as generating more product per individual person. Enhancing the lives of these persons is a main economic goal of society. This enhancement properly consists of enabling these individuals to develop themselves more fully, and this is seen as directly requiring rights to more education. Education becomes both a production and a consumption good for society: The good society requires individual education and produces it. Education is an individual right and a duty, a societal need and obligation.

Consider the model embodied here and the extraordinary modern culture it establishes. There is the creation of an imagined community called "society" (Anderson 1983): Other civilizational systems emphasized the gods, families, imperial elites, and so on. Society is an action system with the purpose of generating a product, and it is virtuous inasmuch as it does so. Other systems might envision a community (without a product, and in service to its history or its gods) rather than an action system. Society is made up of individual persons, is produced by them, and is evaluated in terms of their welfare. Other systems might conceive of society as made up of feudal elites and their territories as produced by history and culture rather than individuals, and as evaluated in terms of religious or military considerations rather than individual welfare.

Figure 14.1
Two Cultural Models of Society

a. The Modern Action System, Made up of Individuals

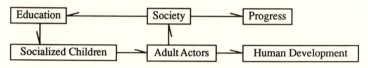

b. One Traditional Version

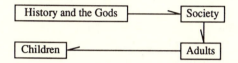

John Richardson, as well as Francisco Ramirez and Marc Ventresca, makes abundantly clear the social and cultural discipline imposed on individuals by such models as these. The social action project made up of individuals gives great attention to the analysis and classification of such individuals in ways that stabilize society and improve its product. Normality takes on meaning if the individual is no longer a natural peasant but a core ingredient in society as a project: The polity expands, and with it classifications of individuals in modern terms. Along with normality, more forceful conceptions of the management of deviants arise as well.

The first panel of Figure 14.1 depicts the relevant aspects of modern society as a model (Meyer 1977). Rationalized society produces educational arrangements that generate the appropriate childhood socialization to create adults who are both fulfilled and socially productive. The second panel of the figure depicts one of the possible alternatives: Society, not a system, and without goals, derives from history and the gods, and it imposes its proper order on adults, who are authoritative models for children. Little schooling results.

I do not review in this chapter the elaborate literature discussing the rise of modern (Western) models of society as an action system made up of individual persons, and their worldwide spread (see, e.g., Mann 1986; Meyer 1989). My point here has been to indicate the underlying cultural form within which education becomes a collective good.

13. With the rise of a model of human society that reflects a purposive action system made up of individual persons as model actors, education becomes a collective good and a legitimated pursuit of societies, interests, and individuals themselves.

An answer to our second great issue—accounting for the rise of education as grounding social stratification—becomes apparent. If, in individualist logic, education makes better (more socially productive) individuals who contribute more to the collective good, rewards and status should be distributed on the basis of education. This is both a matter of incentives (building the appropriate reward structure through the distribution of status and income) and effective functioning (properly distributing power and authority). Other forms of stratification (e.g., on the basis of familial or ethnic community) are both unjust and inefficient. Furthermore, if more educated individuals are themselves more developed persons, and if this is a social desideratum in itself, educated individuals are in themselves carriers of social value.

14. Thus, with the rise of models of human society as an action system made up of individual persons, education becomes the core ingredient of legitimate stratification—hence many additional incentives for its legitimate pursuit by individuals, interests, and societies arise.

We may note that the importance of education in producing collective goods (but especially the importance of education as a direct element of individual welfare) leads to an extraordinary emphasis throughout the modern world on educational equality. Equalizing the welfare of the individuals in society is an important modern desideratum: As education is seen as both a criterion and an instrument for individual opportunity, demands for its equalization are legitimated.

DOMAINS OF THE EXPANSION OF SOCIETY AND, THUS, EDUCATION

In important respects, our emphasis on the example of the economic benefits of education for society is misleading (see also the chapters by Mitch and Boli). In fact, the conception of society as prominently built around an economic action project is relatively late in coming to the core: It really rises only in the eighteenth century and develops slowly in the nineteenth. Something of an economy and a tax base are seen as relevant very early in Western history (Tilly 1975), but the incorporation of individual actors comes later. Only in the modern period— with the rise of the human capital revolution and the detailed analysis of society as an individual-based productive economy—is it more completely elaborated.

Correspondingly, the collective legitimation of education as an economic good comes relatively late. And the use of education as a main element in economic stratification (e.g., the assignment of occupations, income, and economic authority) is primarily a feature of the twentieth century (Collins 1979).

This leads to a more general point. Public society has never comprehended all of recognized social life. More and more domains have been included in public society over time, in a long progression. Thus, in the current period, many expansions of the public order into formerly communal or familial life have been common: Gender, class, and ethnicity have been undercut by public citizenship; age and generation categories of family life have similarly been penetrated by public regulation; and all sorts of "service sector" activities have come under regulation. With each of these changes, new domains of society are created, new collective goods are developed, new aspects of the individual recognized, and inevitably new dimensions of education created. All of these changes produce expanded models along the lines depicted in Figure 14.1. There is an expanded conception of society as a purposive action project, which expands needed socialization to produce adults who are more developed personally (the individual welfare that is collectively valued) and who also contribute more to the social system. The social penetration of child rearing, for instance, leads to efforts at education for family relations, which is thought to produce better children. These children grow up to be better adults who live better lives and are more socially productive.

New aspects of education as a public good are constructed, along with elaborated motives for educational participation and further pressures for educational expansion. Naturally, education expands, both in the domains it includes (in terms of content) and in terms of potential participants. Sorca O'Connor describes in detail one specific dimension—the current educational penetration of earlier childhood, accompanying the general conception of family relations and childhood as components of society and its collective good. One could usefully refer to other studies emphasizing the rise of adult education, educational training for organizational life, education for retirement, education for death, and so on. In each of these instances, the modern conception of society as an action project made up of individuals expands, and with it the perceived value of education. In each case, new legitimate motives for organized actors are created.

Mitch and Boli give some historical overview of the entire process. The earliest Western conceptions of education as a collective good seem to arise in the religious domain (then including political elements), turned in more secular directions by both Reformation and counter-Reformation. To a surprising extent, even much early nation-state emphasis on education stressed the basically religious aspects of recognized society. Forms of schooling emphasized basic religious and moral training and touched little on education for practical work activity, for instance.

More differentiated political elements come later, with nation-states (and their associated incorporation of individuals into their projects) emphasizing citizenship and national culture. As we have noted, the conception of society as a rationalized and individualistic economy seems to come still later. And only in the twentieth century do family and interpersonal relations come under scrutiny.

In short, Western education in earlier periods was more directed to dimensions of social rationalization that tied the individual more closely to religious and political society as a control system. Only later does it absorb the twin themes of (1) maximizing the means-ends productivity of the individuals in society and (2) maximizing personal development. Education as social incorporation and control tends to predate education as improving action efficiency. The parallels here with the evolution of the nation-state and citizenship are direct (e.g., Marshall 1948; Bendix 1964).

The history of this is best written in terms of the curriculum of mass education, which expands following just such lines (see Benavot et al. 1991; Wong 1991). Language and religion come early, mathematics and history a little later, science around the turn of the century, and social studies, art, and physical education only more recently.

For our purposes here, implications for the expansion of education must be stressed.

15. As new domains enter models of society and the collective good, more aspects of education as a collective good are constructed, along with more individual, organizational, and societal motives for its expansion. Thus, the motives expanding education themselves expand and change over time. As a result, education expands at an increasing rate into the available populations and also expands into the new domains.

There are implications here for educationally based stratification as well. The creation of new domains in public society creates new opportunities for legitimate stratification and bases them on education. For example, we observe the rise of the modern service sector in every national society—domains of occupational activity far extended from traditional economic production or political management. These tend to become part of society, to get organized in terms of societal stratification systems, to become rooted in education.

Consider a few examples: (1) Medical activity is removed from family and then from traditional professional arrangements. It is located in societally structured organization around a host of new occupations and organizational roles. All of these are rooted in education and are stratified by education. (2) The same process tends to go on with local governmental activity, which comes to be organized more professionally and bureaucratically. Education expands, and educationally based stratification is extended. (3) The same process is now going on with child rearing—the rise of organizations and professions in this arena, increasingly education-based, is striking.

16. The expansion of public society into more domains creates new dimensions of public stratification, which come to be rooted in education. Motives for educational participation and expansion are increased, as individuals, organizations, and societies seek the advantages involved.

WHAT STOPS EDUCATIONAL EXPANSION?

Given our review of the enormous pressures for educational expansion built into the modern system, we need to consider why it has not gone further. The chapters of this book take a limited view of this question. They stress situations in which powerful status groups, acting on self-interest more than a modern conception of the public good, may restrict opportunities for others (see the chapters by Walters, Rubinson and Fuller, Mitch, and Boli). And they stress the role of the strong Western state, which may choose to restrict educational inflation in something of the same spirit stressing the good of the state over the virtuous expansion of society (see the chapters by Hage and Garnier, and Rubinson and Fuller). Finally, McMahon discusses limitations of cost and foregone time, energy, and labor; however, he does note the many ways in which schooling costs are quite variable.

We may note one other process, which is briefly discussed by Rubinson and Fuller. The modern system stresses the collective good, but as one component of this good, individual welfare is emphasized. The individuals involved clearly come under the principle of educational equality. As we have noted, equality is an important theme in all modern educational discourse and is part of the emphasis on the universalization of education. One process slowing educational expansion can be the institutionalization of principles of equality: This works against educational stratification and its effects, and it can reduce incentives for educational expansion as a means of enhancing individual or organizational interests. Emphasis on equality may simply block educational inflation but may also lower the legitimacy of the striving and competition involved.

17. The institutionalization of educational equality tends to lower the implementation of competitive pressures for educational expansion.

Such an institutionalization can take many forms: (1) tight restrictions on access to education beyond some norm; (2) the tying of advanced educational opportunities to very specialized occupations with limited demand, as in traditional European arrangements; (3) blocking the use of education for many dimensions of stratification (as in the resistance by traditional universities to modern training programs). As has often been noted, the liberal (or, now, American) form of education as a linear sequence with open opportunities and links to society is an exceptionally expansive form. The hegemony of this form in education around the world since 1945 is clearly one force for educational expansion (Benavot 1983).

CONCLUDING COMMENTS

Research reported in this book is strongest in dealing with the motives for schooling expansion, given institutionalization of the value of education as a collective good and in the stratification system. Under these conditions people push for more participation, organizations compete to expand education, and so do national societies and states. And these are the conditions that have prevailed throughout most of contemporary history. As immediate explanations, they account well for the massive educational expansion that has occurred.

We do less well in accounting for the rise of the conditions themselves. This chapter has suggested some exploratory ideas about why education became, in the Western system, such a central cultural ingredient and dimension of stratification. We have stressed the importance of peculiar models of society and the individual according to which individual education contributes both to social progress and to socially valued individual development.

Much more research is needed (1) to examine the links between emergent models of society as an action system based on individuals and the resultant ideological (and consequently competitive) pressures for schooling, (2) to study the evolution of the domains of recognized public society and the consequent pressures for education, and (3) to examine the roles of the professionals and other ideologues developing and institutionalizing the connections.

The real contribution of the studies here is to show with great clarity the impact of such legitimated principles. Under these principles, the widest variety of motives held by the widest variety of participants will fuel educational expansion. Modern history is filled with both the motives and the resultant expansion. The problem researchers face is that so many reasons—and so many groups—are involved. Every road toward modernization and every participant group pressure, it seems, leads to more education. The proponents have the collective good on their side, the legitimacy of their own interests, their authorized power to express these interests, and the reality of their own motives for individual, group, and national success. They also, it turns out, have a right: Education is practically everywhere a social right, well established in national societies and now in the world system (McNeely 1989).

References

Most foreign titles have been translated into English. Please consult authors for authentic titles of works published in other languages.

Åberg, Alf. 1979. *When the Villages Were Shattered*. Stockholm: Natur och kultur.
Abernethy, David B. 1969. *The Political Dilemma of Popular Education: An African Case*. Stanford: Stanford University Press.
Agrell, Jan. 1977. "Permanent Rural Schools in Malmöhus County before 1842: An Overview." Pp. 107–18 in *Individualism and Sociability: Essays in Honor of Wilhelm Sjöstrand*, edited by Thor Nordin and Björn Sjövall. Lund: Doxa.
Altick, Richard. 1957. *The English Common Reader*. Chicago: University of Chicago Press.
American Federation of Labor. 1911. *Report of Proceedings of the Thirty-First Annual Convention*. Washington, DC: Law Reporter Printing Company.
———. 1915. *Report of Proceedings of the Thirty-Fifth Annual Convention*. Washington, DC: Law Reporter Printing Company.
Amin, Samir. 1975. "What Education for What Development?" *Prospects* 5:48–52.
Anderson, Benedict. 1983. *Imagined Communities*. London: Verso Press.
Anderson, James D. 1988. *The Education of Blacks in the South, 1860–1935*. Chapel Hill: University of North Carolina Press.
Anderson, Robert D. 1975. *Education in France*. Oxford: Clarendon Press.
Apple, Michael W. 1982. *Education and Power*. Boston: Routledge and Kegan Paul.
Aquilonius, Klas. 1942. *The Swedish Common School System 1809–1860*. Vol. 2 of *A History of the Swedish Common School*, edited by Viktor Fredriksson. Stockholm: Bonnier.
Archer, Margaret. 1979. *Social Origins of Educational Systems*. Beverly Hills: Sage.
Armer, J. Michael, and Richard Rubinson. 1988. "Educational Expansion and Economic Growth in Taiwan, 1951–1985." Paper presented at the annual meetings of the American Sociological Association, Atlanta, GA.

Armstrong, W. A. 1972. "The Use of Information about Occupation in Nineteenth Century Society." Pp. 191–318 in *Nineteenth Century Society*, edited by E. A. Wrigley. Cambridge: Cambridge University Press.

Arnold, Guy. 1977. *Modern Nigeria*. London: Longman.

Arnove, Robert F., and Harvey Graff. 1987. "Introduction." Pp. 1–28 in *National Literacy Campaigns in Historical and Comparative Perspective*, edited by Robert F. Arnove and Harvey Graff. New York: Plenum.

Arrow, Kenneth. 1973. "Higher Education As a Filter." *Journal of Public Economics* 2:193–216.

Atonakaki, K. 1955. *Greek Education: Reorganization of the Administrative Structure*. New York: Columbia University Teachers College.

Ayres, Leonard. 1909. *Laggards in Our Schools*. New York: Russell Sage Foundation.

Bairoch, Paul. 1981. "The Main Trends in National Economic Disparities since the Industrial Revolution." Pp. 3–18 in *Disparities in Economic Development since the Industrial Revolution*, edited by P. Bairoch and M. Levy-Leboyer. New York: St. Martin's Press.

Banks, Arthur. 1971. *Cross Polity Time Series Data*. Cambridge, MA: MIT Press.

Barbagli, Marzio. 1982. *Educating for Unemployment: Politics, Labor Markets, and the School System—Italy, 1859–1973*. New York: Columbia University Press.

Becker, Gary. 1964. *Human Capital*. New York: Columbia University Press.

Bell, Rudolph. 1979. *Fate and Honor, Family and Village*. Chicago: University of Chicago Press.

Benavot, Aaron. 1983. "The Rise and Decline of Vocational Education." *Sociology of Education* 56:63–76.

———. 1989. "Education, Gender, and Economic Development: A Cross-National Study." *Sociology of Education* 62:14–32.

Benavot, Aaron, and Phyllis Riddle. 1988. "National Estimates of the Expansion of Primary Education, 1870–1940." *Sociology of Education* 62:191–207.

Benavot, Aaron, Yun-Kyung Cha, David Kamens, John Meyer, and Suk-Ying Wong. 1991. "Knowledge for the Masses: World Models and National Curricula, 1920–1986." *American Sociological Review* 56:85–100.

Bendix, Reinhard. 1964. *Nation-Building and Citizenship*. New York: Wiley.

Berg, Ivar. 1971. *Education and Jobs: The Great Training Robbery*. Boston: Beacon Press.

Best, Harry. 1914. *The Deaf, Their Position in Society and the Provision for Their Education in the United States*. New York: Thomas Y. Crowell Company.

Bettelheim, Ruth, and Ruby Takanishi. 1976. *Early Schooling in Asia*. New York: McGraw-Hill.

Beutow, Harold A. 1970. *Of Singular Benefit*. London: Macmillan.

Bidwell, Charles, and John Kasarda. 1980. "Conceptualizing and Measuring the Effects of School and Schooling." *American Journal of Education* 88:401–30.

Biennial Survey of Education. 1930. Washington, DC: U.S. Government Printing Office.

Blaug, Mark. 1970. *An Introduction to the Economics of Education*. London: Penguin Books.

Blodgett, James. 1894. "Parochial Schools." Pp. 349–425 of *Annual Reports of the Commissioner of Education 1894–95*.

Boli, John. 1989. *New Citizens for a New Society: The Institutional Origins of Mass Schooling in Sweden*. Oxford: Pergamon.

Boli, John, and Francisco O. Ramirez. 1986. "World Culture and the Institutional De-
velopment of Mass Education." In *Handbook of Theory and Research in the
Sociology of Education*, edited by John Richardson. Westport, CT: Greenwood
Press.

Boli, John, Francisco Ramirez, and John W. Meyer. 1985. "Explaining the Origins and
Expansion of Mass Education." *Comparative Education Review* 29:145–70.

Boli-Bennett, John, and John Meyer. 1978. "The Ideology of Childhood and the State:
Rules Distinguishing Children in National Constitutions." *American Sociological
Review* 43:797–812.

Bond, Horace Mann. 1934. *The Education of the Negro in the American Social Order*.
New York: Octagon Books.

Boocock, Sarane. 1977. "A Cross-Cultural Analysis of the Child Care System." Pp. 71–
103 in *Current Topics in Early Childhood Education*. vol. 1, edited by Lilian G.
Katz. New York: Ablex.

Bornschier, Volker, and Christopher Chase-Dunn. 1985. *Transnational Corporations and
Underdevelopment*. New York: Praeger.

Boudon, Raymond. 1974. *Education, Opportunity and Social Inequality*. New York:
Wiley.

Bowen, Howard R. 1948. *Toward Social Economy*. New York: Rinehart & Co.

Bowles, Samuel. 1968. *Planning Educational Systems for Economic Growth*. Cambridge,
MA: Harvard University Press.

Bowles, Samuel, and Herbert Gintis. 1976. *Schooling in Capitalist America: Educational
Reform and the Contradictions of Economic Life*. New York: Basic Books.

———. 1986. *Democracy and Capitalism*. New York: Basic Books.

Briggs, John. 1978. *An Italian Passage*. New Haven: Yale University Press.

British Parliamentary Papers. Various years.

Brooks, Jeffrey. 1985. *When Russia Learned to Read: Literacy and Popular Literature,
1861–1917*. Princeton: Princeton University Press.

Buchanan, James M. 1966. *The Demand and Supply of Public Goods*. Chicago: Rand
McNally.

Bullock, Henry Allen. 1967. *A History of Negro Education in the South*. Cambridge,
MA: Harvard University Press.

Callahan, Raymond E. 1962. *Education and the Cult of Efficiency*. Chicago: University
of Chicago Press.

Cameron, Rondo. 1985. "A New View of European Industrialization." *Economic History
Review* 38:1–23.

Cardoso, Fernando. 1972. "Dependency and Underdevelopment in Latin America." *New
Left Review* 74:83–98.

Carlsson, Sten. 1956. *The Peasant in Swedish History*, vol. 3. Stockholm: Lantbruck-
förbundet.

———. 1961. *Swedish History 2: The Period after 1718*. 3d ed. Stockholm: Svenska
Bokförlaget.

Carnoy, Martin. 1982. "Education for Alternative Development." *Comparative Education Review* 26:160–77.

Carnoy, Martin, and Henry Levin. 1985. *Schooling and Work in the Democratic State*.
Stanford, CA: Stanford University Press.

Chodorow, Nancy. 1980. *The Reproduction of Mothering*. Berkeley: University of California Press.

Cipolla, Carlo. 1969. *Literacy and Development in the West*. Harmondsworth, England: Penguin Books.

Clignet, Remi. 1974. *Liberty and Equality in the Educational Process*. New York: Wiley.

Cohen, Sol. 1968. "The Industrial Education Movement, 1906–17." *American Quarterly* 20:95–110.

Collins, Randall. 1979. *The Credential Society: A Historical Sociology of Education and Stratification*. New York: Academic Press.

Committee for Economic Development. 1987. *Children in Need*. New York: Committee for Economic Development.

Cooper, B. 1982. "Nonpublic Schools." *International Encyclopedia of Education* 6:3561–66.

Craig, John. 1981. "The Expansion of Education." Pp. 151–213 in *Review of Research in Education*, vol. 9, edited by David C. Berliner. Washington, DC: American Educational Research Association.

Cressy, David. 1980. *Literacy and the Social Order*. Cambridge: Cambridge University Press.

Cross, Robert D. 1958. *The Emergence of Liberal Catholicism in America*. Cambridge, MA: Harvard University Press.

Cubberly, Ellwood P. 1920. *The History of Education*. Cambridge, MA: Riverside Press.

David, Miriam, and Irene Lezine. 1976. *Early Child Care in France*. London: Gordon and Breach.

Delacroix, Jacques, and Charles Ragin. 1978. "Modernizing Institutions, Mobilization and Third World Development: A Cross-National Study." *American Journal of Sociology* 84:123–49.

Denison, Edward F. 1964. *Measuring the Contribution of Education and the Residual to Economic Growth*. Paris: Organization for Economic Cooperation and Development.

DeVries, Jan. 1976. *The Economy of Europe in an Age of Crisis*. New York: Cambridge University Press.

DiMaggio, P., and W. Powell. 1983. "The Iron Cage Revisited: Institutional Isomorphism and Collective Rationality in Organizational Fields." *American Sociological Review* 48:147–60.

Dolan, Jay P. 1987. *The American Catholic Parish*, vols. 1 and 2. New York: Paulist Press.

Donald, James. 1985. "Beacons of the Future: Schooling, Subjection, and Subjectification." In *Subjectivity and Social Relations*, edited by V. Beechey and J. Donald. Philadelphia: Open University Press.

Dreeben, Robert. 1968. *On What Is Learned in School*. Reading, MA: Addison Wesley.

DuBois, W.E.B. [1903] 1968. *The Souls of Black Folk: Essays and Sketches*. Greenwich, CT: Fawcett.

Dumont, Louis. 1965. "The Modern Conception of the Individual: Notes on Its Genesis and That of Concomitant Institutions." *Contributions to Indian Sociology* 8 (October):13–61.

Duncan, Wendy. 1989. *Engendering School Learning*. Studies in Comparative and International Education, no. 16. Stockholm: Institute of International Education.

Durkheim, Emile (trans. Sherwood Fox). 1956. *Education and Sociology*. Glencoe, IL: Free Press.

Eastmond, J. 1964. "A Progress Report on Efforts to Attain the Enrollment Goals of

Primary Education in Northern Nigeria.'' Kaduna: Ministry of Education. Mimeographed.

Eklof, Ben. 1986. *Russian Peasant Schools: Officialdom, Village Culture, and Popular Pedagogy, 1861–1914.* Berkeley: University of California Press.

Fiala, Robert, and Francisco Ramirez. 1984. ''Dependence, Service Sector Growth, and Economic Development, 1960–1975.'' *Comparative Social Research* 7:339–424.

Field, Alexander J. 1976. ''Educational Expansion in Mid-Nineteenth Century Massachusetts: Human Capital Formation or Structural Reinforcement?'' *Harvard Educational Review* 46:521–52.

Fishlow, Albert. 1966. ''Levels of Nineteenth-Century American Investment in Education.'' *Journal of Economic History* 26:418–36.

Fitzpatrick, David. 1986. ''A Share of the Honeycomb: Education, Emigration and Irishwomen.'' *Continuity and Change* 1:217–34.

Fleury, M., and P. Valmary. 1957. ''Le Progrès de l'Instruction Elémentaire de Louis XIV à Napoleon III d'Après l'Enquête de Louis Maggiolo (1877–1879).'' *Population* 12:71–92.

Flinn, Michael W. 1981. *The European Demographic System, 1500–1820.* Baltimore: Johns Hopkins University Press.

Flora, Peter, and Jens Alber. 1983. *State, Economy, and Society in Western Europe, 1815–1975: A Data Handbook in Two Volumes.* Chicago: St. James Press.

Flynt, J. Wayne. 1979. *Dixie's Forgotten People: The South's Poor Whites.* Bloomington: Indiana University Press.

Fogarty, Gerald P. 1985. *The Vatican and the American Hierarchy from 1870 to 1965.* Wilmington, DE: Michael Glazier.

Fortes, Meyer. 1978. ''Parenthood, Marriage, and Fertility in West Africa.'' *Journal of Developmental Studies* 14:121–49.

Frank, André G. 1967. *Capitalism and Underdevelopment in Latin America.* New York: Monthly Review Press.

Fried, Robert. 1963. *The Italian Prefects: A Study in Administrative Politics.* New Haven: Yale University Press.

Fuller, Bruce. 1983. ''Youth Job Structure and School Enrollment, 1890–1920.'' *Sociology of Education* 56:145–56.

———. 1987. ''What School Factors Raise Achievement in the Third World?'' *Review of Educational Research* 57:255–92.

———. 1991. *Growing up Modern: The Western State Builds Third World Schools.* New York: Routledge.

Fuller, Bruce, John Edwards, and Kathleen Gorman. 1986. ''When Does Education Boost Economic Growth: School Expansion and Quality in Mexico.'' *Sociology of Education* 59:167–81.

Fuller, Bruce, Maurice Garnier, and Jerald Hage. 1990. ''State Action and Labor Structure Change in Mexico.'' *Social Forces* 68:1165–89.

Fullerton, Ronald. 1977. ''Creating a Mass Book Market in Germany: The Story of the Colporteur Novel, 1870–1890.'' *Journal of Social History* 10:265–83.

Furet, François, and Jacques Ozouf. [1977] 1982. *Reading and Writing: Literacy in France from Calvin to Jules Ferry.* Cambridge: Cambridge University Press.

Gallagher, Charles S. 1979. *Education and Society in Twentieth-Century Spain.* Hanover, NH: American University Field Staff.

Gallagher, Mark, and Osita Ogbu. 1989. ''Public Expenditures, Adjustment and the

Provision of Social Services in Africa.'' World Bank Working Paper, Draft of May 22. Washington, DC: World Bank, Africa Division.

Gardner, Phil. 1984. *The Lost Schools of Victorian England: The Peoples Education.* London: Croon Helm.

Garnier, Maurice, and Jerald Hage. 1990. ''Education and Economic Growth in Germany.'' *Research in Sociology of Education and Socialization* 9:25–53.

Garnier, Maurice, Jerald Hage, and Bruce Fuller. 1989. ''The Strong State, Social Class, and Controlled School Expansion in France, 1881–1975.'' *American Journal of Sociology* 95:279–306.

Garrido, José Luis García. 1986. *International Yearbook of Education*, vol. 38. Geneva: Unesco.

Geertz, Clifford, (ed.). 1963. *Old Societies and New States: The Quest for Modernity in Asia and Africa.* New York: Free Press.

Gelb, Steven A., and Donald T. Mizokawa. 1986. ''Special Education and Social Structure: The Commonality of 'Exceptionality'.'' *American Educational Research Journal* 23:543–57.

Georgia Department of Education. 1911. *Thirty-Ninth Annual Report of the Department of Education to the General Assembly of the State of Georgia for the School Year Ending December 31, 1910.* Atlanta: Chas. P. Byrd.

Gerger, Torvald, and Göran Hoppe. 1980. *Education and Society: The Geographer's View.* Stockholm: Almqvist & Wiksell.

Germino, Dante, and S. Passigli. 1968. *The Government and Politics of Contemporary Italy.* New York: Harper and Row.

Gerschenkron, Alexander. 1962. ''Economic Backwardness in Historical Perspective.'' Pp. 5–30 in *Economic Backwardness in Historical Perspective*, edited by Alexander Gerschenkron. Cambridge: Harvard University Press.

Giddens, Anthony. 1984. *The Constitution of Society.* Berkeley: University of California Press.

Gildea, Robert. 1983. *Education in Provincial France 1800–1914.* Oxford: Oxford University Press.

Gobalet, Jeanne, and Larry Diamond. 1979. ''Effects of Investment Dependence on Economic Growth.'' *International Studies Quarterly* 23:412–44.

Goodnow, Jacqueline, and Ailoa Burns. 1984. ''Factors Affecting Policies in Early Childhood Education: An Australian Case.'' Pp. 189–208 in *Current Topics in Early Childhood Education*, vol. 5, edited by Lilian G. Katz. New York: Ablex.

Goody, Esther N. 1982. *Parenthood and Social Reproduction: Fostering and Occupational Roles in West Africa.* Cambridge: Cambridge University Press.

Graff, Harvey J. 1987. *The Legacies of Literacy.* Bloomington: Indiana University Press.

Grafteaux, Serge. [1975] 1985. *Mme. Santerre: A French Woman of the People.* Translated by Louise A. Tilly and Kathryn L. Tilly. New York: Schocken Books.

Grubb, Norton, and Marvin Lazerson. 1988. *Broken Promises.* Chicago: University of Chicago Press.

Guest, Avery, and Stewart Tolnay. 1985. ''Agricultural Organization and Education Consumption in the United States in 1900.'' *Sociology of Education* 58:201–12.

Gustafsson, Berndt. 1973. *Swedish Church History.* 5th ed. Stockholm: Verbum.

Haber, Samuel. 1964. *Efficiency and Uplift: Scientific Management in the Progressive Era 1890–1920.* Chicago: University of Chicago Press.

Hage, Jerald, and Maurice A. Garnier. 1990. ''Education and Economic Growth in

Germany.'' Pp. 25–54 in *Research in Sociology of Education and Socialization*, vol. 9, edited by Ronald G. Corwin. Greenwich, CT: JAI Press.

Hage, Jerald, Maurice A. Garnier, and Bruce Fuller. 1988. ''The Active State, Investment in Human Capital, and Economic Growth: France, 1825–1975.'' *American Sociological Review* 53:824–37.

Hage, Jerald, Robert Hanneman, and Edward T. Gargen. 1989. *State Responsiveness and State Activism*. London: Unwin Hyman.

Hall, Jacquelyn Dowd, James Leloudis, Robert Korstad, Mary Murphy, Lu Ann Jones, and Christopher B. Daly. 1987. *Like a Family: The Making of a Southern Cotton Mill World*. Chapel Hill: University of North Carolina Press.

Hanf, T., K. Ammann, P. Dias, M. Fremerey, and H. Weiland. 1975. ''Education: An Obstacle to Development?'' *Comparative Education Review* 19:68–87.

Hansard's Parliamentary Debates. 1847. 3d ser., vol. 91. London: Hansard.

Harbison, Frederick H., and Charles A. Myers (eds.). 1964. *Education, Manpower, and Economic Growth: Strategies of Human Resource Development*. New York: McGraw-Hill.

Harbison, Ralph, and Eric Hanushek. 1990. *School Achievement among the Rural Poor: The Case of Northeast Brazil*. Washington, DC: World Bank.

Harlan, Louis R. 1958. *Separate and Unequal: Public School Campaigns and Racism in the Southern Seaboard States 1901–1915*. Chapel Hill: University of North Carolina Press.

Hazard, Paul. 1964. *The European Mind, 1680–1715*. London: Penguin.

Heal, Ambrose. 1947. *Signboards of Old London Shops*. London: Batsford Press.

Hennesey, James S. J. 1981. *American Catholics*. New York: Oxford University Press.

Hicks, Norman. 1980. *Economic Growth and Human Resources*. World Bank Staff Working Paper no. 408. Washington, DC: World Bank.

Higham, John. 1955. *Strangers in the Land*. New Brunswick, NJ: Rutgers University Press.

Hogan, David. 1985. *Class and Reform: School and Society in Chicago, 1880–1930*. Philadelphia: University of Pennsylvania Press.

Houston, Rab. 1985. *Scottish Literacy and the Scottish Identity*. Cambridge: Cambridge University Press.

Hurd, Henry M., ed. [1916–1917] 1973. *The Institutional Care of the Insane in the United States and Canada*. Baltimore, MD: Johns Hopkins University Press.

Hurn, Christopher J. 1985. *The Limits and Possibilities of Schooling*. Boston: Allyn and Bacon.

Hurt, John S. 1971. ''Professor West on Early Nineteenth-Century Education.'' *Economic History Review* 2d. ser. 24:624–32.

Hyde, J. K. 1979. ''Some Uses of Literacy in Venice and Florence in the Thirteenth and Fourteenth Centuries.'' *Transactions of the Royal Historical Society*, 5th ser., 29:109–28. London: Offices of the Royal Historical Society.

Hyde, Karin A. L. 1989. ''Improving Women's Education in Sub-Saharan Africa: Review of the Literature.'' Mimeograph. Washington, DC: World Bank.

Inkeles, Alex, and D. Smith. 1974. *Becoming Modern*. London: Heinemann Education Books.

International Encyclopedia of Education. 1985. New York: Pergamon Press.

Irizarry, Rafael L. 1981. ''Dependency, Industrialization and Overeducation in the Underdeveloped Countries.'' Ed.D. diss., Harvard Graduate School of Education.

Isling, Åke. 1980. *Social Structure and School Organization*. Vol. 1 of *The Struggle for and against a Democratic School*. Stockholm: Sober.

Jaffe, E. D. 1982. *Child Welfare in Israel*. New York: Praeger.

Jaffee, David. 1985. "Export Dependence and Economic Growth: A Reformulation and Respecification." *Social Forces* 64:102–18.

James, David R., and Pamela Walters. 1990. "The Supply Side of Public Schools: Local-State Determinants of School Enrollment Patterns in the U.S." Pp. 81–110 in *Research in Sociology of Education and Socialization*, vol. 9, edited by Ronald G. Corwin. Greenwich, CT: JAI Press.

Jancar, Barbara. 1981. "Women in Communist Countries: Comparative Public Policy." Pp. 139–58 in *Women and World Change*, edited by N. Black and A. Cottrell. Beverly Hills, CA: Sage.

Janet, Mary. 1949. *Catholic Secondary Education*. Washington, DC: Ransdell, Inc., for the National Catholic Welfare Conference.

Jeong, Insook. 1988. "Educational Effects on Economic Growth in the Republic of Korea, 1955–1985." Master's thesis, Department of Sociology, Florida State University, Tallahassee.

Jepperson, Ronald L. 1991. "Institutions, Institutional Effects, and Institutionalism." Pp. 143–63 in *The New Institutionalism in Organizational Analysis*, edited by Walter W. Powell and Paul J. DiMaggio. Chicago: University of Chicago Press.

Jimenez, Emmanuel, and Marlaine E. Lockheed (eds). 1991. *Private vs. Public Education: An International Perspective*. Special issue of *International Journal of Education* 15:353–498.

Johansson, Egil. 1981. "The History of Literacy in Sweden." Pp. 151–82 in *Literacy and Social Development in the West: A Reader*, edited by Harvey J. Graff. Cambridge: Cambridge University Press.

Johansson, K. H. 1937. "Self-Government in the Swedish Parish 1686–1862." Ph.D. diss. University of Lund.

Johnson, Charles S. 1934. *Shadow of the Plantation*. Chicago: University of Chicago Press.

Jones, Thomas Jesse. 1917. *Negro Education: A Study of the Private and Higher Schools for Colored People in the United States*. 2 vols. U.S. Department of the Interior, Bureau of Education, Bulletins 38 and 39. Washington, DC: Government Printing Office.

Jorgenson, Dale. 1984. "The Contribution of Education to Economic Growth, 1948–1973." Pp. 95–162 in *Education and Economic Productivity*, edited by E. Dean. Cambridge, MA: Ballinger.

Jorgenson, Lloyd P. 1987. *The State and the Non-Public School 1825–1925*. Columbia: University of Missouri Press.

Kaelble, Hartmut. 1989. "Was Prometheus Most Unbound in Europe? The Labour Force in Europe during the Late XIXth and XXth Centuries." *Journal of European Economic History* 18:65–104.

Kaestle, Carl. 1985. "The History of Literacy and the History of Readers." Pp. 11–53 in *Review of Research in Education*, vol. 12, edited by Edmund W. Gordon. Washington, DC: American Educational Research Association.

Kärre, Marianne, et al. 1973. "Social Rights in Sweden before School Starts." Pp. 303–19 in *Child Care: Who Cares?*, edited by Pamela Roby. New York: Basic Books.

Katz, Michael B. 1968. *The Irony of Early School Reform: Educational Innovation in*

Mid-Nineteenth-Century Massachusetts. Cambridge, MA: Harvard University Press.

Katznelson, Ira, and Margaret Weir. 1985. *Schooling for All: Class, Race, and the Decline of the Democratic Ideal*. New York: Basic Books.

Key, V. O., Jr. 1949. *Southern Politics*. New York: Vintage.

Khalakdina, Margaret. 1979. *Early Child Care in India*. London: Gordon and Breach.

King, Elizabeth, and Lillard, L. 1987. "Education Policy and School Attainment in Malaysia and the Philippines." *Economics of Education Review* 6:167–81.

Knight, Edgar W. 1922. *Public Education in the South*. Boston: Ginn & Co.

Knight. J. B., and R. H. Sabot. 1987. "The Rate of Return on Educational Expansion." *Economics of Education Review* 6:255–62.

Kousser, J. Morgan. 1974. *The Shaping of Southern Politics: Suffrage Restriction and the Establishment of the One-Party South, 1880–1910*. New Haven: Yale University Press.

Kurian, George. 1988. *World Encyclopedia of Education*. 3 vols. New York: Facts on File.

Kwack, Sung Yeung. 1986. "The Economic Development of the Republic of Korea, 1965–1981." Pp. 65–133 in *Models of Development: A Comparative Study of Economic Growth in South Korea and Taiwan*. edited by Lawrence J. Lau. San Francisco: Institute for Contemporary Studies Press.

Laqueur, Thomas. 1976. "The Cultural Origins of Popular Literacy in England 1500–1850." *Oxford Educational Review* 2:255–75.

Larkin, E. 1976. *The Historical Dimensions of Irish Catholicism*. Washington, DC: Catholic University of America Press.

Larwood, Jacob, and John Camden. 1870. *The History of Signboards from Earliest Times to the Present Day*. 7th ed. London: Chatto and Windus.

Lazerson, Marvin. 1977. "Understanding American Catholic Educational History." *History of Education Quarterly* 17:297–317.

Lee, James Michael. 1967. *Catholic Education in the Western World*. South Bend, IN: University of Notre Dame Press.

Leiner, Marvin. 1987. "The 1961 National Cuban Literacy Campaign." Pp. 173–96 in *National Literacy Campaigns: Historical and Comparative Perspectives*, edited by Robert F. Arnove and Harvey Graff. New York: Plenum Press.

Lieberson, Stanley. 1980. *A Piece of the Pie: Black and White Immigrants since 1880*. Berkeley: University of California Press.

Lockheed, Marlaine, Dean Jamison, and Lawrence Lau. 1980. "Farmer Education and Farmer Efficiency: A Survey." Pp. 111–52 in *Education and Income*, edited by T. King. Washington, DC: World Bank.

Lockheed, Marlaine, Adriaan Verspoor, et al. 1991. *Improving Primary Education in Developing Countries*. New York: Oxford University Press.

Löfberg, David. 1949. *National-Economic Motives in Swedish Pedagogy in the 18th Century*. Uppsala, Sweden: Appelberg.

Maddison, Angus. 1982. *Phases of Capitalist Development*. Oxford: Oxford University Press.

Maillet, Jean. 1974. "L'évolution des effectifs de l'enseignement secondaire de 1809 à 1961." In *La Scolarisation en France depuis un Siècle*, edited by Pierre Chevallier. Paris: Mouton.

Malmström, Per. 1813. *Essai sur le système militaire de la Suède*. Stockholm: Charles Delén.

Mandle, Jay R. 1978. *The Roots of Black Poverty: The Southern Plantation Economy after the Civil War*. Durham: Duke University Press.

Mann, Michael. 1986. *The Sources of Social Power*. Cambridge: Cambridge University Press.

———. 1987. "Ruling Class Strategies and Citizenship." *Sociology* 21:339–54.

Margo, Robert A. 1987. "Accounting for Racial Differences in School Attendance in the American South: The Role of Separate-but-Equal." *Review of Economics and Statistics* 4:661–66.

———. 1990. *Race and Schooling in the South, 1880–1950*. Chicago: University of Chicago Press.

Marshall, Alfred. 1890. *Principles of Economics*. London: Macmillan and Company.

Marshall, T. H. 1948. *Class, Citizenship and Social Development*. Garden City, NY: Doubleday.

Massachusetts, Commonwealth of. 1852. *An Act Concerning the Attendance of Children at School*. Ch. 240, Sec. 1–4.

Massachusetts Board of Education. 1911. *Seventy-Fourth Annual Report of the Board of Education*. Boston: Wright & Potter Printing Co.

Maxcy, Spencer J. 1981. "Progressivism and Rural Education in the Deep South, 1900–1950." In *Education and the Rise of the New South*, edited by Ronald K. Goodenow and Arthur O. White. Boston: G. K. Hall and Co.

Maynes, Mary Jo. 1977. "Schooling the Masses: A Comparative Social History of France and Germany, 1750–1850." Ph.D. diss., University of Michigan.

———. 1985. *Schooling for the People*. New York: Holmes & Meier.

McCarren, Edgar Patrick. 1966. *The Origin and Early Years of the National Catholic Educational Association*. Washington, DC: Catholic University of America Press.

McGreevey, William. 1968. "Recent Research on the Economic History of Latin America." *Latin American Research Review* 3:89–117.

McMahon, Walter W. 1970. "An Economic Analysis of the Major Determinants of Expenditures on Public Primary and Secondary Education." *Review of Economics and Statistics* 52:242–52.

———. 1975. "Economic and Demographic Effects on Investment in Education." *The Southern Economic Journal* 41:506–14.

———. 1976. "Influences on Investment by Blacks in Higher Education." *American Economic Review* 66:32–44.

———. 1984. "Why Families Invest in Education." Pp. 75–91 in *The Collection and Analysis of Economic and Consumer Behavior Data*. Champaign: University of Illinois Press.

———. 1987. "The Relation of Education and R&D to Productivity Growth in the Developing Countries of Africa." *Economics of Education Review* 6:183–94.

McNeely, Connie L. 1989. "Cultural Isomorphism among Nation-States: The Role of International Organizations." Ph.D. diss., Stanford University.

Meyer, John. 1977. "The Effects of Education as an Institution." *American Journal of Sociology* 83:340–63.

Meyer, John, and Michael T. Hannan (eds.). 1979. *National Development and the World System: Educational, Economic, and Political Change*. Chicago: University of Chicago Press.

Meyer, John, Francisco Ramirez, and Yasemin Soysal. 1991. "World Expansion of Mass Education, 1870–1980." *Sociology of Education*. Forthcoming.

Meyer, John, and Brian Rowan. 1977. "Institutionalized Organizations: Formal Structure as Myth and Ceremony." *American Sociological Review* 83:340–63.

Meyer, John W. 1989. "Conceptions of Christendom: Notes on the Distinctiveness of the West." Pp. 395–413 in *Cross-National Research in Sociology*, edited by M. Kohn. Sage: Newbury Park.

Meyer, John W., David Tyack, Joane Nagel, and Audri Gordon. 1979. "Public Education and Nation-Building in America: Enrollments and Bureaucratization in the American States, 1870–1930." *American Journal of Sociology* 85:591–613.

Mialaret, Gaston. 1976. *World Survey of Preschool Education*. Education Studies and Documents, no. 14. Paris: Unesco.

Mitch, David. 1982. "The Spread of Literacy in Nineteenth Century England." Ph.D. diss., University of Chicago.

———. 1991. *The Rise of Literacy in Victorian England: The Influence of Private Choice and Public Policy*. Philadelphia: University of Pennsylvania Press.

Mitchell, Brian. 1983. *International Historical Statistics: The Americas and Australasia*. Detroit, MI: Gale Research Company.

Monica, Maria Filomena. 1978. *Educacao E Sociedad E No Portugal De Salazar: a Escola Primaria Salazarista 1926–1939*. Lisbon: Editoria Presenza.

Monroe, Paul. 1927. *Essays in Comparative Education*. New York: Teachers College.

Moore, P. Laurance. 1986. *Religious Outsiders and the Making of Americans*. New York: Oxford University Press.

Morawetz, David. 1976. *Twenty-five Years of Economic Development, 1950 to 1975*. Washington, DC: World Bank.

Morgan, William R., and J. Michael Armer. 1988. "Islamic and Western Educational Accommodation in a West African Society: A Cohort-Comparison Analysis." *American Sociological Review* 53:634–39.

Müller, Detlef, Fritz Ringer, and Brian Simon. 1987. *The Rise of the Modern Educational System: Structural Change and Social Reproduction, 1870–1920*. New York: Cambridge University Press.

Myrdal, Alva, and Viola Klein. 1968. *Women's Two Roles*. London: Routledge and Kegan Paul.

National Catholic Educational Association. 1901. *Minutes of the 3rd Annual Conference of NCEA, Chicago*, vol. 3. Washington, DC: NCEA.

———. 1905. *Proceedings and Addresses*, vol. 2. Washington, DC: NCEA.

———. 1915. *Minutes of the 11th Annual Conference of NCEA, Atlantic City, NJ*, vol. 11. Washington, DC: NCEA.

Nisbet, Robert. 1980. *A History of the Idea of Progress*. New York: Basic Books.

O'Connor, Sorca. 1988. "Women's Labor Force Participation and Preschool Enrollment, 1965–1980." *Sociology of Education* 61:15–28.

Offe, Claus. 1984. *Contradictions of the Welfare State*. Cambridge, MA: MIT Press.

Official Catholic Directory. Vol. 1870–1930. New York: P. J. Kennedy and Sons.

Parsons, Talcott. 1951. *The Social System*. Glencoe, IL: Free Press.

———. 1959. "The School Class as a Social System: Some of its Functions in American Society." *Harvard Educational Review* 29:297–318.

Paulsson, Per. 1866. *A History of Popular Education in Sweden*. Stockholm: Bonnier.

Perkin, Harold. 1957. "The Origins of the Popular Press." *History Today*. 7:425–35.

Perlmann, Joel. 1988. *Ethnic Differences: Schooling and Social Structure among the Irish, Italians, Jews, and Blacks in an American City, 1880–1935.* Cambridge: Cambridge University Press.

Plenary Council of Baltimore. 1866. *In Ecclesia Metropolitana Baltimorensi, a die VII., ad diem XII. Octobris, A.D. MDCCCLXVI., habiti, et a Sede Apostolica recogniti, Decreta.* Baltimore: Sede Apostolica.

Portes, A. 1976. "On the Sociology of National Development." *American Journal of Sociology* 82:55–85.

Prost, Antoine. 1968. *Histoire de L'Enseignement en France 1800–1967.* Paris: National Catholic Education Association.

Psacharopoulos, George. 1985. "Returns to Education: A Recent Updated International Comparison." *Journal of Human Resources* 20:583–97.

———. 1989. "Time Trends of the Returns to Education: Cross National Evidence." *Economics of Education Review* 8:225–31.

Quadagno, Jill. 1987. "Theories of the Welfare State." *Annual Review of Sociology* 6:151–74. Greenwich, CT: JAI Press.

Rabinowitz, Howard N. 1974. "Half a Loaf: The Shift from White to Black Teachers in the Negro Schools of the Urban South, 1865–1890." *Journal of Southern History* 40:565–94.

Ralph, John H., and Richard Rubinson. 1980. "Immigration and the Expansion of Schooling in the United States, 1890–1970." *American Sociological Review* 45:943–54.

Ramirez, Francisco, and John Boli. 1987. "The Political Construction of Mass Schooling: European Origins and Worldwide Institutionalization." *Sociology of Education* 60:2–17.

Ramirez, Francisco, and Richard Rubinson. 1979. "Creating Members: The Political Incorporation and Expansion of Education." In *National Development and the World System*, edited by John Meyer and Michael Hannan. Chicago: University of Chicago Press.

Ransom, Roger L., and Richard H. Sutch. 1977. *One Kind of Freedom: The Economic Consequences of Emancipation.* Cambridge: Cambridge University Press.

Ravitch, Diane. 1974. *The Great School Wars, New York City, 1805–1973: A History of the Public Schools as Battlefield of Social Change.* New York: Basic Books.

Reese, William J. 1986. *Power and the Promise of School Reform: Grass-Roots Movements during the Progressive Era.* Boston: Routledge and Kegan Paul.

Report of the Commissioner of Education. 1901. "Truant Schools," pp. 85–219. Washington, DC: U.S. Government Printing Office.

———. Various years. Washington, DC: U.S. Government Printing Office.

Richardson, John G. 1984. "The American States and the Age of School Systems." *American Journal of Education* 92:473–502.

———. 1987. "Town vs. Countryside and Systems of Common Schooling." *Social Science History* 2:401–32.

Ringer, Fritz. 1979. *Education and Society in Modern Europe.* Bloomington: Indiana University Press.

Rothman, David J. 1971. *The Discovery of the Asylum, Social Order and Disorder in the New Republic.* Boston: Little Brown.

Rubinson, Richard. 1986. "Class Formation, Political Organization, and Institutional

Structure: The Case of Schooling in the United States." *American Journal of Sociology* 92:519–48.

Rubinson, Richard, and Deborah Holtzman. 1981. "Comparative Dependence and Economic Development." *International Journal of Comparative Sociology* 32:86–101.

Rubinson, Richard, and John Ralph. 1984. "Technical Change and the Expansion of Schooling in the United States, 1890–1970." *Sociology of Education* 57:134–51.

Sanderson, Michael. 1972. "Literacy and Social Mobility in the Industrial Revolution in England." *Past and Present* 56:75–104.

Sandin, Bengt. 1988. "Education and Popular Culture in Stockholm between 1600 and the 1840s." *Continuity and Change* 3:363–85.

Sandström, Carl Ivar. 1978. *A History of Educational Ideas: On the Impact of Social Change on the Purposes of Education in Sweden and Abroad.* Stockholm: Aldus.

Sarason, Seymour B., and John Doris. 1979. *Educational Handicap, Public Policy, and Social History: A Broadened Perspective on Mental Retardation.* New York: Free Press.

Schelin, Margitta. 1978. *Official Statistics on Schooling in Sweden, 1847–1881.* Umeå: Pedagogiska Monografier, Universitetet i Umeå.

Schofield, Roger S. 1968. "The Measurement of Literacy in Pre-Industrial England." Pp. 311–25 in *Literacy in Traditional Societies*, edited by Jack Goody. Cambridge: Cambridge University Press.

Schultz, T. Paul. 1988. "Expansion of Public School Expenditures and Enrollments: Intercountry Evidence on the Effects of Income, Prices, and Population Growth." *Economics of Education Review* 7:167–84.

Schultz, Theodore W. 1961. "Investment in Human Capital." *American Economic Review* 51:1–16.

Selowsky, Marcelo. 1976. "A Note on Preschool Age Investment in Human Capital in Developing Countries." *Economic Development and Cultural Change* 24:707–20.

Sewell, William. 1985. *Structure and Mobility: The Men and Women of Marseille, 1820–1870.* Cambridge: Cambridge University Press.

Shils, Edward H. 1981. *Tradition.* Chicago: University of Chicago Press.

Simon, Joan. 1968. "Was There a Charity School Movement?" Pp. 55–100 in *Education in Leicestershire, 1540–1940*, edited by Brian Simon. Leicester: University of Leicestershire Press.

Sjöstrand, Wilhelm. 1961. *Sweden and Her Nordic Neighbors in the Age of Liberty and the Gustavian Period.* Vol. 1 of *A History of Pedagogy III.* Malmö: Gleerup.

Skocpol, Theda, and Edwin Amenta. 1986. "States and Social Policies." Pp. 131–57 in *Annual Review of Sociology*, vol. 12, edited by R. H. Turner and J. F. Short, Jr. Palo Alto, CA: Annual Reviews.

Skowronek, Stephen. 1982. *Building a New American State: The Expansion of National Administrative Capacities, 1877–1920.* New York: Cambridge University Press.

Smith, Adam. [1776] 1976. *The Wealth of Nations.* 2 vols. edited by R. H. Campbell, A. S. Skinner, and W. B. Todd. Oxford: Oxford University Press.

Smith, Timothy L. 1967. "Protestant Schooling and American Nationality, 1800–1850." *Journal of American History* 53:679–95.

Soltow, Lee, and Edward Stevens. 1981. *The Rise of Literacy and the Common School in the United States: A Socioeconomic Analysis to 1870*. Chicago: University of Chicago Press.

Sommerville, John. 1982. *The Rise and Fall of Childhood*. Beverly Hills, CA: Sage.

Spiers, Edward F. 1951. *The Central Catholic High School*. Washington, DC: Catholic University of America Press.

Spufford, Margaret. 1979. "First Steps in Literacy: The Reading and Writing Experiences of the Humblest Seventeenth-Century Spiritual Autobiographers." *Social History* 4:407–35.

Stinchcombe, Arthur L. 1965. "Social Structure and Organizations." Pp. 142–93 in *Handbook on Organizations*, edited by James G. March. Chicago: Rand McNally.

Stone, Lawrence. 1969. "Literacy and Education in England, 1640–1900." *Past and Present* 42:69–139.

Stone, Philip. 1972. "Child Care in Twelve Countries." Pp. 249–64 in *The Uses of Time*, edited by A. Szalui. Paris: Mouton.

Suggs, Glen W. 1977. "National Religious Administrative Districts: A Test of the Size-Density Hypothesis." Master's thesis, Western Washington State College, Bellingham, WA.

Suleiman, Ezra. 1976. *Les Hauts Fonctionnaires et la Politique*. Paris: Editions du Seuil.

Sundbärg, Axel Gustav. 1907. *Swedish Population Statistics 1750–1910: Some Major Findings*. Stockholm: Norstedt.

Sutherland, Gillian. 1971. *Elementary Schooling in the Nineteenth Century*. London: Historical Association.

Sutton, John. 1988. *Stubborn Children: Controlling Delinquency in the United States, 1640–1981*. Berkeley: University of California Press.

Talbott, John E. 1969. *The Politics of Educational Reform in France 1918–1940*. Princeton: Princeton University Press.

Thompson, A. R. 1981. *Education and Development in Africa*. New York: St. Martin's Press.

Thurow, Lester. 1974. *Generating Inequality: Mechanisms of Distribution in the U.S. Economy*. New York: Basic Books.

Tilly, Charles. 1973. "Population and Pedagogy in France." *History of Education Quarterly* 13:113–28.

———, (ed.). 1975. *The Formation of National States in Western Europe*. Princeton: Princeton University Press.

Tilly, Louise, and Joan W. Scott. 1978. *Women, Work and Family*. New York: Praeger.

Torpson, Nils. 1888. *The Development of Swedish Popular Education from the Reformation to 1842*. Stockholm: Norstedt.

Tropp, Asher. 1950. *The School Teachers*. New York: Macmillan.

Tullos, Allen. 1989. *Habits of Industry: White Culture and the Transformation of the Carolina Piedmont*. Chapel Hill: University of North Carolina Press.

Tyack, David (ed.). 1967. *Turning Points in American Educational History*. Waltham, MA: Blaisdell Publishing.

———. 1974. *The One Best System: A History of American Urban Education*. Cambridge, MA: Harvard University Press.

Tyack, David, and Elisabeth Hansot. 1982. *Managers of Virtue: Public School Leadership in America, 1820–1980*. New York: Basic Books.

Tyack, David, Thomas James, and Aaron Benavot. 1987. *Law and the Shaping of Public Education, 1785–1954*. Madison: University of Wisconsin Press.

Ullmann, Walter. 1966. *The Individual and Society in the Middle Ages.* Baltimore, MD: Johns Hopkins University Press.

Unesco. Various years. *Statistical Yearbook.* Paris: Unesco.

———. 1971. *World Survey of Education,* vols. 2 and 5. Geneva: Unesco.

———. 1983. *Trends and Projections of Enrollment by Level of Education and Age, 1960–2000.* Paris: Unesco.

U.S. Bureau of Education. 1893. *Report of the Commissioner of Education for the Year 1888–89.* Washington, DC: Government Printing Office.

———. 1911. *Report of the Commissioner of Education for the Year 1909–10.* Washington, DC: Government Printing Office.

U.S. Department of Education. 1990. *National Goals for Education.* Washington, DC: Government Printing Office.

U.S. Department of Labor, Bureau of Labor Statistics. 1916. *Summary of the Report on the Condition of Woman and Child Wage Earners in the United States.* Bulletin 175. Washington, DC: Government Printing Office.

Van der Woude, A. M. 1980. "De Alfabetisering." *Algemene Geschiednis der Nederlanden* 7:263.

Van Sickle, J. H., L. Witmer, and L. P. Ayres. 1911. "Provision for Exceptional Children in Public Schools." *U.S. Bureau of Education Bulletin*, no. 14. Washington, DC: Government Printing Office.

Vaughn, Michalina, and Margaret Archer. 1971. *Social Conflict and Educational Change in England and France 1789–1848.* Cambridge: Cambridge University Press.

Vinao Frago, Antonio. 1990. "The History of Literacy in Spain: Evolution, Traits and Questions." *History of Education Quarterly* 30:573–99.

Vincent, David. 1989. *Literacy and Popular Culture, England 1750–1914.* Cambridge: Cambridge University Press.

Vovelle, M. 1975. "Y-a-t'il Eu une Révolution Culturelle au XVIIIe Siècle? A Propos de l'Education Populaire en Provence." *Revue d'Histoire Moderne et Contemporaine* 22:89–141.

Wallerstein, Immanuel. 1974. *The Modern World System,* vol. 1. New York: Academic Press.

Walters, Pamela. 1984. "Occupational and Labor Market Effects on Secondary and Postsecondary Educational Expansion in the United States: 1922 to 1979." *American Sociological Review* 49:659–71.

Walters, Pamela, Holly J. McCammon, and David R. James. 1990. "Schooling or Working? Public Education, Racial Politics, and the Organization of Production in 1910." *Sociology of Education* 63:1–26.

Walters, Pamela, and Philip J. O'Connell. 1988. "The Family Economy, Work, and Educational Participation in the United States, 1890–1940." *American Journal of Sociology* 93:1116–52.

Walters, Pamela, and Richard Rubinson. 1983. "Educational Expansion and Economic Output in the United States, 1890–1969." *American Sociological Review* 48:480–93.

Ward, Katherine. 1985. *Women in the World System.* New York: Praeger.

Wardle, David. 1971. *Education and Society in Nineteenth Century Nottingham.* Cambridge: Cambridge University Press.

Weber, Adna. [1899] 1963. *The Growth of Cities in the Nineteenth Century: A Study in Statistics.* Ithaca, NY: Cornell University Press.

Weiler, Hans. 1978. "Education and Development: From the Age of Innocence to the Age of Skepticism." *Comparative Education* 14:179–98.

West, E. G. 1975. *Education and the Industrial Revolution.* London: Batsford Press.

Wheeler, David. 1980. *Human Resource Development and Economic Growth in LDC's.* World Bank Staff Working Paper no. 407. Washington, DC: World Bank.

Wilensky, Harold L. 1976. *The New Corporation: Centralization and the Welfare State.* London: Sage.

Williams, Raymond. 1966. *The Long Revolution.* Rev. ed. New York: Harper Torchbook Edition.

Wong, Suk-Ying. 1991. "The Evolution of Social Science Instruction, 1980–86." *Sociology of Education* 64:33–47.

World Bank. 1983, 1988. *World Tables.* 3d and 4th eds. New York: Oxford University Press.

———. 1988. *World Development Report.* Washington, DC: World Bank.

World Health Organization. 1980. "Health and Status of Women Background Paper for the World Conference of the United Nations Decade for Women: Equality, Development and Peace." Copenhagen: United Nations.

Wormald, C. P. 1977. "The Uses of Literacy in Anglo-Saxon England and Its Neighbours." *Transactions of the Royal Historical Society*, 5th ser., 27:95–114. London: Offices of the Royal Historical Society.

Index

About the Editors and Contributors

BRUCE FULLER is Associate Professor, Harvard University, Graduate School of Education. His work centers on how the state attempts to touch the school institution—its expansion, quality, and social rules within classrooms. He is the author of *Growing Up Modern* (1991).

RICHARD RUBINSON is Professor of Sociology, Emory University. He is presently investigating the political determinants and economic consequences of educational change in East Asia. He also focuses on the role of politics and class in shaping the influence of the state.

J. MICHAEL ARMER is Professor of Sociology, Florida State University. In addition to his work on the effects of Islamic and Western schooling in Nigeria, Armer is currently working on the contribution of educational expansion to economic growth in East Asia.

DAVID P. BAKER is Associate Professor of Sociology, Catholic University of America, Washington, D.C. His research interests include Catholic schooling, immigration and the labor market, and international comparisons of school organization and student achievement.

AARON BENAVOT is Lecturer in Sociology, Hebrew University of Jerusalem, and Assistant Professor, University of Georgia. He is currently investigating the historical impact of different curricular areas on economic growth.

JOHN BOLI is Senior Research Associate, University of Uppsala, and Visiting

Scholar, University of Lund. His chapter draws from his most recent book, *New Citizens for a New Society: The Institutional Origins of Mass Schooling in Sweden* (1989).

MAURICE GARNIER is Professor of Sociology, Indiana University. He is working with Jerald Hage on an empirically based theory of educational expansion and its consequences, using historical data from Britain, France, Germany, and Italy.

JERALD HAGE is Professor of Sociology in the Political Economy Program, University of Maryland. He is coauthor of two recent books on the state's influence in the social sectors and the economy: *State Responsiveness and State Activism* (with Robert Hanneman and Edward Gargan, 1989) and *State Intervention in Health Care* (with J. Rogers Hollingsworth and Robert Hanneman, 1989).

WALTER W. McMAHON is Professor of Economics and Education, University of Illinois. His work involves the contribution of education to productivity growth in the United States and in developing countries, and he has combined academic research with frequent project-design efforts for a variety of international agencies.

JOHN W. MEYER is Professor of Sociology, Stanford University. He is involved in comparative research on educational and political institutions and the formal and symbolic structure of organizations. He is currently completing a crossnational historical study of the world's primary school curricula, and his book with Michael Hannan, *National Development in the World System* (1979), spurred work on the institutional causes and consequences of mass schooling.

DAVID MITCH is Associate Professor of Economics, University of Maryland, Baltimore County. An economic historian, he also works on occupational mobility in England and the development of distributional systems in the United States.

WILLIAM R. MORGAN is Professor and Chair, Department of Sociology, Cleveland State University. He held a professorship at Bayero University, Kano, Nigeria, and his current research involves a field experiment on the provision of Afrocentric education to schoolchildren in Cleveland.

SORCA O'CONNOR is Associate Professor in the School of Education, Portland State University. She is currently completing a study of contrasting forms of leadership and administration of kindergartens at the turn of the century.

FRANCISCO O. RAMIREZ is Professor of Education and Sociology (by courtesy), Stanford University. His most recent book is *Rethinking the Nineteenth Century: Contradictions and Movements* (Greenwood Press, 1988).

JOHN G. RICHARDSON is Professor of Sociology, Western Washington University. He is working on the historical roots and growth of special education.

MARC J. VENTRESCA is completing his Ph.D. in sociology at Stanford University. His dissertation examines the modern population census as state practice, scientific initiative, and cultural form, and looks at the cultural organization of the modern state and government tools.

PAMELA BARNHOUSE WALTERS is Associate Professor of Sociology, Indiana University, Bloomington. With David J. James, she is currently studying the relationship between class structure and racial inequality in education in the American South from the late nineteenth century to the present.